The Perfect Game

Edited by Mark Alvarez

Foreword by Bill James

Taylor Publishing Company
Dallas, Texas

Published by Taylor Publishing Company
1550 West Mockingbird Lane
Dallas, Texas 75235

The articles herein were previously published in *The National Pastime,*
The Baseball Research Journal, and *The SABR Review of Books.*

All photos courtesy of the National Baseball Library with the exception
of the photo of Dolf Luque, which is courtesy of Peter C. Bjarkman.

Designed by Hespenheide Design

Library of Congress Cataloging-in-Publication Data
The Perfect game / edited by Mark Alvarez.
        p. cm.
    ISBN 0-87833-815-2
    1. Baseball—United States—History. I. Alvarez, Mark.
GV863.A1P46 1993
796.357′0973—dc20   92-39487
                                              CIP

Printed in the United States of America
10 9 8 7 6 5 4 3 2 1

This book is printed on acid-free recycled paper.

CONTENTS

LOOKING BACK

FOREWORD

The government, as far as I know, does not fund baseball research. Hey, Senator, I want to know what Babe Ruth's career batting average was against left-handed pitchers . . . can you spare me a couple hundred thousand? Doesn't work. Baseball research is funded by enthusiasm and directed by obsession.

That's where SABR comes in, see; SABR feeds the enthusiasm and channels the obsessions. SABR, the Society for American Baseball Research. Research is that which creates knowledge. If you want to know something about baseball, SABR puts you in touch with the other people who want to know the same types of things.

Let me propose a paradox: the great value in baseball research is that it is inherently meaningless. It doesn't *matter* who wins a baseball game, or a pennant race, or who gets into the Hall of Fame. It doesn't matter, but we choose to care.

What you have, then, is clean vision. For almost anything else that we study, there is a political impact, and therefore there are political positions. Want to study the impact of television on attitudes about war? There's a political impact to that, which fogs the truth. It is hard for a Whig to find a Tory's answer; let the Tories pay for their own study.

Baseball research is clean, apolitical, and we care a lot about it, and that creates the possibility that you can see things that you otherwise might miss. I'll give you a specific example. I have noticed, in casually flipping through baseball encyclopedias for a few thousand hours, that players whose careers peak early also tend to die early, and vice versa. Take the case of Sparky Adams, a Babe Ruth-era infielder who didn't come to the majors until he was almost thirty, but who led the National League in doubles at age thirty-seven. He lived to be ninety-four. That seems to happen a lot.

It would be a reasonably simple thing to do to study players' careers, figure out at what age they reach their peak, and then record that and also the age at which they pass away. I haven't done the research, but let's say it's true. What if. If *baseball players* who peak early in their careers also tend to die early, then might one not guess that the same was true of basketball players? What about football players? What about soldiers? What about mechanics? What about accountants?

Wouldn't it be interesting if you studied it, and found out that the age at which a person peaks professionally is a strong predictor of the age at which he will die? The government would probably pay for that study, but I don't care about that part of it; I just want to do the baseball bit. I'll do that sometime, and write up the results, and publish it in some little SABR publication or something similar. If it works out well it might end up in a collection like this one someday.

Baseball research is often like that: what is true about baseball players *might* be true about all of us. We just happen to see it because we care about the baseball players, and also because there is no political fog to fight through. SABR has no left or right, no liberal or conservative, no elephants and only a normal number of jackasses. Our battles are clean; we only fight over nothing.

—BILL JAMES

INTRODUCTION

Did you know that the original plan called for Jackie Robinson to be only one of several black players brought into baseball simultaneously by Branch Rickey?

Or that a home movie exists that seems to show that Babe Ruth really *did* call his shot in the 1932 World Series?

Or that teams loaded with future Hall of Fame players are usually not very good teams?

Intrigued? Read on. You'll find out more about these topics—and about many more just as interesting—in this collection of articles from the publications of the Society for American Baseball Research (SABR).

SABR was founded in 1971, and now has over 6000 members around the world. SABR members have broken new ground in correcting records, analyzing the game, and sorting historical fact from long-held fiction. In fact, the hardest thing about editing a collection like this is that there are dozens more fascinating articles in the SABR canon than we can fit in a single volume.

You don't have to be a serious researcher to join SABR. Membership is open to all, and it includes a subscription to the publications from which these articles have been taken. They range from the largely statistical *Baseball Research Journal* to the mainly historical *National Pastime,* and they cover virtually every other baseball area of interest along the way. For more information, write to SABR at P.O. Box 93183, Cleveland, OH 44121.

I hope to hear from you—and until then, good reading!

Mark Alvarez
Publications Director
The Society for American Baseball Research

The Best Year Any Hitter Ever Had

LARRY THOMPSON

♦ ♦ ♦

One of the most enduring and interesting of baseball controversies is a comparison of hitters playing in different eras. How do Babe Ruth's 60 home runs in 1927 compare with Ty Cobb's .420 batting average in 1911? Did Ted Williams and Honus Wagner in their best years equal Ruth and Cobb? How do the moderns—Rod Carew, George Brett, and Mike Schmidt—compare with the great hitters of the past? To compare hitters from different eras (or even different years in the same era) two measurements are required. First, we need a number that expresses the total offensive performance of a player in a given year. All the conventional statistics—batting average, home runs, runs batted in, slugging average—are deficient in expressing overall hitting performance. Second, once we find a measurement of total offensive performance, we must find a way of comparing the different conditions facing a hitter in, for example, 1911 and 1927.

The first question is the more difficult, and over the years baseball experts have developed a number of measurement schemes designed to compare the value of an apple (i.e., a home run) with the value of an orange (a stolen base). To date, the best resolution of the apples and oranges problem is John Thorn and Pete Palmer's complex study in their book *The Hidden Game of Baseball* (Doubleday, 1984). Aided by a computer simulation of every game since 1901, Thorn and Palmer developed a formula called Linear Weights (LWTS) that assigns a numerical value to each offensive event as follows:

Single (1B)—.46; Double (2B)—.80; Triple (3B)—1.02; Home run (HR)—1.40; Base on balls (BB) and Hit by pitch (HBP)—.33; Stolen base (SB)—.30; Caught stealing (CS)—.60

The sum of a hitter's performance using the LWTS formula, which is presented here only in part, is runs. An average single in an average game results in .46 runs, an average double results in .80 runs, etc. The best hitter produces more runs in a career or a season than his competition.

The LWTS formula, if we accept its validity, opens up endless possibilities for tinkering. A minor difficulty is that the end result of an LWTS calculation is not recognizable to a baseball fan as a "statistic." It will be a long time before the public becomes aware that an LWTS of 80 runs above average in a single season is exceptional. A second minor difficulty is that the LWTS formula uses statistics (caught stealing and hit by pitch) that are not available to the average fan. To become universally computable, the LWTS formula requires some simplification, hopefully without doing violence to the elegant original.

A third and more serious difficulty for single-season comparisons is that LWTS measures runs, but runs are a function of plate appearances. All other things being equal, a batter with 700 plate appearances will cause more runs than another batter with 600 plate appearances. Hitters of the last two decades, aided by a 162-game schedule, have a 4 percent advantage over their predecessors who played 154 games per year. Likewise hitters who compile impressive statistics in a single season but, for one reason or another, fail to accumulate a large number of plate appearances are less likely to achieve a high LWTS rating. Brett's injury-ridden 1980 season (507 ABs and BBs), Williams' 1957 season (539 ABs and BBs) and Schmidt's strike-shortened 1981 season are examples. Finally, in "Guns of August" heavy-hitting years, a player will have more plate appearances than his counterpart in years of hitting feebleness. In 1927 Ruth accumulated 678 plate appearances (ABs and BBs) in 151 games; in 1908 Wagner totaled 622 plate appearances—or 56 fewer—in 151 games. In other words the Babe had 9 percent more opportunities to produce runs in the same number of games played.

Summing up, LWTS measures total batting output. For single-season comparisons it would seem preferable to measure batting efficiency, the measure of success per plate appearance. The LWTS formula can be adapted to serve this purpose.

Let's first make a cosmetic change in the LWTS formula to convert values for offensive events into a more recognizable number and to eliminate from the formula the relatively insignificant statistics for HBP and CS. The revised values are:

1B—1.0; 2B—1.7; 3B—2.2; HR—3.0; BB—.7; SB—.3

We have changed the value of each offensive event but not the relationships among those values. In the LWTS formula a double equaled 1.7 singles (.80 ÷ .46 = 1.696), a triple equaled 2.2 singles, etc. However, the .3 value of a stolen base requires some explanation. In the LWTS formula a net value (SB minus CS) for stolen bases of the equivalent of .3 would require a success ratio of 80 percent. Consequently, a value of .3 for a stolen base may undervalue the stolen base on a few occasions (Max Carey's 51 successful steals in 53 attempts in 1922) and overvalue it on many others. Still, a .3 value for a stolen base is a reasonably comfortable figure. A large number of stolen bases—even if the success ratio is less than 80 percent—implies that the player will also take an extra base now and then on a teammate's hit and thereby contribute in a statistically unmeasurable way to his own offensive importance. The stolen base is also relatively unimportant in total offensive performance and a slight misjudgment of its value has only a minor impact.

Now we can unveil our revised LWTS formula:

$$\frac{1B\ (1.0) + 2B\ (1.7) + 3B\ (2.2) + HR\ (3.0) + BB\ (.7) + SB\ (.3)}{AB + BB}$$

The result of this lengthy but simple calculation is a measure of batting efficiency most closely akin to the slugging average. However, slugging average overvalues extra-base hits (2.0 for a 2B compared with a "real" value of only 1.7, etc.) and does not take into account walks and stolen bases, both undeniably of value. Because every statistic needs a name we'll call the figure obtained from our revised formula a Real Slugging Average (RSA). Now we'll compute the RSA for a real player in a real year—Honus Wagner in his great 1908 season with the Pittsburgh Pirates. His statistics that year read as follows:

G	AB	H	2B	3B	HR	BB	SB	BA	SA
151	568	201	39	19	10	54	53	.354	.542

Not a bad set of numbers. If Wagner were playing in the 1980s, his 1908 season would make him a strong contender—possibly a shoo-in—for MVP honors. Converting these totals into RSA, we get a .5222 figure for Wagner. To simplify things we'll move the decimal point three spaces to the right and call Wagner's 1908 RSA 522.2.

For comparative purposes let's look at Ruth's record for 1927—the year he hit 60 home runs:

G	AB	H	2B	3B	HR	BB	SB	BA	SA
151	540	192	29	8	60	138	7	.356	.772

Using the revised formula, we find that the Babe had a 649.9 RSA that year. Thus his 1927 performance seems clearly superior to Wagner's 1908 season. Ruth hit 60 home runs, Wagner only 10; Ruth exceeded Wagner in batting average, slugging average, and bases on balls. But wait a minute. Everybody hit more home runs in 1927 than in 1908. The American League's batting average in 1927 was .285 and its slugging average .399. In 1908 the National League batted only .239 and the slugging average was an anemic .306. A direct comparison of Ruth's and Wagner's RSAs would only be valid if they played in the same league in the same year. They didn't, and conditions changed mightily between 1908 and 1927. To compare Ruth and Wagner we need a method to equate their RSAs.

Baseball experts have suggested a number of ways to make the cross-era and cross-league comparisons of different players. The solution offered here is simple though laborious. We compare Wagner's 1908 RSA with the RSA of the National League that season and Ruth's with the RSA of the American League in 1927. Then we can determine which was better (expressed in percentage terms) compared with the average hitting accomplishment in his league. The formula is: A player's RSA divided by the league RSA equals the player's relative performance.

To calculate league RSA we need the number of AB, H, 2B, 3B, HR, RBI, and SB in a given year. *The Baseball Encyclopedia* does not list total league at bats and hits, but *The Sports Encyclopedia: Baseball* does. Calculating league RSA in the same way as individual RSA produces a 323.8 RSA for the National League in 1908 and a 396.1 figure for the American League in 1927.

Applying the formula for determining a player's relative hitting performance, we find that Wagner winds up with 161.3 and Ruth with 164.1. In other words, Ruth was 64.1 percent better than the average American League hitter in 1927 and Wagner was 61.3 percent better than the average National League hitter of 1908. Ruth's offensive performance exceeded that of Wagner, but the application of a relative comparison substantially reduced the difference between the two. Wagner's 1908 batting record was almost as good as Ruth's in 1927. (It could, of course, be argued that Wagner's defensive contribution at shortstop more than made up the hitting difference between the two and that Wagner was the more valuable player. But that's another study.)

The outstanding single-season hitting performances listed in the accompanying table were calculated in the same manner as the aforemen-

The Bambino connects for one in 1920

tioned examples. All of the hitters compiled seasons at least 50 percent better than average—or in other words accomplished more in two plate appearances than the average hitter accomplished in three plate appearances.

Best Hitting Seasons Since 1900

Player - Year	Player's RSA	League RSA	Relative Performance
1. Babe Ruth - 1920	699.3	385.9	181.2
2. Babe Ruth - 1921	698.7	401.5	174.0
3. Babe Ruth - 1923	662.1	388.2	170.6
4. Ted Williams - 1957	636.5	376.1	169.2
5. Ted Williams - 1941	645.3	386.0	167.2
6. Ty Cobb - 1910	553.4	332.7	166.3
7. Babe Ruth - 1927	649.9	396.1	164.1
8. Babe Ruth - 1926	640.2	390.7	163.9
9. Lou Gehrig - 1927	648.3	396.1	163.7
10. Ty Cobb - 1911	600.6	370.3	162.2
11. Ty Cobb - 1917	549.5	338.8	162.2
12. Babe Ruth - 1924	640.5	395.6	161.9
13. Ted Williams - 1946	592.1	365.8	161.9
14. Rogers Hornsby - 1925	649.6	401.7	161.7
15. Rogers Hornsby - 1924	620.3	384.2	161.5
16. Ted Williams - 1942	585.0	362.5	161.4
17. Honus Wagner - 1908	522.2	323.8	161.3
18. Mickey Mantle - 1957	604.5	376.1	160.7
19. Stan Musial - 1948	607.5	378.8	160.4
20. Jimmie Foxx - 1932	634.8	396.5	160.1
21. Rogers Hornsby - 1922	630.2	395.9	159.2
22. Nap Lajoie - 1904	518.1	326.8	158.5
23. Carl Yastrzemski - 1967	552.5	349.2	158.2
24. Babe Ruth - 1919	577.9	365.4	158.2
25. Ty Cobb - 1909	524.2	331.7	158.0
26. Richie Allen - 1972	546.4	346.0	157.9
27. Hank Aaron - 1971	574.2	363.6	157.9
28. Babe Ruth - 1931	616.3	390.5	157.8
29. Willie McCovey - 1969	575.7	366.0	157.3
30. Mickey Mantle - 1956	612.1	389.2	157.3
31. Jimmie Foxx - 1933	604.6	386.1	156.6
32. Ted Williams - 1947	575.7	367.7	156.6
33. Ty Cobb - 1912	567.1	363.5	156.0
34. Mike Schmidt - 1981	572.4	367.7	156.0
35. Nap Lajoie - 1901	580.4	373.8	155.3
36. Lou Gehrig - 1934	613.7	395.8	155.1
37. Babe Ruth - 1928	606.0	391.1	154.9
38. Babe Ruth - 1930	630.9	407.4	154.9
39. Joe Morgan - 1976	562.8	364.2	154.5
40. Mickey Mantle - 1961	595.6	385.7	154.4
41. Frank Robinson - 1966	557.3	361.0	154.4
42. Honus Wagner - 1904	516.9	336.4	153.7
43. Ty Cobb - 1915	532.6	346.7	153.6
44. Norm Cash - 1961	592.0	385.7	153.5
45. Lou Gehrig - 1930	624.8	407.4	153.4
46. Willie Mays - 1965	560.3	365.8	153.2

Best Hitting Seasons Since 1900 (cont.)

Player - Year	Player's RSA	League RSA	Relative Performance
47. Chuck Klein - 1933	546.7	357.1	153.1
48. Ty Cobb - 1913	541.2	353.8	153.0
49. George Brett - 1980*	595.7	390.6	152.5
50. Tris Speaker - 1912	553.6	363.5	152.3
51. Joe Jackson - 1911	562.7	370.3	152.0
52. Nap Lajoie - 1910	505.2	332.7	151.8
53. Ted Williams - 1949	584.1	385.5	151.5
54. Cy Seymour - 1905	522.5	344.9	151.5
55. Ted Williams - 1954	561.4	373.2	150.4
56. Joe Jackson - 1912	546.8	363.5	150.4
57. Jimmie Foxx - 1939	602.9	401.4	150.2

* Except for the designated-hitter rule in the American League, Brett's 1980 season would rank higher on the list—perhaps about twenty-fifth.

Thorn and Palmer calculated a list of best single-season hitting performances using their LWTS formula. The question arises whether my refinement of their work is necessary. Obviously, I would not have repeated their efforts unless I considered my adjustments of their benchmark study to be significant. Why? (1) Calculating single-season performances using my formula is easier and within the capability of the average person with easily available references. (2) My list has better balance. Thorn and Palmer's results highlight players in the heavy-hitting 1920s and 1930s. My list includes more hitters from both the dead-ball and modern eras. (3) Thorn and Palmer omit stolen bases from their calculation of single-season performances because of the unavailability of caught-stealing statistics for all years. My approximation of stolen-base value may be misleading in a few instances, but it seems logical that a good runner such as Cobb deserves credit for base stealing in comparison to a "thunder-foot" like Ted Williams, who stole only 24 bases in his entire career. (4) Thorn and Palmer apply a "park adjustment factor" to hitters. This is a complex calculation and I remain to be convinced that its application to individuals always produces good results. And (5) in Wagner's day about 30 percent of total "offense" consisted of unearned runs; in recent times only 10 percent of all runs are unearned. In calculating a player's run production superiority above the average hitter, does the LWTS formula account for a differing ratio of earned to unearned runs? I'm not sure.

But one thing is sure as the best present measurements can make it— the Babe had baseball's greatest offensive year.

Hall-of-Fame Teams: A Study in Paradox

JEREMY GILLER AND HENRY BERMAN

♦ ♦ ♦

Although much is written about Hall-of-Fame players, little is written about the teams they have played on together. Fans who know the answer to questions like, "Which teams have won (or lost) the most games?" or "Which teams have hit the most home runs?" don't know which teams had the most Hall-of-Fame players and how well those teams did. This article will answer these questions and discuss some of the interesting teams that we studied in the process of doing this analysis. It also will show that, with extraordinarily few exceptions, the teams with the most future Hall of Famers were not successful teams. They were rarely championship teams and seldom even won pennants; a number finished in the second division.

We gathered our data by studying all National and American League teams from 1901 to the present; although a case can be made for including teams before 1901, we felt we had more consistency by restricting our study to the "modern baseball era." The last teams with Hall of Famers through 1988 were the 1983 Red Sox (Carl Yastrzemski) and Reds (Johnny Bench), preceded by the 1982 Pirates (Willie Stargell), the 1980 Giants (Willie McCovey), and the 1979 Yankees (Catfish Hunter). Hall of Famers who played after 1969 were so few that we ended our study that year, although at the end of the article we will look at some of the great teams of the 1970s to see how many future Hall of Famers they may have had.

Seventy-eight times a team has had five Hall of Famers for at least part of the season. Four of these had eight such players: the 1930–1933 Yankees. A look at these four teams demonstrates two points. The first, not surprisingly, is the Hall's preponderance of players from the late 1920s and early 1930s, presumably because of that era's inflated batting averages. The other, very surprisingly, is the lack of direct correlation between having many Hall of Famers and outstanding success. Although 1930–1933 fall within the Yankee dynasty years (1921–1964), the Yanks won only one pennant during those years (1932). Their world championship teams of 1936 through 1939, in contrast, had "only" five Hall of Famers.

Seven teams had seven Hall of Famers: the 1927 and 1929 Giants, the 1933 Cardinals, the 1934 Pirates, the 1927 and 1928 Athletics, and the 1928 Yankees. The two principles mentioned above apply. All of these teams are in that same era, and the Giants in particular show a pattern they continued into the 1960s of having a large number of Hall of Famers with little to show for it.

Of the sixteen teams with six Hall of Famers, all but two—the 1912 Athletics and the 1956 Dodgers—played from 1923 to 1934. True to form, those Athletics did not win the pennant, and the 1956 Dodgers, although pennant-winners, did not win the World Series; it was their predecessors in 1955, with five Hall of Famers, who had broken the Dodger drought.

If we need further evidence of these patterns, we need look no further than the Reds of 1932–1935. Each of these teams had four Hall of Famers. Yet in the first three of those years the Reds finished last, and in 1935 they finally escaped the cellar to reach sixth place. Indeed, except for the Black Sox's opponents, the only Cincinnati team to win the World Series in the era under consideration was the 1940 Reds, with only one Hall of Famer. To understand how unusual that is, consider that only two other teams (excluding the 1943–1945 wartime championship teams) ever won the World Series with only one Hall of Famer: the 1960 Pirates (which will no longer be the case once Bill Mazeroski is awarded his rightful place in Cooperstown) and the 1906 White Sox—the famous "Hitless Wonders."

Overall, of the forty National League teams with five or more Hall of Famers, fifteen won pennants, and five of those won the World Series. The American League teams were a bit more successful: of 38 such teams, 13 won pennants, and 10 of those won the World Series. The latter in large part owed to the success of those 1936–1939 Yankees. To learn more about these teams, and about their relative lack of success despite their superstars, we did a more detailed study of the teams.

We originally decided that to construct the data base for our more thorough analysis, we would define a "Hall-of-Fame team" as one with four or more Hall of Famers. That left us with the heavy bias toward the 1920s and 1930s that we have discussed.

Number of "Hall-of-Fame teams"

Decade	National League	American League
1901–09	9	6
1910–19	7	10
1920–29	27	24
1930–39	34	24
1940–49	7	9
1950–59	10	11
1960–69	2	0

Rather than assume that the players were actually that much better from 1920 to 1939, we decided that it made more sense for us to adjust our criterion to reflect the obvious bias that has been shown to the players of that era, when a .300 hitter was only an average player. To do that, we looked at how our data would come out if we kept the same criterion for "Hall-of-Fame teams" of 1920–1939, but made the criterion for before and after those years three or more Hall of Famers. This made our table look like this:

Number of "Hall-of-Fame teams" (adjusted)

Decade	National League	American League
1901–09	20	23
1910–19	21	24
1920–29	27	24
1930–39	34	24
1940–49	23	15
1950–59	19	20
1960–69	22	10

This adjustment gives us a reasonably equal distribution of "Hall-of-Fame teams" by decade, which is consistent with our intuitive sense that there should be about the same number of Hall of Famers in one decade as another. From here on, we will use this as our data base, since it corrects for the bias toward the two "hitting decades."

Top "Hall-of-Fame teams" by Decade

To study further this phenomenon of "Hall-of-Fame teams" not being as successful as we had expected, we developed a list of the top Hall-of-Fame teams of each decade. Since a number of future Hall of Famers who played in the 1960s have yet to be voted into the Hall, we ended this study in 1959. The list looks like this:

Decade	National League	American League
1900	1904 Giants (5)*	1907–08 Athletics (5)
1910	1917 Phillies (5)	1912 Athletics (6)
1920	1927, 1929 Giants (7)	1927–28 Athletics 1928 Yankees**(7)
1930	1933 Cardinals 1934 Pirates (7)	1930, '31, '32**, '33 Yankees (8)
1940	1948 Dodgers (5)	1940–41 Red Sox 1949 Indians (5)
1950	1956 Dodgers (6)*	Nine Yankee teams 1950, 1955 Indians (4)

* pennant winner only   ** world champion

Not counting the cluster of Yankee teams from 1950 to 1959, there are twenty-three teams on this list. Of those, only the 1928 and 1932 Yankees were world champions; the 1956 Dodgers were pennant winners and World Series losers, and the 1904 Giants were pennant winners who refused to play in a World Series. Let's look in more detail at some of these unsuccessful "Hall-of-Fame teams."

1906–1914 Athletics

Player	'06	'07	'08	'09	'10	'11	'12	'13	'14
Bender	y	y	y	y	y	y	y	y	y
Plank	y	y	y	y	y	y	y	y	y
E. Collins	y	y	y	y	y	y	y	y	y
Waddell	y	y	n	n	n	n	n	n	n
J. Collins	n	y	y	n	n	n	n	n	n
Baker	n	n	y	y	y	y	y	y	y
Coveleski	n	n	n	n	n	n	y	n	n
Pennock	n	n	n	n	n	n	y	y	y
Total	4	5	5	4	4	4	6	5	5
Standings	**4th**	**2nd**	**6th**	**2nd**	**1st**	**1st**	**3rd**	**1st**	**1st**

y = yes (played on team that year); n = no

A closer look at the players' stats shows that Pennock and Coveleski both broke in with the Athletics, contributing little to the 1912–1914 teams but much to their subsequent teams. Waddell won 19 games in

1907, but was sold to the Browns in February of 1908; he won 19 again in 1908, but was out of baseball two years later. Jimmy Collins joined the Athletics at the end of his career, contributing little in 1908. Baker was a rookie with 31 at bats in 1908; once he got going, in 1909, and in concert with the nucleus of Bender, Plank, and Eddie Collins, the Athletics finished first four times, second once, and third once in six years. The next teams we will examine, however, show a much different pattern:

1923–1932 Giants

Player	'23	'24	'25	'26	'27	'28	'29	'30	'31	'32
Bancroft	y	n	n	n	n	n	n	y	n	n
Kelly	y	y	y	n	n	n	n	n	n	n
Youngs	y	y	y	y	n	n	n	n	n	n
Frisch	y	y	y	y	n	n	n	n	n	n
Jackson	y	y	y	y	y	y	y	y	y	y
Terry	y	y	y	y	y	y	y	y	y	y
Lindstrom	n	y	y	y	y	y	y	y	y	y
Ott	n	n	n	y	y	y	y	y	y	y
Grimes	n	n	n	n	y	n	n	n	n	n
Hornsby	n	n	n	n	y	n	n	n	n	n
Roush	n	n	n	n	y	y	y	n	n	n
Hubbell	n	n	n	n	n	y	y	y	y	y
Schalk	n	n	n	n	n	n	y	n	n	n
Hoyt	n	n	n	n	n	n	n	n	n	y
Total	6	6	6	6	7	6	7	6	5	6
Standings	**1st**	**1st**	**2nd**	**5th**	**3rd**	**2nd**	**3rd**	**3rd**	**2nd**	**6th**

Although the Giants won the pennant the first two of these years, they did not win the World Series, which they had won in 1921 and

The 1924 Giants infield: George Kelly, Frankie Frisch, Travis Jackson, Heinie Groh

1922 with fewer Hall of Famers. After that there were no more pennants until 1933, when they were down to four Hall of Famers (Jackson, Terry, Ott, and Hubbell). Although several of the players the Giants had added to this nucleus were winding down their careers—Bancroft, Schalk, Hoyt—two, Grimes and Hornsby, clearly were not.

Hornsby, after hitting .361 with 26 home runs, 133 runs scored, and 125 RBIs in his year with the Giants (1927), was traded to the Braves for Shanty Hogan and Jimmy Welsh. Both Hogan and Welsh were .300 hitters, but in an era when that was commonplace; together the next year they drove in 125 runs and scored the same number in 887 at bats. Hornsby, in contrast, hit .387 in 1928 and .380 in 1929 for the Cubs, with 39 HRs, 149 RBIs, and 156 runs scored. Grimes, after winning 19 games for the Giants in 1927, was traded to the Pirates for Vic Aldridge, a pitcher the same age who had won 15 games in 1927. Aldridge won four games in 1928 (ERA 4.83), while Grimes won 25 games for the Pirates with an ERA of 2.99.

This was just the first group of unsuccessful "Hall-of-Fame teams" that the Giants produced. The Giants of 1943 and those of 1964 and 1965 also had many Hall of Famers with no pennants. The 1943 Giants still had Hubbell and had added Johnny Mize, Joe Medwick, and Ernie Lombardi but finished last. Poor Lombardi: he was a member of those 1932–1934 Reds teams with four Hall of Famers that finished last three consecutive years. (On the other hand, in a nice touch of poetic justice, he was the only Hall of Famer on the 1940 Reds.) And the Giants of 1964–1965, by now in San Francisco, added first Duke Snider and then Warren Spahn to their Hall-of-Fame triumvirate (1960–1972) of Willie Mays, Willie McCovey, and Juan Marichal, only to finish fourth and second.

1925–1932 Athletics

Player	'25	'26	'27	'28	'29	'30	'31	'32
Simmons	y	y	y	y	y	y	y	y
Foxx	y	y	y	y	y	y	y	y
Cochrane	y	y	y	y	y	y	y	y
Grove	y	y	y	y	y	y	y	y
Cobb	n	n	y	y	n	n	n	n
E. Collins	n	n	y	y	y	y	n	n
Wheat	n	n	y	n	n	n	n	n
Speaker	n	n	n	y	n	n	n	n
Hoyt	n	n	n	n	n	n	y	n
Total	4	4	7	7	5	5	5	4
Standings	**2nd**	**3rd**	**2nd**	**2nd**	**1st**	**1st**	**1st**	**2nd**

Although the Athletics were a very successful team through these years, their only pennants came after their complement of Hall of Famers had been reduced from seven to five. Cobb, forty when he joined the team in 1927, hit .357 with 104 runs scored and 93 RBIs; his last year in baseball, 1928, he kept his average up, at .323, but his production fell to 54 runs and 40 RBIs. Wheat in 1927 and Speaker in 1928 finished their careers with the A's, contributing little. Hoyt, on the other hand, won 10 games in half a season for the 1931 A's and went on pitching reasonably productively for another half a decade, for three other teams.

1926–1934 Yankees

Player	'26	'27	'28	'29	'30	'31	'32	'33	'34
Combs	y	y	y	y	y	y	y	y	y
Gehrig	y	y	y	y	y	y	y	y	y
Hoyt	y	y	y	y	y	n	n	n	n
Pennock	y	y	y	y	y	y	y	y	n
Ruth	y	y	y	y	y	y	y	y	n
Coveleski	n	n	y	n	n	n	n	n	n
Dickey	n	n	y	y	y	y	y	y	y
Gomez	n	n	n	n	y	y	y	y	y
Ruffing	n	n	n	n	y	y	y	y	y
Sewell	n	n	n	n	n	y	y	y	n
Grimes	n	n	n	n	n	n	n	n	y
Total	5	5	7	6	8	8	8	8	6
Standings	**1st**	**1st**	**1st**	**2nd**	**3rd**	**2nd**	**1st**	**2nd**	**2nd**

The Yankees were certainly a strong team these years, but for the most part these were not their glory years. And, in particular, the "all-time Hall-of-Fame teams," with eight such stars, won only one pennant in the four years from 1930 to 1933. Admittedly, Gomez pitched only 60 innings in his rookie year, but he won 21 in 1931. Sewell was winding down his career, but he scored 102, 95, and 87 runs in each of his years with the Yankees to make a reasonable contribution. It almost seems as if there is a limit to how many Hall of Famers can be on a given team if it is to be successful. The 1936–1939 Yankees, winning four consecutive world championships while losing a total of three World Series games, had gotten down to a streamlined five: Gehrig, Dickey, Gomez, Ruffing, and DiMaggio.

1926–1934 Cardinals

Player	'26	'27	'28	'29	'30	'31	'32	'33
Haines	y	y	y	y	y	y	y	y
Bottomley	y	y	y	y	y	y	y	n

1926–1934 Cardinals (cont.)

Player	'26	'27	'28	'29	'30	'31	'32	'33
Hafey	y	y	y	y	y	y	n	n
Alexander	y	y	y	y	n	n	n	n
Hornsby	y	n	n	n	n	n	n	y
Frisch	n	y	y	y	y	y	y	y
Maranville	n	y	y	n	n	n	n	n
Dean	n	n	n	n	y	n	y	y
Grimes	n	n	n	n	y	y	n	y
Medwick	n	n	n	n	n	n	y	y
Vance	n	n	n	n	n	n	n	y
Total	5	6	6	5	6	5	5	7
Standings	**1st**	**2nd**	**1st**	**4th**	**1st**	**1st**	**7th**	**5th**

These Cardinals were another successful team, but not in 1932 or 1933, even though the latter year found NL-record-tying seven Hall of Famers. Hornsby played only 46 games for the Cards in 1933, but hit .325; Vance, winding down his career, pitched 99 innings, and was 6–2 that year. Grimes pitched in just four games that year and four more the next. In truth, only Dean, Frisch, and Medwick were at the Hall-of-Fame level in 1933, so the figures in a sense misrepresent how many Hall-of-Famer performances were delivered. Nevertheless, the pattern continues. Teams do not have their most successful results with the most Hall of Famers.

1933–1939 Pirates

Player	'33	'34	'35	'36	'37	'38	'39
Hoyt	y	y	y	y	y	n	n
Lindstrom	y	y	n	n	n	n	n
Traynor	y	y	y	n	y	n	n
L. Waner	y	y	y	y	y	y	y
P. Waner	y	y	y	y	y	y	y
Vaughan	y	y	y	y	y	y	y
Grimes	n	y	n	n	n	n	n
Manush	n	n	n	n	n	y	y
Klein	n	n	n	n	n	n	y
Total	6	7	5	4	5	4	5
Standings	**2nd**	**5th**	**4th**	**4th**	**3rd**	**2nd**	**6th**

The Pirates of this era were not a very successful team. Adding Lindstrom, a marginal Hall of Famer, in 1933, Grimes in 1934, and Manush in 1938, did nothing for the team. The latter two retired after playing a handful of games, while Lindstrom contributed two ordinary years before winding down with the Cubs (1935) and the Dodgers (1936).

The only reason Klein is in the Hall of Fame is his outstanding seasons from 1929 through 1933. During those five years, he averaged 224 hits, 46 doubles, 36 home runs, 132 runs scored and 139 RBIs while hitting between .337 and .386 and slugging between .584 and .687. The rest of his career, which dragged on to 1944, was only average; the 1939 Pirates had him for 85 games during a season in which he hit 12 home runs with 56 RBIs.

The other interesting observation to emerge from studying these teams is that Lloyd Waner was no Hall-of-Fame player. After an excellent first three years (1927–1929) he never again scored 100 runs or drove in more than 57. During his career, which looks more like an infielder's, the outfielder had only 28 home runs. And he didn't make up for it anywhere else offensively—he stole only 67 bases lifetime and never walked more than 40 times in a season. His outstanding achievement was that he rarely struck out: 173 times in 7772 at bats! And he had a remarkable statistic his rookie year—he scored 133 runs, while driving in only 27. It is hard to imagine that that "feat" has ever been duplicated.

1936–1942 Red Sox

Player	'36	'37	'38	'39	'40	'41	'42
Cronin	y	y	y	y	y	y	y
Grove	y	y	y	y	y	y	n
Foxx	y	y	y	y	y	y	y
Ferrell	y	y	n	n	n	n	n
Manush	y	n	n	n	n	n	n
Doerr	n	y	y	y	y	y	y
Williams	n	n	n	y	y	y	y
Total	5	5	4	5	5	5	4
Standings	**6th**	**5th**	**2nd**	**2nd**	**4th**	**2nd**	**2nd**

It is not surprising that one of the franchises that led a decade in nonwinning Hall-of-Fame teams would be the Red Sox, who seem never to have shaken the bad luck that started when they sold Babe Ruth. Admittedly, Lefty Grove was at the end of his glorious career by 1940 and 1941; but in 1939 he went 15–4 and led the league with an ERA of 2.54. Williams was a mere rookie that year, so he hit only .327, with 31 home runs, 131 runs scored, and 145 RBIs! Foxx led the league in homers and slugging percentage that year, while hitting .360; Doerr hit .318 and Cronin .308, with 97 runs and 107 RBIs. Yet the Sox finished second to the Yankees.

We all know that the dominant team in baseball from 1948 to 1956 was the Yankees with seven pennants, six world championships, and an average of 97 wins a year. But which team during those years won one world championship, never winning fewer than 88 games and averaging 94 wins a season? The answer is not the Dodgers, who won only 84 games in 1948, but the Indians, a great team that had the misfortune to compete with the Yankees year after year. From 1951 to 1956, the Indians finished second five times and first once, winning 111 games in 1954.

1948–1956 Indians

Player	'48	'49	'50	'51	'52	'53	'54	'55	'56
Boudreau	y	y	y	n	n	n	n	n	n
Feller	y	y	y	y	y	y	y	y	y
Lemon	y	y	y	y	y	y	y	y	y
Paige	y	y	n	n	n	n	n	n	n
Wynn	n	y	y	y	y	y	y	y	y
Kiner	n	n	n	n	n	n	n	y	n
Total	4	5	4	3	3	3	3	4	3
Standings	**1st**	**3rd**	**4th**	**2nd**	**2nd**	**2nd**	**1st**	**2nd**	**2nd**

Once again we see that the pattern holds. The two pennant-winning teams did not have the most Hall of Famers for the franchise. Admittedly, Kiner joined the team for his last year. However, he was not unproductive: in 321 at bats, he hit 18 home runs, with 56 runs scored, 54 RBIs, and 65 walks. Paige was forty-two (at least) when he joined the Indians and pitched only 155 innings in the two years but was reasonably effective. Boudreau, too, was at the end of his career with productivity dropping sharply after his 1948 MVP season. But the Indians of those years also had Larry Doby, who drove in over 100 runs four times between 1950 and 1954; Mike Garcia, who won 79 games from 1951 to 1954; Al Rosen, who drove in over 100 runs every year from 1950 through 1954; and Bobby Avila, who averaged .307 during those five years. The same problem plagued these Indians as the 1936–1942 Red Sox and 1925–1932 Athletics: the New York Yankees.

1948–1958 Dodgers

Player	'48	'49	'50	'51	'52	'53	'54	'55	'56	'57	'58
Reese	y	y	y	y	y	y	y	y	y	y	y
Robinson	y	y	y	y	y	y	y	y	y	n	n
Snider	y	y	y	y	y	y	y	y	y	y	y
Campanella	y	y	y	y	y	y	y	y	y	y	n
Vaughan	y	n	n	n	n	n	n	n	n	n	n
Koufax	n	n	n	n	n	n	n	y	y	y	y

1948–1958 Dodgers (cont.)

Player	'48	'49	'50	'51	'52	'53	'54	'55	'56	'57	'58
Drysdale	n	n	n	n	n	n	n	n	y	y	y
Total	5	4	4	4	4	4	4	5	6	5	4
Standings	**3rd**	**1st**	**2nd**	**2nd**	**1st**	**1st**	**2nd**	**1st**	**1st**	**3rd**	**7th**

With the exception of Vaughan, finishing his career in 1948, of these exceptional teams we find no has-beens coming on to finish their careers. Campanella and Snider made peripheral contributions in 1948, but for the next eight years, until Robinson retired, the Dodgers had a core of four Hall of Famers playing together during their prime years. Koufax pitched only 41, 58, and 104 innings in 1955, 1956, and 1957, and Drysdale only 99 innings in 1956. Don Newcombe, however, was a Hall-of-Fame-caliber pitcher from 1949 through 1956, winning 112 and losing 48, while missing 1952 and 1953 in the military. But even here, with a team that won five pennants and lost the 1950 and 1951 pennants on the last day of the season, their only team with six Hall of Famers was not their only championship team, in 1955, but rather their 1956 team.

The Yankees here follow a similar pattern to the Dodgers with whom they are forever twinned for this era (the two were Series opponents six times from 1947 to 1956, the Dodgers winning only in 1955). Berra, Ford, and Mantle played together for more than a decade—through 1963. Hall of Famers Mize, then Slaughter, played productively in supportive roles to round out the team. Why were these Yankees able consistently to turn back the challenges of the Indians in their own league and the Dodgers come October? Possibly it was because the Indians' Hall-of-Fame teams consisted almost exclusively of pitchers and the Dodgers almost exclusively of hitters. Perhaps Whitey Ford, with his record of 207–83 from 1953 to 1964, was the real key to the extraordinary success of these teams. Only the Yankees had Hall-of-Fame hitting, pitching, and fielding those years, and only these Yankees have been able to break out of the pattern of having their "Hall of Fame teams" be losers.

1949–1959 Yankees

Player	'49	'50	'51	'52	'53	'54	'55	'56	'57	'58	'59
DiMaggio	y	y	y	n	n	n	n	n	n	n	n
Berra	y	y	y	y	y	y	y	y	y	y	y
Mize	y	y	y	y	y	n	n	n	n	n	n
Ford	n	y	n	n	y	y	y	y	y	y	y
Mantle	n	n	y	y	y	y	y	y	y	y	y
Slaughter	n	n	n	n	n	y	y	y	y	y	y
Total	3	4	4	3	4	4	4	4	4	4	4
Standings	**1st**	**1st**	**1st**	**1st**	**1st**	**2nd**	**1st**	**1st**	**1st**	**1st**	**3rd**

There is one additional pattern that can be discerned by a careful examination of the most successful "Hall-of-Fame teams"—the presence of a Hall-of-Fame catcher. Using Bill James's rankings in his updated *Historical Baseball Abstract,* the top catchers in baseball history are Yogi Berra, Johnny Bench, Mickey Cochrane, Gary Carter, Carlton Fisk, Gabby Hartnett, Bill Dickey, Ernie Lombardi, and Roy Campanella. With the exception of Carter and Fisk, both of whom are still active, only Hartnett does not figure prominently on Hall-of-Fame teams. Bench, we will see, starred on the team that is apt to end up with the most Hall of Famers in the 1970s—the Big Red Machine. And one of the strongest teams of the 1980s, the New York Mets, did not win a pennant until they added Carter.

The 1960s and 1970s

It is too soon to come to conclusions about these decades—too many Hall of Famers are yet to be voted in. But we have already discussed the 1964 and 1965 Giants, losers despite four Hall of Famers. The election of Ferguson Jenkins to Cooperstown makes the 1970 Cubs a four-Hall-of-Famer team (with Banks, Williams, and Wilhelm). If Ron Santo is added (.277 BA, .464 SA, 342 HRs, 1331 RBIs), that would make five for this second-place team. On the other hand, another team that could have five—the 1967 Cardinals—were world champions. That team had Lou Brock and Bob Gibson, already in the Hall; Steve Carlton, a shoo-in once eligible; Orlando Cepeda, with 379 home runs, a .297 BA, and a .499 SA; plus Roger Maris. Of course if Cepeda makes the Hall, he will join his 1964 and 1965 Giant teammates. With Gaylord Perry, that gives those Giant teams that finished fourth and second six Hall of Famers.

It does appear that the 1970s may break the pattern of the best teams not having the most Hall of Famers. That decade was dominated by two teams: the Oakland A's in the American League, who won five straight divisional championships from 1971 to 1975 and three consecutive world championships from 1972 to 1974; and the Cincinnati Reds in the National League, who won six divisional championships, four pennants, and two world championships. Let's see how these teams might chart out:

1970–1976 A's

Player	'70	'71	'72	'73	'74	'75	'76
Hunter	y	y	y	y	y	n	n
Jackson	y	y	y	y	y	y	n
Fingers	y	y	y	y	y	y	y

1970–1976 A's (cont.)

Player	'70	'71	'72	'73	'74	'75	'76
Williams	n	n	n	n	n	y	y
McCovey	n	n	n	n	n	n	y
Campaneris	y	y	y	y	y	y	y
Total	4	4	4	4	4	4	4
Standings	**2nd**	**1st**	**1st**	**1st**	**1st**	**1st**	**2nd**

Hunter, Williams, McCovey, and Fingers are already in the Hall; Jackson will probably be admitted. Campaneris may well be elected; he played shortstop on the best team of the early '70s, had 2249 hits, and stole 649 bases while leading the league six times. In addition, he was remarkably consistent, getting between 135 and 177 hits every year from 1965 to 1977.

1970–1979 Reds

Player	'70	'71	'72	'73	'74	'75	'76	'77	'78	'79
Rose	y	y	y	y	y	y	y	y	y	n
Bench	y	y	y	y	y	y	y	y	y	y
Perez	y	y	y	y	y	y	y	n	n	n
Concepcion	y	y	y	y	y	y	y	y	y	y
Morgan	n	n	y	y	y	y	y	y	y	y
Seaver	n	n	n	n	n	n	n	y	y	y
Total	4	4	5	5	5	5	5	5	5	5
Standings	**1st**	**4th**	**1st**	**1st**	**2nd**	**1st**	**1st**	**2nd**	**2nd**	**1st**

Morgan and Bench are in the Hall. Rose may eventually be allowed in the door; Perez is worthy. Concepcion seems likely to be elected for similar reasons to Campaneris: shortstop on the best team of the decade, .268 hitter with 2326 hits, between 1973 and 1979 hit between .271 and .301 each year and stole between 19 and 41 bases. These teams are reminiscent of the Dodgers of the 1950s—Hall of Famers galore in the field but none on the mound until Seaver joined the team just as Perez left.

The 1980s

The team of the '80s with the most potential Hall of Famers would seem to be the New York Mets. According to *The 1988 Bill James Baseball Abstract,* both Carter and Hernandez could be elected on the basis of their career credentials. Gooden and Strawberry still have a chance, though they both had off years in 1992.

Why do so few teams with many Hall of Famers win the world championship or even the pennant? There could be many explanations but the most likely is a lack of team chemistry. A team with six or seven great stars could also be a team with six or seven great egos—perhaps the individuals can't work with each other for the benefit of the team. (This phenomenon does not seem unique to baseball, because "dream backfields" of Earl Campbell and George Rogers, or Tony Dorsett and Herschel Walker, or "Hall-of-Fame" combinations of Wilt Chamberlain, Elgin Baylor, and Jerry West, or Ralph Sampson and Akeem Olajuwon have also proved not to work out.) Or perhaps the rest of the players wait around for the superstars to carry the team. Or some of the Famers are aborning or over the hill. Without recounting every case history, it's safe to say that the splendid work old Johnny Mize did for the 1949–1953 Yankees and Enos Slaughter did for the 1954–1959 Yankees were the exceptions rather than rule.

In any case, we feel the facts clearly speak for themselves: maximizing the number of future Hall of Famers on a team is not the key to success. If any specific strategies can be learned from our study, they are the following: do not add a future Hall of Famer at the end of his career, and find yourself a catcher with great potential. The Mets of the 1980s did do the latter and to date have not made the mistake of doing the former.

Little-Known Facts

Horseshoe Brown, former St. Louis shortstop, played seventeen consecutive games in 1909 while suffering from a severe headache. . . . Wally Norton, Boston third baseman, slipped and fell three times in one inning without hurting himself. . . . A baseball, even though it appears round, is not a true geometric sphere.

Conrad Horn

WHO WOULD HAVE WON THIS "BEST PITCHER" TROPHY IN THE YEARS BEFORE IT WAS GIVEN?

Retroactive Cy Young Awards

LYLE SPATZ

♦ ♦ ♦

On the morning of November 29, 1956, the sports section of *The New York Times*, otherwise almost completely devoted to the Melbourne Olympics, carried a baseball story. Buried on page five, the story announced that the Cleveland Indians had selected Kerby Farrell as their new manager. In the notes that followed, it was revealed that the Baseball Writers Association of America had named Brooklyn's Don Newcombe the Major League Pitcher of the Year. It was the first year for the citation, officially called the Cy Young Award in honor of the legendary pitcher. At that time pitchers from both leagues competed against one another, with only one award given. This practice continued through 1966. For the 1967 season an award was given to the best pitcher in each league. Despite suggestions that the honor be split further, between starters and relievers, that is still the way it's done. Since the award's inception, the prestige it bestows and the interest it generates have come to approach that of the Most Valuable Player awards. In recognition of this interest, SABR conducted a survey to determine pre-1967 winners of the Cy Young Award. Retroactive winners were selected in the National League for the years 1900–1955, 1958, 1959, and 1961; and in the American League for 1901–1957, 1960, 1962, 1963, 1965, and 1966. The selections for the years 1956–66 were for a Cy Young Award winner in the league not represented by the BBWAA winner. The voting was done on the BBWAA's 5-3-1 point basis for first, second, and third places. The winners are presented in the accompanying table. It should come as no surprise that the pitchers with the most awards are those generally regarded as the game's all-time best. Christy Mathewson with seven and Pete Alexander and Warren Spahn (including one from the BBWAA) with six each had the most in the NL, while Lefty Grove and Walter Johnson each had six to lead the AL. Mathewson had two seconds and a third to go with his seven wins, and Johnson had five second-place finishes with his six wins.

In 1912, Johnson finished second despite a won-lost record of 32–12, a league-leading earned run average of 1.39, and a 16-game winning streak. Up in Boston, however, Smokey Joe Wood was compiling his own 16-game winning streak on

Bob Feller

his way to a 34–5 record and the Cy Young Award. In 1916, Johnson again finished second to a young Red Sox ace, Babe Ruth. Grove won six consecutive awards between 1928 and 1933 after finishing fourth in 1927. Following an injury-plagued year in 1934, his first with the Red Sox, he bounced back to finish second in 1935 and 1936 and fourth in 1937, 1938, and 1939. The most consecutive awards won in the National League were four, by Mathewson in 1907–1910 and Sandy Koufax in 1963–1966 (three from the BBWAA, one from SABR). Those who won three years in a row include Cy Young himself (1901–1903), Walter Johnson (1913–1915), Pete Alexander (1915–1917), Bob Feller (1939–1941), and Hal Newhouser (1944–1946).

The relationship between Feller and Newhouser is an intriguing one. Feller was baseball's premier pitcher—the winner of three straight Cy Young Awards—when World War II interrupted his career. The four years that he lost could well have yielded up to 100 wins in addition to his lifetime total of 266. Four more years could conceivably have resulted in four more Cy Young Awards (1942–1945), giving him seven straight.

In 1944 and 1945 Newhouser took Feller's place as baseball's dominant pitcher. He went 29–9 in 1944 and 25–9 in 1945. His earned run average was 2.22 in 1944 and a league-best 1.84 in the pennant-winning 1945 season. He not only won the Cy Young Award those two years but the American League's Most Valuable Player Award. Still, there were those who downgraded Newhouser's accomplishments because they had come against "wartime" players. The critics awaited 1946 to see if he could continue to be as successful pitching against DiMaggio, Williams, and the other returning veterans.

Feller too had something to prove: that he could come back from his long naval service and regain his prewar form. Both men succeeded. Newhouser led the league in wins for a third straight year (26–9) and again in ERA (1.94). Feller tied Newhouser for most wins with 26 (losing 15) and had an ERA of 2.18. In an extremely close vote Newhouser edged Feller to win his third straight Cy Young Award. Dave Ferriss, who went 25–6 for the pennant-winning Red Sox, finished a distant third. The All-Star game played at Fenway Park that year is best remembered for Ted Williams leading the American Leaguers to a crushing 12–0 victory. But let's not forget that Feller, Newhouser, and Jack Kramer of the Browns shut out the National Leaguers on just three singles. The confrontations between Feller and Newhouser were among the most anticipated and exciting pitching match-ups in history.

In many years one pitcher clearly was the best in his league and the overwhelming choice of the voters. For many other years, however, the "best pitcher" was far from obvious. The five closest races were: Al Orth over Addie Joss (AL 1902), Christy Mathewson over Mordecai Brown (NL 1909), Larry Benton over Dazzy Vance (NL 1928), Tex Hughson over Ernie Bonham (AL 1942), and Hank Wyse over Charley (Red) Barrett (NL 1945). Barrett, who started the '45 season with Boston, had a record of 2–3 when he was traded to the Cardinals. He went 21–9 to finish with a league-leading 23 wins. If he had won the Cy Young that year, he would have been the only winner to have pitched for two teams in his award season. Brown's close loss to Matty in 1909 was the second of three consecutive years in which he finished runner-up to his arch rival. No one else had three consecutive second-place finishes, although Carl Hubbell finished second on four separate occasions (1932, 1934, 1935, and 1937), the most in the National League.

Other close years: Bill Donovan over Noodles Hahn (NL 1901), Pat Malone over Dazzy Vance (NL 1930), Johnny Antonelli over Robin Roberts (NL 1954), and Jim Perry over Chuck Estrada (AL 1960). In 1965 Jim Grant barely defeated AL rivals Sam McDowell and Mel Stottlemyre in the closest three-man race ever.

Cy Young Winners 1900–1966

National League		American League	
1900 Joe McGinnity	BKN	1900 ———	—
1901 Bill Donovan	BKN	1901 Cy Young	BOS
1902 Jack Chesbro	PIT	1902 Cy Young	BOS
1903 Christy Mathewson	NY	1903 Cy Young	BOS
1904 Joe McGinnity	NY	1904 Jack Chesbro	NY
1905 Christy Mathewson	NY	1905 Rube Waddell	PHI
1906 Mordecai Brown	CHI	1906 Al Orth	NY
1907 Christy Mathewson	NY	1907 Addie Joss	CLE
1908 Christy Mathewson	NY	1908 Ed Walsh	CHI
1909 Christy Mathewson	NY	1909 George Mullin	DET
1910 Christy Mathewson	NY	1910 Jack Coombs	PHI
1911 Pete Alexander	PHI	1911 Walter Johnson	WAS
1912 Rube Marquard	NY	1912 Joe Wood	BOS
1913 Christy Mathewson	NY	1913 Walter Johnson	WAS
1914 Bill James	BOS	1914 Walter Johnson	WAS
1915 Pete Alexander	PHI	1915 Walter Johnson	WAS
1916 Pete Alexander	PHI	1916 Babe Ruth	BOS
1917 Pete Alexander	PHI	1917 Ed Cicotte	CHI
1918 Jim Vaughn	CHI	1918 Walter Johnson	WAS
1919 Jesse Barnes	NY	1919 Ed Cicotte	CHI
1920 Pete Alexander	CHI	1920 Jim Bagby	CLE
1921 Burleigh Grimes	BKL	1921 Red Faber	CHI
1922 Eppa Rixey	CIN	1922 Eddie Rommel	PHI
1923 Dolf Luque	CIN	1923 George Uhle	CLE
1924 Dazzy Vance	BKN	1924 Walter Johnson	WAS
1925 Dazzy Vance	BKN	1925 Stan Coveleski	WAS
1926 Ray Kremer	PIT	1926 George Uhle	CLE
1927 Jesse Haines	STL	1927 Waite Hoyt	NY
1928 Larry Benton	NY	1928 Lefty Grove	PHI
1929 Pat Malone	CHI	1929 Lefty Grove	PHI
1930 Pat Malone	CHI	1930 Lefty Grove	PHI
1931 Bill Walker	NY	1931 Lefty Grove	PHI
1932 Lon Warneke	CHI	1932 Lefty Grove	PHI
1933 Carl Hubbell	NY	1933 Lefty Grove	PHI
1934 Dizzy Dean	STL	1934 Lefty Gomez	NY
1935 Dizzy Dean	STL	1935 Wes Ferrell	BOS
1936 Carl Hubbell	NY	1936 Tommy Bridges	DET
1937 Jim Turner	BOS	1937 Lefty Gomez	NY
1938 Bill Lee	CHI	1938 Red Ruffing	NY

Cy Young Winners 1900–1966 (cont.)

National League			American League		
1939	Bucky Walters	CIN	1939	Bob Feller	CLE
1940	Bucky Walters	CIN	1940	Bob Feller	CLE
1941	Whit Wyatt	BKN	1941	Bob Feller	CLE
1942	Mort Cooper	STL	1942	Tex Hughson	BOS
1943	Mort Cooper	STL	1943	Spud Chandler	NY
1944	Bucky Walters	CIN	1944	Hal Newhouser	DET
1945	Hank Wyse	CHI	1945	Hal Newhouser	DET
1946	Howie Pollett	STL	1946	Hal Newhouser	DET
1947	Ewell Blackwell	CIN	1947	Bob Feller	CLE
1948	Johnny Sain	BOS	1948	Gene Bearden	CLE
1949	Warren Spahn	BOS	1949	Mel Parnell	BOS
1950	Jim Konstanty	PHI	1950	Bob Lemon	CLE
1951	Sal Maglie	NY	1951	Ed Lopat	NY
1952	Robin Roberts	PHI	1952	Bobby Shantz	PHI
1953	Warren Spahn	MIL	1953	Bob Porterfield	WAS
1954	Johnny Antonelli	NY	1954	Bob Lemon	CLE
1955	Robin Roberts	PHI	1955	Whitey Ford	NY
1956	Don Newcombe*	BKN	1956	Herb Score	CLE
1957	Warren Spahn*	MIL	1957	Jim Bunning	DET
1958	Warren Spahn	MIL	1958	Bob Turley*	NY
1959	Sam Jones	SF	1959	Early Wynn*	CHI
1960	Vern Law*	PIT	1960	Jim Perry	CLE
1961	Warren Spahn	MIL	1961	Whitey Ford*	NY
1962	Don Drysdale*	LA	1962	Ralph Terry	NY
1963	Sandy Koufax*	LA	1963	Whitey Ford	NY
1964	Sandy Koufax	LA	1964	Dean Chance*	LA
1965	Sandy Koufax*	LA	1965	Jim Grant	MIN
1966	Sandy Koufax*	LA	1966	Jim Kaat	MIN

* Choice of BBWAA

Games won was the category most connected to winning the award. Forty-eight of the sixty NL winners and fifty-three of the sixty-two AL winners either led or tied for most wins in their league. In ERA only twenty-two of sixty NL and seventeen of sixty-two AL leaders won the award. This is somewhat surprising, since ERA is usually considered a better gauge of performance than games won.

None of the retroactive winners pitched for a team that finished in last place. Three American League winners pitched for seventh-place clubs: Walter Johnson for the 1911 Washington Senators, Red Faber for the 1921 Chicago White Sox, and Ed Rommel for the 1922 Philadelphia Athletics. In the National League Dazzy Vance (for Brooklyn in 1925) and Sandy Koufax (for Los Angeles in 1964) pitched for teams that finished tied for sixth. Twenty-eight National League winners and twenty-six American League winners helped lead their team to pennants.

In twelve of those years both winners came from the pennant-winning team. One conjures up images of the opening World Series game with the best pitcher in each league facing one another. In the retroactive period this has happened only twice: in 1938, when Red Ruffing of the Yankees bested Bill Lee of the Cubs 3–1, and in 1963, when Sandy Koufax of LA defeated Whitey Ford and the Yanks 5–2. Oddly, both of those Series ended in four-game sweeps, with Ruffing and Koufax again beating Lee and Ford in Game Four. The only other Cy Young Series matchup during this period was Game Five of the 1943 Series, when Spud Chandler defeated Mort Cooper 2–0 as the Yankees won the Series four games to one over St. Louis. Recent history has seen Cy Young Award winners facing each other in the World Series on several other occasions. In 1968, Bob Gibson of the Cardinals won the opener and the fourth game over the Tigers and Denny McLain. The following year the Orioles' Mike Cuellar (co-winner with McLain) won Game One over Tom Seaver and the Mets. In Game Four Seaver defeated the Orioles, but Baltimore starter Cuellar was not involved in the decision.

Since the award was established in 1956, only Fernando Valenzuela, in 1981, has won it in his rookie year. SABR's retroactive survey produced three rookie winners: Pete Alexander of the 1911 Phillies, Jim Turner of the 1937 Boston Bees (Braves), and Gene Bearden of the 1948 Indians.

In 1904, three-quarters of a century before Gaylord Perry became the first to win the award in each league, Jack Chesbro had accomplished this feat. He won a record-setting 41 games as a member of the AL New York Highlanders, a team he had joined a year earlier. He had earned his first award in 1902 for the Pittsburgh Pirates.

Detroit's Willie Hernandez won the 1984 Cy Young Award amid much controversy, the usual refrain for a Cy Young relief pitcher. No matter how outstanding a Mike Marshall or Rollie Fingers or Bruce Sutter might be, a significant number of fans and sportswriters oppose giving the award to a reliever. Yet as far back as Doc Crandall of the 1910 New York Giants, pitchers who were primarily or exclusively relievers were included in the retroactive balloting. The importance of the relief pitcher has greatly increased over the last twenty years, but earlier bullpen aces such as Fred Marberry, Joe Page, and Hugh Casey were important members of their teams too. SABR members understood their importance. In 1952 Hoyt Wilhelm of the Giants and Joe Black of Brooklyn, both relievers and rookies, finished second and third behind winner Robin Roberts. Still, the only relief pitcher to win a pre-BBWAA Cy Young Award was Jim Konstanty of the 1950 Phillies, who also won the National League's

Most Valuable Player Award. All of Konstanty's 74 regular-season appearances were in relief. His only start was a 1–0 loss to the Yankees' Vic Raschi in the World Series opener. Konstanty, who was thirty-three in 1950, had made his big league debut in 1944 and continued to pitch until 1956, but he never again approached his 1950 brilliance.

If there is any winner who could be classified as a one-year wonder, however, it would have to be Bill James. Breaking in with the Boston Braves in 1913, he went 6–10. The following year he was 26–7 and helped lead the "Miracle Braves" to the National League pennant. World Series performance doesn't count in the voting, but James pitched a 2-hit shutout in the 1914 Series as the Braves swept the heavily favored Philadelphia Athletics. In the balloting he defeated Pete Alexander and teammate Dick Rudolph. James was never again an effective pitcher. In 1916 he fell off to 5–4, suffered a shoulder injury, pitched one game in 1915, and then was gone.

There are some years worth noting because of the dominance of a particular team's pitching staff. In 1906 Mordecai Brown, Ed Reulbach, and Jack Pfiester of the Cubs finished first, second, and fourth in the voting. The Giants' Mathewson won the following year, but the Cubs had five pitchers in the top seven (Orval Overall, Brown, Carl Lundgren, Pfiester, and Reulbach). The Cubs won pennants in 1906, 1907, and 1918, when Jim Vaughn won the award and teammates George Tyler and Claude Hendrix finished third and fourth. In 1925 Eppa Rixey, Pete Donohue, and Dolf Luque of Cincinnati finished second, third, and fourth behind Dazzy Vance.

The late, lamented St. Louis Browns were the only team never to have a Cy Young Award winner. Second-place finishes by Urban Shocker in 1923 (to George Uhle), and Ned Garver in 1951 (to Ed Lopat) were the best they could do.

Although the 1920 Chicago White Sox were the first team to have four 20-game winners, the Cy Young Award that year went to Jim Bagby, who won 31 for Cleveland. The only other team to have four 20-game winners was the 1971 Baltimore Orioles. The American League's Cy Young winner that year was Vida Blue of the Oakland Athletics.

There were several teams whose pitchers finished one-two in the voting. In 1920 Stan Coveleski was second to Cleveland teammate Jim Bagby; five years later and now pitching for Washington, Coveleski won and Walter Johnson finished second. Some other teammates who finished one-two include: Joe McGinnity and Mathewson of the 1904 Giants, Pat Malone and Charley Root of the 1929 Cubs, Wes Ferrell and

Lefty Grove of the 1935 Red Sox, Bucky Walters and Paul Derringer of the 1939 Reds, and Hal Newhouser and Dizzy Trout of the 1944 Tigers.

In two cases pitchers from the same team took the top three slots. Bob Lemon, Early Wynn, and Mike Garcia finished one-two-three for the Indians' 1954 pennant winners. This was the team that set an American League record for games won (111) and broke a Yankee streak of five straight world championships. In the World Series, however, they were swept by the Giants, who had their own Cy Young winner in Johnny Antonelli. The only other team to capture win, place, and show was the 1905 Philadelphia Athletics, with Rube Waddell, Eddie Plank, and Andy Coakley, finishing first, second, and third. They too were beaten in the World Series by the Giants, four games to one, every game a shutout. The A's Chief Bender pitched one to even the Series after they were blanked by Mathewson in the opener. Mathewson, McGinnity, and Matty again shut out Philadelphia in Games Three, Four, and Five, giving John McGraw his first World Series championship.

Eddie Plank, second that year, had finished third two years earlier. It's interesting that Plank, a Hall of Famer who won 306 games in the American League (and 21 in the 1915 Federal League), was never considered the league's best pitcher. Don Sutton and Phil Niekro are not the only 300-game winners never to have won a Cy Young Award.

Other pitchers who reached the Hall of Fame without having won the award are Plank's Philadelphia teammate Bender, Red Sox and Yankee star Herb Pennock, and longtime White Sox ace Ted Lyons. This in no way detracts from their reputations among the game's all-time best pitchers. It is, however, indicative of how keen the competition for the award is and how much pitchers like Johnson and Grove dominated their respective eras.

Several pitchers who won neither Cy Young Awards nor Hall-of-Fame plaques are also worth mentioning. Consider Pirate great Wilbur Cooper. A lefthander who pitched in the majors for fifteen years, he never played for a pennant winner despite winning 216 games and retiring with a 2.89 ERA. Of all pitchers with more than 3000 innings, only seven have better lifetime ERA's. From 1917 to 1924, Cooper never won fewer than 17 games, and four times won more than 20.

Some others who seem to have slipped through the cracks of fame include Deacon Phillipe, Jess Tannehill, Vic Willis, and Urban Shocker. Perhaps the greatest value of this project is the extent to which it made us look not only at Mathewson, Johnson, and Grove, but at players like Newhouser, Cooper, and Willis.

WHICH KID WAS BEST FROM 1900 TO 1948?

Retroactive Rookie-of-the-Year Awards

LYLE SPATZ

◆ ◆ ◆

The tradition of a Rookie of the Year in the major leagues dates back to 1946. Late that year *The Sporting News* introduced a new award honoring the top freshman performer and chose outfielder Del Ennis of the Philadelphia Phillies as the initial recipient. The following year the Baseball Writers' Association of America also began naming the majors' top rookie. Both the BBWAA and *The Sporting News* picked first baseman Jackie Robinson of the Brooklyn Dodgers in 1947. Two years later TSN and the BBWAA each began choosing the No. 1 rookie in each league. *The Sporting News* split the honor even further starting in 1957 by selecting a rookie player and rookie pitcher for each league.

But, many of us wondered, who were the best rookies in the seasons prior to 1946? Were Walter Johnson in 1907 and Babe Ruth in 1915 the outstanding American League rookies for those years? Did National League greats Paul Waner, Mel Ott, and Dizzy Dean rate as the best first-year men in 1926, 1927, and 1932, respectively? And what about Carl Hubbell, Lefty Grove, Stan Musial, and Ted Williams? Following a conversation several years ago between Marty Appel, then of the Commissioner's office, and SABR founder Bob Davids, it was decided to conduct a poll to determine who the leading rookies were for each league in each pre-1949 season.

Over the course of several years, ballots listing the top several rookies for each year in both leagues were sent to the SABR membership, which responded in a most enthusiastic manner. The winners who were chosen by the collective wisdom of SABR are presented in the accompanying table. The voting was done on a 5-3-1 point basis for first, second, and third places, the same method used in the BBWAA's current selection process. To be considered a rookie, a player could not have had more than 90 official at bats or have pitched more than 45 innings in previous major league seasons. Thus, Joe Jackson, who batted .408 for Cleveland in his first full year, 1911, was not eligible for consideration because he had accumulated 115 at bats in the previous three seasons. The winners have included such Hall of Famers as the aforementioned Ruth, Waner, Dean, and Williams, as well as Christy Mathewson, Rogers Hornsby, Joe DiMaggio, and others. They also have included such relatively obscure players as Glen Liebhardt, Homer Smoot, Tommy Long, and Ed Morris. They have ranged in age from twenty-year-olds like Ruth, Hornsby, Mathewson, and Chief Bender to Joe Berry, who was thirty-nine in his rookie season of 1944.

For many winners their rookie year was the best they experienced in the major leagues. This category would include American League winners Russ Ford, Scott Perry, Hugh Bedient, Homer Summa, Wilcy Moore, and Jake Powell. Some National League winners whose rookie year was their finest were Jack Pfiester, George McQuillan, Larry Cheney, Jim Viox, Hack Miller, Dick Cox, and Cy Blanton.

Although Grover Alexander in 1911 had what is considered to be the best rookie season of any pitcher, his selection by SABR voters was not unanimous. Nor were those of Ruth, Williams, DiMaggio, Hornsby, the Waners, Hal Trosky, or Joe Vosmik. They are among the winners who were chosen on all but a handful of the hundreds of ballots cast. Some races were so close they weren't decided until the last few ballots had been counted. Several examples would be Nap Rucker over Mike Mitchell (NL 1907), Lefty Williams over Jim Bagby (AL 1916), Paul Dean over Curt Davis (NL 1934), Hoot Evers over Bob Dillinger (AL 1946), and Spec Shea over Sam Mele (AL 1947).

It is probably not surprising that pitchers won the award for almost half of the years surveyed—23 in the NL and 22 in the AL. Their dominance was most pronounced in the era of the alleged "dead ball," with hurlers being selected 13 times in the NL and 14 in the AL between 1901 and 1919. Pitchers won the award in both leagues each year during the 1907–1912 period.

By contrast, Billy Sullivan of Boston, the National League winner in 1900, was the only fulltime catcher so honored. Rudy York, the AL winner in 1937, split his defensive duties between catcher and third base. Sullivan's win was accomplished against a small and mediocre field. The National League had reduced from twelve teams to eight in 1900, resulting in a scramble for jobs and limited opportunities for rookies.

The World War II year of 1944 arguably produced the American League's poorest rookie crop. Honors went to thirty-nine-year-old relief pitcher Joe Berry of the Philadelphia Athletics, who edged thirty-five-year-old pitcher Sig Jakucki of the pennant-winning St. Louis Browns in a close race. However, without a doubt the weakest group ever were the National League rookies of 1919. In this postwar year the winner among three candidates was Cardinal relief pitcher Oscar Tuero, who had a 5–7 won-lost record. Tuero had pitched 44⅓ innings for St. Louis in 1918 and thus barely qualified as a rookie in 1919. In 1920, after pitching only two-thirds of an inning, he was back in the minor leagues, where he continued to pitch until 1941, finishing with 269 minor league wins.

At the other extreme there were seasons in which many future greats came up to the big leagues together. Such a year was 1925 in the AL when future Hall of Famers Earle Combs, Mickey Cochrane, and Lou Gehrig ranked 1-2-3 in the voting. Finishing seventh in that year's poll was the man who would go on to become the greatest left-handed pitcher in the league's history—Lefty Grove. Another banner rookie year for the American League was 1929. Behind winner Dale Alexander were Wes Ferrell, Earl Averill, Bill Dickey, and Roy Johnson in that order.

In the National League rookie race of 1902 the St. Louis Cardinals' trio of center fielder Homer Smoot, pitcher Mike O'Neill, and left fielder George Barclay finished 1-2-3. This sweep was surpassed by the 1924 Pittsburgh Pirates, who had the top four finishers: Kiki Cuyler (lf), Glenn Wright (ss), Emil Yde (p), and Ray Kremer (p). All four also had excellent sophomore seasons in helping the Pirates to the 1925 world championship.

The Cardinals led the NL in rookie-of-the-year selections for the 1900–1948 period with 11. The St. Louis club's domination was especially noticeable in the early 1940s. In 1941 Redbirds Ernie White (p), Frank Crespi (2b), and Howie Krist (p) finished 2-3-4 behind Cincinnati pitcher Elmer Riddle. In 1942 Cardinal pitcher John Beazley was the winner, edging teammate Stan Musial. During the next three years the Cards had two winners—second baseman Lou Klein in 1943 and pitcher Ken Burkhart in 1945—and one runner-up, pitcher Ted Wilks in 1944. These products of Branch Rickey's extensive farm system helped lead St. Louis to four pennants and three World Series titles between 1942 and 1946. Notable Cardinal winners from previous years included Rogers Hornsby, Dizzy and Paul Dean, and Johnny Mize.

Rookies of the Year, 1900–1948
American League

Year	Player	Pos.	Team
1900	Not a major league		
1901	Socks Seybold	rf	Phila.
1902	Addie Joss	p	Clev.
1903	Chief Bender	p	Phila.
1904	Fred Glade	p	St.L.
1905	George Stone	lf	St.L.
1906	Claude Rossman	1b	Clev.
1907	Glen Liebhardt	p	Clev.
1908	Ed Summers	p	Det.
1909	Harry Krause	p	Phila.
1910	Russ Ford	p	N.Y.
1911	Vean Gregg	p	Clev.
1912	Hugh Bedient	p	Bos.
1913	Reb Russell	p	Chi.
1914	George Burns	1b	Det.
1915	Babe Ruth	p	Bos.
1916	Claud Williams	p	Chi.
1917	Joe Harris	1b	Clev.
1918	Scott Perry	p	Phila.
1919	Dickie Kerr	p	Chi.
1920	Bob Meusel	of/3b	N.Y.
1921	Joe Sewell	ss	Clev.
1922	Herman Pillette	p	Det.
1923	Homer Summa	rf	Clev.
1924	Al Simmons	cf	Phila.
1925	Earle Combs	cf	N.Y.
1926	Tony Lazzeri	2b	N.Y.
1927	Wilcy Moore	p	N.Y.
1928	Ed Morris	p	Bos.
1929	Dale Alexander	1b	Det.
1930	Smead Jolley	rf	Chi.
1931	Joe Vosmik	lf	Clev.
1932	Johnny Allen	p	N.Y.
1933	Pinky Higgins	3b	Phila.
1934	Hal Trosky	1b	Clev.
1935	Jake Powell	cf	Wash.
1936	Joe DiMaggio	lf	N.Y.
1937	Rudy York	c/3b	Det.
1938	Ken Keltner	3b	Clev.
1939	Ted Williams	rf	Bos.
1940	Walt Judnich	cf	St.L.
1941	Phil Rizzuto	ss	N.Y.

Rookies of the Year, 1900–1948 (cont.)
American League

Year	Player	Pos.	Team
1942	Johnny Pesky	ss	Bos.
1943	Dick Wakefield	lf	Det.
1944	Joe Berry	p	Phila.
1945	Dave Ferriss	p	Bos.
1946	Hoot Evers	cf	Det.
1947	Frank Shea	p	N.Y.
1948	Gene Bearden	p	Clev.

National League

Year	Player	Pos.	Team
1900	Billy Sullivan	c	Bos.
1901	Christy Mathewson	p	N.Y.
1902	Homer Smoot	cf	St.L.
1903	Jake Weimer	p	Chi.
1904	Harry Lumley	rf	Bkn.
1905	Ed Reulbach	p	Chi.
1906	Jack Pfiester	p	Chi.
1907	Nap Rucker	p	Bkn.
1908	George McQuillan	p	Phila.
1909	Babe Adams	p	Pitt.
1910	King Cole	p	Chi.
1911	Grover Alexander	p	Phila.
1912	Larry Cheney	p	Chi.
1913	Jim Viox	2b	Pitt.
1914	Jeff Pfeffer	p	Bkn.
1915	Tommy Long	rf	St.L.
1916	Rogers Hornsby	3b/ss	St.L.
1917	Leon Cadore	p	Bkn.
1918	Charlie Hollocher	ss	Chi.
1919	Oscar Tuero	p	St.L.
1920	Fred Nicholson	of	Pitt.
1921	Ray Grimes	1b	Chi.
1922	Hack Miller	lf	Chi.
1923	George Grantham	2b	Chi.
1924	Kiki Cuyler	lf	Pitt.
1925	Dick Cox	rf	Bkn.
1926	Paul Waner	rf	Pitt.
1927	Lloyd Waner	cf	Pitt.
1928	Del Bissonette	1b	Bkn.
1929	Johnny Frederick	cf	Bkn.
1930	Wally Berger	lf	Bos.
1931	Paul Derringer	p	St.L.

National League (cont.)

Year	Player	Pos.	Team
1932	Dizzy Dean	p	St.L.
1933	Frank Demaree	cf	Chi.
1934	Paul Dean	p	St.L.
1935	Cy Blanton	p	Pitt.
1936	Johnny Mize	1b	St.L.
1937	Jim Turner	p	Bos.
1938	Johnny Rizzo	lf	Pitt.
1939	Hugh Casey	p	Bkn.
1940	Babe Young	1b	N.Y.
1941	Elmer Riddle	p	Cin.
1942	Johnny Beazley	p	St.L.
1943	Lou Klein	2b	St.L.
1944	Bill Voiselle	p	N.Y.
1945	Ken Burkhart	p	St.L.
1946	Del Ennis	lf	Phila.
1947	Jackie Robinson	1b	Bkn.
1948	Alvin Dark	ss	Bos.

The Cubs, who were the only NL team to have the leading rookie in three consecutive years (1921–23), had ten winners in all. Brooklyn had nine and Pittsburgh eight, including the Waner brothers, Paul and Lloyd, who were the picks for 1926 and 1927, respectively.

Following the selection of Mathewson in 1901, the Giants did not have another winner until journeyman first baseman Babe Young was chosen in 1940. Pitcher Bill Voiselle, in 1944, was the only other Giant choice.

Cleveland (with eleven) and the Yankees (with ten) were the biggest winners in the AL for the pre-1949 period.

Although no American League team matched the "sweeps" of the 1902 Cardinals and the 1924 Pirates, the 1905 St. Louis Browns came close. In addition to the winner, left fielder George Stone, three other Browns finished third, fourth, and sixth. In the closely contested race of 1946, Brownies Bob Dillinger (3b), Chuck Stevens (1b) and Cliff Fannin (p) rated 2-3-4 behind Hoot Evers of Detroit. In the previously mentioned 1925 AL race when Combs and Gehrig wound up first and third, another Yankee, outfielder Ben Paschal, finished fourth. The selections of Tony Lazzeri in 1926 and Wilcy Moore in 1927 gave the Yankees the distinction of being the only AL team to have winners in three consecutive seasons.

New York's domination of the American League that produced seven pennants and six world championships in eight years in 1936–1943 can be traced to an exceptional group of rookies that joined the club during that period. Joe DiMaggio was the runaway winner for 1936. The next year Tommy Henrich and Spud Chandler finished second and third. Joe Gordon was the runner-up in '38, as was Charlie Keller in '39. Atley Donald and Marius Russo also made their debuts that year, and Ernie Bonham did so in 1940. The next three years brought Phil Rizzuto, the winner in 1941, and runners-up Hank Borowy in 1942 and Billy Johnson in 1943.

In only eleven seasons in each league did the Rookie of the Year play for a pennant-winning team, and only in 1927, 1947, and 1948 did both World Series participants have their league's best rookies.

Little-Known Facts

President William Howard Taft refused to throw out the first ball at the opening game in 1909, thereby terminating the season. . . . James (Ferriswheel) Finnegan, Philadelphia first baseman in 1916, played thirteen games for Chicago by mistake. . . . Ty Cobb, who holds the all-time record for most runs scored, lifetime, never touched second base. . . . Oddball (Don) Ryan, St. Louis outfielder, reported for 1969 spring training a year early.

Conrad Horn

Cobb on a Rampage

LARRY AMMAN

♦ ♦ ♦

There was good news for Detroit Tiger fans from spring training in 1911. The team's volatile star, Tyrus R. Cobb, was on speaking terms again with shortstop Donie Bush and right fielder Sam Crawford. The two men hit second and fourth respectively around Cobb. Having the three working together was important if the Tigers were to finish first. After winning three straight pennants, the Bengals had finished third in 1910, 18 games behind the Philadelphia A's.

The Detroiters won the 1911 season opener 4–1 at Detroit's Bennett Park against Chicago. Cobb was 1-for-4, with a home run off spitballer Ed Walsh.

By the end of April batting averages and scoring were up all over the majors. Writers used the term "lively ball" to describe the new cork-centered baseball. Ty was having trouble bunting. Instead he had three home runs and four game-winning RBIs to go with his .379 average.

Cobb opened May in grand style as the Bengals swept a four-game set in St. Louis. Ty made two spectacular catches in center field, and twice got himself into rundowns deliberately and beat them out. Cobb could do this solo, but often he would perform the trick with Bush ahead of him or with Crawford behind him, giving them a chance to advance.

On May 7, Cobb and Company opened a series in the new Comiskey Park and beat Chicago 5–4. Cobb went 4-for-5 against veteran southpaw Doc White. It had taken Cobb several years to learn to hit White's drop ball. This day he drove in the tying and winning runs. The Detroit *Free Press* called it the "turning point of the year."

Several other games in May stand out: New York was the Tiger opponent on the twelfth at Bennett Park. In the first inning Ty scored from

37

first on a Crawford single. In the sixth, Cobb scored from second on a wild pitch. The next frame he doubled in two runs to tie the game. Yankee catcher Ed Sweeney was furious over the call at the plate. The *New York Times* reported:

> Sweeney began to protest. Pitcher Caldwell and the rest of the infield flocked to the plate to help. Cobb, observing that third base was unguarded, trotted amiably there. No one saw him. So he tiptoed gingerly along toward the group at the plate. He did not come under observation until he was about ten feet from the plate, where for a few seconds he stood practically still, peering into the cluster of disputants, looking for an opening to slide through. All at once there was a white streak, a cry of warning, a cloud of dust and Cobb was picking himself up on the other side of the plate as safe as a murderer in Mexico.

A youthful Ty Cobb

The *Times* added dryly: "Ty Cobb once again demonstrated his claim to be the most original of all players."

On May 15 Ty's 40-game hitting streak began with two hits off Boston's Joe Wood. In the tenth inning Wood gave Cobb an intentional walk. Two hitters later Jim Delahanty won the game. Cobb only received two other intentional passes all season, as Sam Crawford, hitting behind him, enjoyed the highest average of his career at .378.

On May 19 against Philadelphia, the Tigers won, 9–8. Cobb contributed a triple and scored twice.

In the fifth Ty prevented the A's from going ahead with one of his special defensive stunts. Frank Baker was on first when Harry Davis hit a soft liner to center. Baker went to second, fearing Cobb would let the ball fall in and force him (a much faster runner than Davis) at second. Ty, however, was thinking one step ahead of his opponent. He caught the ball in the air and doubled the hapless Baker off first.

Four days later Detroit won another 9–8 game, against Washington. In the eighth Ty came to the plate with the bases loaded against Walter Johnson in relief. Cobb was already 3-for-4 with three stolen bases. This time he "pranced and danced around at the plate like a hen on a hot rock," and the Big Train walked Cobb to force in what proved to be the winning game.

Cobb hit .428 for the month, with at least one hit in each of the last fifteen games. His team won twenty of twenty-nine games. Detroit was in first, far ahead of the world champion A's.

In June Cobb hit safely in all twenty-three games.

On the eighteenth Ty went 5-for-6.

On June 19 at Bennett Park against the White Sox, Cobb equaled Bill Bradley's American League consecutive-game hitting streak of 29 set in 1902. After singling in the second inning off Irv Young, he scored from first on another single.

Ty set the new milestone of 30 the next day with a single against Cleveland's Willie Mitchell in the second inning. It was a high chopper to shortstop Ivy Olson, whose throw to first was too late.

In the first game of the July 4 doubleheader, Ed Walsh of the White Sox held Cobb hitless in four trips to the plate. Both the *Chicago Tribune* and the Detroit *Free Press* noted that the 40-game hitting streak was over. Neither paper gave any particulars of the four times at bat except to say that Cobb grounded into a double play once.

It must be pointed out that no one was conscious of the streak while it was in progress. The Detroit *News* said absolutely nothing about it. The Detroit *Free Press* only mentioned it on July 5 when it was over, as did the *Chicago Tribune*. The Cleveland *Plain Dealer* said nothing when the 40-game mark was reached on July 2. Ty fell four games short of the major league mark Willie Keeler had established in 1897, but Wee Willie and his record were never mentioned by sportswriters in 1911.

This key fact probably renders moot the question of whether Cobb's hitting streak was aided by official scorers or umpires.

Note that in the twenty-seventh, thirtieth, and thirty-ninth games of the streak, Ty had only one hit—an infield single. In all four cases the newspapers in the opposing team's city did not dispute the scoring, even by implication.

The list of pitchers victimized includes Hall of Famers Walter Johnson, Ed Plank, Ed Walsh, and Cy Young. Jack Coombs, Joe Wood, and Ed Cicotte are other great hurlers who gave up hits.

Cobb's 1911 Hit Streak

Game	Date	Score	W–L	Opp	AB	R	H	Pitcher
	May 14	6–5	W	Bos	4	0	0	Collins
1	May 15	5–4	W	Bos	4	0	2 (2B, SB, RBI)	Wood
2	May 16	7–6	W	Bos	5	2	3 (2 2B)	Karger (2-for-3) Cicotte (1-for-2)
3	May 18	9–4	W	Phi	4	1	1 (SB)	Plank
4	May 19	9–6	W	Phi	3	2	1 (3B, SB, RBI)	Coombs (1-for-1) Russell (0-for-2)
5	May 20	14–12	W	Phi	4	2	3 (2 RBIs)	Coombs (2-for-3)
6	May 21	6–2	L	Phi	3	0	1 (SB)	Krause
7	May 22	7–3	L	Was	4	1	2 (2B)	Walker
8	May 23	9–8	W	Was	4	2	3 (2B, 3 SB, RBI, IFS, CS)	Gray (3-for-4) Johnson (0-for-0)
9	May 24	6–5	W	Was	5	0	2 (2B, IFS)	Groom (2-for-4) Hughes (0-for-1)
10	May 25	6–2	L	Was	4	0	2 (2B)	Johnson
11	May 27	9–3	W	StL	5	2	2 (3 RBIs)	Bailey
12	May 28	12–6	L	StL	5	1	2 (3B, SB, RBI)	Hamilton
13	May 29	7–6	L	Cle	5	1	2 (2B, SB)	Blanding (2-for-4) Gregg (0-for-1)
14	May 30	3–2	W	Cle	5	0	1 (2B)	Mitchell
15	May 30	6–5	W	Cle	3	2	1	Gregg
16	Jun 1	8–7	W	Was	5	0	3 (2B, 3 SB, 2 RBIs)	Walker (1-for-2) Otey (2-for-3)
17	Jun 2	14–7	L	Was	5	2	2 (SB, 2 RBIs)	Hughes
18	Jun 3	7–2	W	Was	5	2	3 (2 3B, 2 RBIs)	Johnson
19	Jun 5	5–1	W	Was	4	1	3 (2 SB, RBI)	Groom
20	Jun 7	4–3	L	Phi	4	1	2 (3B, 2 RBIs)	Coombs
21	Jun 8	8–3	W	Phi	3	2	3 (2 SB, Bunt 1B, CS)	Plant
22	Jun 9	5–4	L	Phi	5	0	1	Krause
23	Jun 10	6–5	L	Bos	4	1	1 (CS)	Wood
24	Jun 12	5–4	W	Bos	4	0	4 (2 2B, 3 RBIs)	Hall
25	Jun 14	5–3	L	NY	5	0	2 (RBI)	Ford
26	Jun 15	5–0	L	NY	4	0	2 (2B)	Fisher
27	Jun 17	3–2	L	NY	4	0	1 (IFS)	Warhop
28	Jun 18	16–15	W	Chi	6	3	5 (3B, 5 RBIs)	White (3-for-3) Olmstead (2-for-2) Walsh (0-for-1)
29	Jun 19	8–5	W	Chi	4	1	2 (SB, RBI)	Young (1-for-2) Lange (1-for-1) Baker (0-for-1)

Cobb's 1911 Hit Streak (cont.)

Game	Date	Score	W–L	Opp	AB	R	H	Pitcher
30	Jun 20	8–3	W	Cle	4	1	1 (2 SB, IFS)	Mitchell (1-for-2) Krapp (0-for-2)
31	Jun 21	5–3	W	Cle	4	1	1 (2 RBIs, HR)	Blanding
32	Jun 22	4–3	L	Cle	3	0	1 (RBI)	West
33	Jun 23	4–2	W	Cle	4	1	2 (SB)	Young
34	Jun 25	8–4	L	Chi	5	1	2	White (2-for-3) Walsh (0-for-2)
35	Jun 26	6–3	W	Chi	3	2	2 (Bunt, 1B)	Young
36	Jun 27	3–0	L	Chi	4	0	1 (IFS, CS)	Walsh
37	Jun 28	3–2	W	StL	4	0	1 (RBI, SB)	Powell
38	Jun 29	6–5	L	StL	3	1	1 (RBI, IFS, SF)	Hamilton
39	Jul 1	8–0	W	StL	3	1	1 (RBI, IFS, SF)	Hamilton
40	Jul 2	14–6	W	Cle	4	3	3 (RBI, CS, SB, 3B)	Krapp (0-for-1) West (2-for-2) James (1-for-1)
	Jul 4	7–3	L	Chi	4	0	0	Walsh

However, Detroit won only twenty-four of the forty games. The early-season luck of the Tigers was beginning to run out.

The hitless game that ended his streak on July 4 was just a brief pause for the Cobb express. The highlight of the month of July was a four-game sweep from Philadelphia in Detroit.

On July 12 in a 9–0 win, Cobb's line score was 1-4-0. Without even a hit he was responsible for four runs. In the first, Ty walked and stole the next three bases, twice beating perfect throws by catcher Ira Thomas. In the third, he was safe on a fielder's choice and scored on a Crawford homer. Two frames later he had a sacrifice fly. Finally, in the seventh, he walked and was sacrificed to second. On a sacrifice fly Cobb came all the way around to score by knocking the ball from the hands of the new catcher, Paddy Livingston.

The next day the Tigers and the A's were tied at 7–7 going into the ninth inning. Earlier in the contest Ty had contributed a three-run double. This time he singled to center. When Jim Delahanty singled to right field, Cobb tried to advance three bases. Harry Davis' throw to Thomas at the plate was on the money, but Ty used the fadeaway slide to get around him after going through a frantic stop sign by coach Hughie Jennings.

Normal rules of baserunning did not apply to this man called "the Dixie Demon."

At the close of July, Ty's average was .419, and his team was still in first. In August, however, the roof fell in on the Detroiters. Their run production declined just enough so that it could no longer compensate for the weakness of the pitching staff. The Tigers were 17–13 and fell far behind Philadelphia. At the end of the month Detroit appeared out of the pennant race.

And at .416 Cobb was in some danger of being overtaken by Joe Jackson of Cleveland.

In September Ty hit .429 to help raise his final average to .420, twelve points ahead of Jackson for the batting title. He led the league in every offensive category except home runs, where he finished second, three behind Home Run Baker. He set a number of American League records.

Looking at the charts, one can see Ty's consistency throughout the season. He hit .418 at home and .422 on the road.

His .383 mark against southpaws is amazing, considering Cobb couldn't hit them at all when he first entered the league six years earlier. Doc White of Chicago made Ty look foolish for several years. In 1911 Cobb was 10-for-17 against White. Two southpaws who were especially tough on Cobb this season were rookies Earl Hamilton and Vern Gregg of St. Louis and Cleveland, respectively. Ty never hit a pitcher well until he had seen him a few times.

Was 1911 Ty Cobb's greatest year?

His 1910 batting average of .385 was actually higher relative to the whole league. The year of his greatest run production was 1917. Nevertheless, 1911 ranks as his best for hitting, fielding, and base-running combined. In the field he exceeded Tris Speaker in total chances per game and in fielding average. On the bases this was Cobb's most successfully daring campaign. His youthful energy combined with a mature baseball wisdom to produce a quality of play never seen before.

Ty Cobb's Hit-Streak Totals in 1911

G	AB	R	H	2B	3B	HR	RBI	BA	SA	SB	CS	IF	Bunt Hits
40	167	40	79	12	8	1	36	.467	.652	23	4	8	2

Cobb's 1911 Records, American League

	Cobb 1911	Old Record			Lasted Until		
TB	367	Lajoie	350	1901	Sisler	398	1920
RBI	144	Lajoie	125	1901	Ruth	171	1921
Hits	248	Lajoie	232	1901	Sisler	257	1920
Runs	147	Lajoie	145	1901	Ruth	177	1921
SB	83	Collins	81	1910	Cobb	96	1915
Hit Streak	40	Bradley	29	1902	Sisler	41	1922

The Runner Wore Skirts

DEBBIE DAGAVARIAN-BONAR

♦ ♦ ♦

For twelve summers Sophie Kurys' legs were bruised and skinned from barreling into bases with nothing but stockings and a short skirt. She stole 201 bases that way in one year, 1946, and 1114 in a career from 1943 to 1954.

No man has ever stolen as many. Rickey Henderson had 936 as of Opening Day 1991. But how many would he swipe wearing short pants?

Sophie's manager in the old All American Girls Professional Baseball League tried taping sliding pads to her legs. "But they were so cumbersome, I told him no, I'd just get the strawberries. I got strawberry upon strawberry, and they got calloused a bit." Almost half a century later she still gets a twinge in her hip when she wakes up in the morning.

Sophie was seventeen when she left Flint, Michigan, in 1943 to join the Racine Belles as a 5'5", 120-pound second baseman in the then new AAGPBL. Opposing runners wore spikes, just as the men used to before Astroturf, adding a dimension of danger to the double-play pivot.

Kurys stole 44 bases in 106 games as an $85-a-week rookie at the sixty-five-foot distance. For the next seven years, although the baselines grew progressively longer, she averaged more than a steal a game. The papers began calling her "the Flint Flash."

In some of those cold midwestern April evenings, the girls shivered in their short skirts, while the fans warmed themselves with thermos jugs of hot coffee. "We were tougher than the men, I'll tell you," Kurys says.

Did they have a good league? "We were the third major league," she says. Cubs manager Charlie Grimm said he'd pay $50,000 for hard-hitting outfielder Dottie Schroeder "if only she were a man." Ex-Yankee first baseman Wally Pipp called Dorothy Kamenshek the best-fielding first baseman he had ever seen; she was later offered a minor league tryout. Kurys' Arizona neighbor, Joanne Winters, hurled 63 straight scoreless innings. In 1989 "I was afraid Orel Hershiser was going to break it," says Sophie, but he didn't.

Kurys' biggest year was 1946. With the distance to second base increased to seventy-two feet, she swiped 201 bases in 203 attempts. To put it another way, she got on first base 191 times on singles and walks, and still stole 201 bases! She must have stolen every time she got on.

"That's about it," she says, grinning. "I had a fast break; I could generate right away."

The fans used to say when Sophie hits a single, it's really a triple. Yes, the distance to second was short, but so was the throw from the catcher.

"It amazes me—I watch Rickey Henderson, and you know, he's cockier than hell of course—anyway, it surprises me that the ballplayers don't steal more than they have.

"If you watch the pitchers and you get a good lead on them, they all have a definite thing when they go to home plate. They show their shoulder more to you when they go to first base.

"Vince Coleman isn't a smart baserunner. Henderson is a lot smarter than Coleman is. Tim Raines is a good runner, too; the White Sox should give Oakland a lot of trouble." The pitching distance was only forty-three feet, sidearm pitching was permitted, and "those balls were coming in there pretty fast." Even so, Sophie batted .286, second-best in the league, according to figures compiled by Sharon Roepke, the leading historian of the league.

No wonder they named Kurys MVP. "Hey, Sophie, where's your trophy?" the bench jockeys called.

In the final championship game that fall—"our World Series," she calls it—Racine came up against Rockford pitcher Carolyn Morris, who hurled a no-hitter for ten innings, and the teams went into the eleventh tied 0–0.

"There were three or four squeeze plays," Kurys says, "girls making spectacular catches. They say Willie Mays made spectacular catches—one girl turned her back to the batter, all of a sudden she turned and leaped and caught the ball. I can still see her to this day."

Still tied 0–0 in the fourteenth, Kurys led off with a single and stole second, her fifth steal of the game. "I was about to steal third, when the batter hit a single on the right-hand side. It went through the infield, and the outfielder was playing shallow." Sophie tore around third. "It was a close play, but I hooked away from the tag" to give Racine the championship, 1–0.

The league president, Hall of Famer Max Carey, declared it was the best game he'd ever seen, bar none.

The AAGPBL was the brainstorm of Cubs owner P.K. Wrigley, who put up $100,000 to start the loop. "I want you to fill the ballparks," he told the girls, "because it looks like they're going to take all our men away in the war." He scoured North America, from Canada to Cuba, for the best girls' softballers and set up teams in four Midwest towns—Racine, Kenosha, Rockford, and South Bend.

Back home in Flint, Sophie had scored 4563 points out of a possible 5000 in the pentathlon: broad jump, high jump, hundred-yard dash, baseball throw, and basketball free-throw shooting. She also ran track. "But they never did time us, none of them even thought about timing us. That came later." She was one of the fortunate few invited to try out.

She demonstrated sliding for Carey, who himself had swiped 738 bases in the major leagues. Yet, she says, Max never offered to give her pointers. She perfected a hook slide but had to do it on her own.

The teams took spring training in Wrigley Field, and in July they played their All Star Game there—under lights—making it the first night game ever played in the Friendly Confines. Seven thousand fans came out to watch, and Sophie drilled three hits in four at bats. They played a second game under lights there in 1944. Thus when the Cubs played their first nighter there in 1988, it was actually the third one. Sophie picked up the phone and called her local newspaper to tell them that she had played in the first Wrigley night game forty-five years earlier.

"Yeah?" said a bored voice on the other end.

"They thought I was nuts," she says.

"I know you don't believe me," she told the reporter, "you think I'm some sort of a kook, but that's the truth."

"Well, thanks for calling," the voice said, hanging up.

"That's the way it goes," she shrugs. "We were always secondary. Right?"

Kurys looks back on the old league fondly. After she got over her homesickness, "We had some wonderful camaraderie. We were housed in family homes. We were their daughters. They went to the ballgame every night; it was a family affair. They treated us royally." Their managers were ex-big leaguers like Jimmie Foxx, who hit 534 home runs, and Bill Wambsganss, who made an unassisted World Series triple play. The young ladies were sent to charm school, and every team had a chaperon. They once smuggled a coach's trousers into the chaperon's locker and had quite a giggle over it.

When the league took spring training in Cuba, they outdrew the Dodgers, who were also there with Jackie Robinson.

The AAGPBL started out playing softball. Gradually they reduced the size of the ball and lengthened the base paths.

In 1950 the mound was fifty-five feet from home, and Sophie smacked five homers to lead the league. Some parks "didn't have fences like the men have, and you'd have to hit it between the fielders and run like the devil. They played you pretty deep."

Four years later the pitching distance was lengthened to sixty feet, only six inches less than the regulation baseball distance, and batting averages zoomed. Sophie hit .307, the best she'd ever hit. The basepath was extended to eighty-five feet, only five feet less than the men's baseball distance. Kurys still averaged more steals, 120, than games, 110.

But that was the end. The Korean War plus increased TV coverage of the major leagues spelled the end of the league. The league folded after the 1954 season. Sophie was only twenty-nine. Ty Cobb was still stealing bases after forty. How many steals did Sophie have left in her legs?

"I reverted to professional softball," Kurys says. She played three years in Chicago and one year in Phoenix. She played against a male team in a charity game. "But they paid us on the side," she says, "because we were professionals."

Then it was back to Racine, where she had an offer to go into business manufacturing automobile, electronic, and aeronautical parts. She's now retired in Scottsdale, Arizona.

In 1988 Kurys and other AAGPBL vets were invited to Cooperstown to inaugurate a special exhibit on the women's league.

At long last, "We're getting recognition," Kurys says. The league has been the subject of a TV documentary, "When Diamonds Were a Girl's Best Friend." And in the summer of 1992 the film *A League of Their Own*, directed by director Penny Marshall and starring Geena Davis, Tom Hanks, and Madonna, opened to rave reviews and triggered a new wave of interest in the league. "People are beginning to realize that there really was a major league for women," she says. "It's still my theory that some of those women should have the chance to be inducted into Cooperstown. After all, we played just as hard as the men."

Sophie Kurys

All American Girls Professional Baseball League 1943–1954
HT: 5'5"   WT: 120   Bats: Right   Throws: Right   Born: May 14, 1925
Hometown: Flint, Michigan

Complete Major League Batting Record

Year	Club	G	AB	R	H	2B	3B	HR	RBI	SB	BB	SO	AVG
1943	Racine Belles	106	383	60	104	8	7	3	59	44	28	21	.271
1944	Racine Belles	116	394	87	96	7	3	1	60	166	69	32	.244
1945	Racine Belles	105	347	73	83	6	2	1	15	115	69	27	.239
1946	Racine Belles	113	392	117*	112	5	6	3	33	201*	93*	31	.286
1947	Racine Belles	112	432	81	99	8	6	2	18	142	49	31	.229
1948	Racine Belles	124	444	97	112	12	5	3	22	172	81	21	.252
1949	Racine Belles	111	416	70	102	3	3	2	26	137	59	19	.245
1950	Racine Belles	110	424	95	130	22	6	7*	42	120	68	18	.307
1952	Battle Creek Belles	17	66	8	21	0	1	0	0	17	6	4	.318
Totals		914	3298	688	859	71	39	22	276	1114*	522	204	.260

*League record

Fielding Totals	G	PO	A	E	PCT	POS
	896	2400	1665	190	.955	2B
	4	7	0	0	1.000	OF

Career Highlights

The only major league ballplayer to steal over 200 bases in a single season. All-Star teams in 1946, 1947, 1948, and 1949. Led league in home runs in 1950. Averaged over 100 stolen bases per season. Stole 1114 bases in 914 games. Between 1944–1950 stole 1053 bases in 791 games for a 1.33-per-game average. Averaged more stolen bases than games played for every season after her rookie year. Eighty percent of the time she got on base she stole at least one base. Virtually no pitcher-catcher combination could stop the "Flint Flash." Newspaper accounts of her 1946 season note that Kurys was thrown out 2 times in 203 attempts for a phenomenal 99-percent success ratio. Currently lives in Scottsdale, Arizona.

Let's Save the Hall of Fame

JOHN MCCORMACK

♦ ♦ ♦

Like the old gray mare, baseball's Hall of Fame ain't what she used to be. What's worse, each passing year has seen the Hall slip further away from what it was intended to be: baseball's Pantheon. Fortunately, the Hall can be saved. Difficult decisions will be needed. Mistakes will have to be admitted and corrected. Selection procedures will have to be changed. But then—and only then—will the Hall become once more a shrine for the game's few true titans, not a mere repository of stars.

Hall of Famers. All-stars. There is a vast difference between them. It's indefinable, but it's there. A Supreme Court justice once stated that while he could not define pornography, he knew it when he saw it. So, too, with Hall of Famers. Hall of Famers, unlike all-stars, are not enshrined as a result of sentimentality, friendship, or election campaigns in their behalf decades after their careers have ended. No wholly objective standards can be set which, if met, would make a player indisputably a Hall of Famer. But when one comes along, he's usually quickly and widely recognized as being Cooperstown bound.

Examples? Stan Musial was, Chick Hafey was not. Paul Waner was, Lloyd Waner was not. Bill Dickey was, Ernie Lombardi was not. Ted Williams was, Kiki Cuyler was not. Lou Gehrig was, George Kelly was not. Al Simmons was, Chuck Klein was not. Why go on? The point is obvious. When they were playing, few fans would have equated Chick Hafey or Lloyd Waner with the game's all-time greats. But everyone soon knew that Musial and Williams were Hall-of-Famers-to-be. One other point is obvious. The Hall of Famers I've mentioned were elected by the Baseball Writers Association of America (BBWAA); the Committee on Veterans (the Committee) chose the all-stars.

Which brings us to the first step that must be taken if the Hall is to regain its rightful grandeur. The Committee must be dissolved and never reconstituted.

The creation in 1937 of a committee to select veterans for the Hall was an excellent move. BBWAA elections had been held in 1936 and 1937. Only players whose careers had ended in the teens or much later (except for Cy Young, who called it a day after the 1911 season) had been elected. There was rightful concern that since most electors had not seen the old-timers play, the game's early greats would be shut out of Cooperstown. The need for a committee to consider players whose careers had ended before 1910 was clear.

The initial old-timers committees served between 1937 and 1952. They did their jobs well. They did not operate on a grind-'em-out-annually basis. In fact no selections were made in eight of those years. Mistakes were made. Morgan J. Bulkeley was a monumental error. Johnny Evers and Joe Tinker, magnificent as they were to Franklin P. Adams, were clearly less than Hall of Famers. Thomas McCarthy was, at best, a dubious choice. But their other thirty-three choices were bona fide Hall of Famers. Those early committees earned high marks and the gratitude of the game's fans.

In 1953 the Committee took over. It too, initially felt no compelling need to produce Hall of Famers every year. It made no selections in four of its first eight years. Unlike its predecessors, however, it selected players other than those whose careers were before (or mostly before) 1910. Through 1966 the Committee selected eight bona fide pre-1910 Hall of Famers (plus Elmer Flick, who wasn't) and eight more who had begun their careers after 1910 and who had been passed over by the BBWAA. Beginning in 1967, with the pre-1910 lode of old-timers about played out, the Committee turned its attention almost exclusively to players the BBWAA had already correctly deemed unqualified. When the Committee selected Lloyd Waner in 1967, it opened the floodgates. The deluge has never stopped.

Waner was a National League center fielder from 1927 to 1945. He was *never* chosen by *The Sporting News* for its major league all-star team. The All Star game was first played in 1933. Waner was then twenty-seven years old, a ballplayer's prime. He never played in an All Star game. Was he unlucky and kept from playing by a succession of true Hall of Famers? Hardly. From 1933 to 1945 starting National League center fielders included Wally Berger, Augie Galan, Frank Demaree, Terry Moore, Pete

Reiser, and Harry Walker. Two Hall of Famers did start a game apiece in center field during Waner's years, Mel Ott in 1938 and Stan Musial in 1944. Each, however, was really a right fielder. 'Nuff said about the caliber of the National League's center fielders when Waner didn't play.

I dwell on Waner at some length not to belittle him. I saw him play many times. He was a good ballplayer. He could hit (mostly singles) and field. He was fast and had an adequate arm. I dwell on Waner to castigate the Committee for selecting him for the Hall. How could the Committee have equated Waner with all-time greatness when he wasn't even an all-star in his own time?

The easy answer is that the Committee made a mistake. Doesn't everyone make mistakes? Of course. But everyone doesn't compound them. Unfortunately, Waner was no isolated slip. The Committee subsequently chose Waite Hoyt, Jesse Haines, Fred Lindstrom, Jim Bottomley, and Hack Wilson to name but a few of its disastrous post-1967 selections. These were titans? Don't be silly.

The Committee's routine has become a virtual ritual. It meets annually in Florida in mid-winter. Judging from reports of its meetings no one is deemed too unqualified to warrant serious consideration for the Hall. Finally several more BBWAA rejects are chosen. Having further defiled the Hall, the Committee then adjourns until the following winter when the process is repeated.

The credibility of the Committee is beyond redemption. If it met in International Falls, Minnesota, in mid-January for the next ten years and chose no one for the Hall, it still would have no credibility. It would still be the group that had loaded the Hall with all-stars and almost-all-stars. The guardians of the Hall must pull their heads out of the sand and end this annual ludicrous, demeaning farce by dissolving the Committee immediately.

If that were done, all selections would thereafter be made by the BBWAA. Once in each decade the BBWAA could conduct a special election to consider any pre-1910 players who somehow have been overlooked in the last fifty years, plus blacks and non-players. Very few non-players (other than managers) even merit consideration, much less admission, to the Hall. Does anyone, except their immediate families and friends, believe that Ford Frick, Warren Giles, and Tom Yawkey (to name but three of the Committee's non-player choices between 1970 and 1980) were super special, the likes of which the game will never see again? They were all good men. They all loved the game. They served it for a long time. All of which are fine qualities, but not enough to warrant enshrinement in the Hall. A Hall of Famer is exceptional. None of these gentlemen was. They should have received wrist watches for their long and meritorious service, not plaques at Cooperstown.

Any fear that dissolving the Committee might mean that there might be years when no one would be inducted should be dismissed. The BBWAA last failed to elect someone in 1971. There will be many bona fide candidates for it to consider in the foreseeable future. It's unlikely there will be many years in which no one will be chosen. But suppose no one was. That would be a magnificent plus for the Hall. It would make clear that selection is a rare honor, not an annual marketing ploy.to promote the Hall. What would happen to the mid-summer festivities if there were no one to induct? Nothing really. It wouldn't take much ingenuity to present a fascinating ceremony built around living Hall of Famers. Such a program would figure to be far more interesting than the predictable acceptance speeches that accompany induction. When one and all finally trooped off to the annual exhibition game, there would be few visitors dissatisfied.

Would having the BBWAA make all selections mean qualified players would be ignored because of petty personal dislikes, lack of knowledge of the game's history, or a general ennui? The record of the last fifty years should dispel any concerns in those respects. No doubt there have been BBWAA voters who have not voted for a qualified candidate for personal reasons. It will happen again. But who has been kept out of the Hall because he was disliked personally? (It is, however, quite likely personal feelings and petty jealousies have affected Committee decisions. How else can some selections be explained?) As for knowledge of the game, the BBWAA has made very few mistakes in its choices. Rabbit Maranville, inventor of the basket catch and colorful and quixotic though he was, was no Hall of Famer. Nor were four other choices since 1971. Five mistakes over fifty years is surely an acceptable margin of error—though, of course, no errors would be infinitely preferable. Since a representative number of its members vote annually, the BBWAA can not be charged with a lack of interest in its Hall-of-Fame duties. One can only conclude the BBWAA has performed its Hall-of-Fame chores faithfully and well. It deserves high marks.

Correcting the sorry situation the Committee has created presents a greater, though fortunately solvable problem: separating the Hall of Famers from the all-stars and near all-stars. It can be done in several ways.

The easier, more practical (but not absolute) solution would be to establish a new section of the Hall—call it Valhalla—restrict it to players, and install therein only the game's truly great. Such a step would be reasonable. It would demean no one. It would bestow on the truly exceptional the honor they deserve.

No matter the special group—presidents, generals, Nobel prize winners, or whatever—all members are not equal. Some are markedly superior. And some few stand alone. That they do does not detract from the others, the rank and file. It honors them. It shows that they indeed are members of a very special group.

So, too, with the Hall. The Ruths, Cobbs, Mayses, Aarons, and a few other truly great stand several notches above the remaining true Hall of Famers and head and shoulders over the Committee's all-stars and near all-stars. These true titans should be recognized. It's shocking to pretend that Joe DiMaggio and Max Carey were equals. To do so reduces the Hall's stature. Valhalla would at least alleviate that problem.

Admission to Valhalla would be gained through special election by the BBWAA. Membership could never exceed 15 percent of the *players* then in the Hall. Elections would be held every five years provided the 15-percent limitation was not then in effect. Only Hall of Famers of ten or more years' standing would be eligible for election. Voters could vote for five players unless the 15-percent limitation would permit only a lesser number to be elected. A player would have to receive not 75 percent of the vote but at least 80 percent of the votes cast to gain Valhalla. It would be difficult. That, however, would be Valhalla's *raison d'être*—to separate the game's gods from its greats and lesser performers.

A cleaner, absolute, though almost surely less acceptable solution would be for the BBWAA to hold every five years recall elections limited to deceased members. To recall a player would require 85 percent of the votes cast; a non-player 60 percent of the votes cast. Voters could vote for ten individuals.

Recall elections would have two positive effects that the creation of Valhalla would not. In time the all-stars, near all-stars and run-of-the-mill non-players would be removed from the Hall. The Hall would once again become a true Hall of Fame. Secondly, once the lesser lights were cleaned out, the contention could no longer be made, alas with justification, that if X is in the Hall, then certainly Y belongs. This is why the Committee's election of ersatz Hall of Famers has had such a wretched effect. It is inevitable that the Hall will eventually be stuck with Y, too. This rationale will almost assure the arrival in Cooperstown of such as Gil Hodges, Nellie Fox, and, probably, Riggs Stephenson and Tony Lazzeri. None belongs. Yet a persuasive X vs. Y argument can be made in behalf of each. (I have long wondered why the members of the George "Hooks" Dauss Marching and Chowder Society have not used the X vs. Y argument and been more forceful in pushing for their man's admission.

His career stats are strikingly similar to [and generally better than] Jesse Haines'. As that bona fide Hall of Famer, Casey Stengel, was wont to say, "You could look it up." While Hooks was shut out in the 1947 BBWAA election, he trailed Haines by but one vote. The Committee in its wisdom elected Haines in 1970. Hooks had died in 1963. He never knew how close he came to Cooperstown.)

Recall elections restricted to deceased members (or even recall elections per se) would quite likely bring the Hall adverse publicity. The most vitriolic of the uninformed would castigate the Hall's guardians as wishy-washy ghouls. Even more restrained criticism would figure to be sharp. While the end would surely justify recall elections, Valhalla would seem more practicable.

I write more in sorrow than in anger. I have the greatest regard for the Hall. I have been a member of The Friends of the National Baseball Hall of Fame and Museum for a number of years. It's far and away the greatest of all athletic halls of fame. I have been fortunate enough to have visited it. Every fan who has the chance should make the pilgrimage to Cooperstown. It's my great affection for the Hall that causes me to be torn apart annually when the Committee announces its latest selections and further defiles the Hall. The havoc wreaked by the Committee has gone on for much too long. It must be stopped. Its misdoings must be corrected. The Hall must be saved. I urge those in a position to do so to take the necessary actions. Now. Please.

THERE ARE, OF COURSE, MANY GREAT PLAYERS
IN THE HALL—AND SOME NOT-SO-GREAT, TOO

Who Belongs in the Hall?

RICHARD KENDALL

♦ ♦ ♦

My purpose in this study is to make an objective determination of players who belong in the Hall of Fame by comparing them to Hall of Famers at their position.

All Hall of Famers were classified by position and their career totals in nine hitting and fielding categories (hits, home runs, runs batted in, batting average, runs created (1), stolen bases, assists, range factor (2), and fielding percentage) were listed. Then, for the players at each position a mean and standard deviation (SD) for each of the nine categories was computed (3). Each player was rated by how many SDs each of his career totals were from the mean of that category for that position.

An equivalent season (4) for those nine categories for each player was computed. Each player was ranked according to his mean and standard deviation for each seasonal stat. This was compared to the mean and SD for Hall of Famers at that position. This moderated some extremes found when rating players by career totals only. Players who had relatively short but brilliant careers ranked somewhat lower than would be expected because their career totals were not especially high. Joe DiMaggio, Roy Campanella, and Hank Greenberg are good examples. On the other hand, a player who compiled large totals because of a long career will rank higher than his equivalent seasons would suggest. Carl Yastrzemski and Pete Rose are good examples of these. Combining career stats and equivalent seasons gives a total of a player's career and peak value.

The positive and negative career and seasonal SDs for each player were added and divided by 18 (the total number of SDs (5) from the mean). This gives a rating of a player relative to the average Hall of Famer at his position. This was computed for players at that position who are not in the Hall. For example—Mike Schmidt's career home run total was 1.82 SDs above the mean for Hall-of-Fame third basemen, his seasonal home run total was 1.71 SDs above the mean, but his BA was 1.11 SDs below the Hall of Fame third basemen's mean, and so forth. Considering those SDs above the mean as positive numbers and those below the mean as negative, Schmidt's total SDs were +5.94. Divide that by 18 and his over- all SD is +0.33, the second highest among third basemen, past or present.

Pitchers were rated in regard to career and seasonal wins, winning per- centage, earned run average, and strikeouts as well as strikeout-to-walk ratio, career shutouts, number of 20-win seasons, winning percentage compared to the team's winning percentage minus their own (some pitchers with modest winning percentages did so while toiling for teams with low winning percentages), and career ERA normalized to the league average and adjusted for home-park factor (this adjusts the rather high ERAs of lively-ball eras and the extremely low ERAs of certain dead-ball eras). I also ranked pitchers according to opponents' batting average and Pitching Runs (6) normalized to the league average.

Among Hall of Famers I did not consider players who spent the major- ity of their careers in the nineteenth century. Seasons were shorter, rules differed, and the statistics for these players skewed the means and SDs rather extremely. I also left out certain players who were elected to the Hall as managers and relief pitchers.

1. $\dfrac{\textbf{(H+BB)(TB)}}{\textbf{AB+BB}}$ = **Runs Created**

2. **Range Factor** equals assists plus putouts divided by games at that position.

3. **Mean** is the average for that category. **Standard Deviation** is the average variance from that mean. The number of standard deviations above or below the mean is a measure of how far above or below the av- erage player a player places in a category. If a player is one SD above (or below) the mean, he is better (or worse) than about ⅔ of all players in that category. If he is two SDs above (or below) the mean, he is better (or worse) than about 95% of all players in that category.

4. **Equivalent seasons** are determined by dividing the player's career total of games by 162. You then divide this number of equivalent seasons into each of the player's career stats to find out what his stats would be if he played a 162-game schedule. Runs Created, Range Factor, and Equiva- lent Seasons are courtesy of *The Bill James Baseball Abstract,* the source of much of my statistical ideas and information.

5. I had only 16 SDs to divide by for catchers and first basemen be- cause I did not include a range factor for them, since range is not espe-

cially important at those positions. Outfielders were rated on career and seasonal assists, career and seasonal putouts, season and career FP.

6. **Pitching Runs** are the Linear Weights measure of runs saved beyond what a league average pitcher might have saved.

The Rankings
Catchers

Bill Dickey	0.36	Johnny Bench	0.25
Yogi Berra	0.27	Carlton Fisk	0.15
Joe Torre	-0.04	Ray Schalk	-1.07
Gary Carter	-0.07	Ernie Lombardi	-1.08
Mickey Cochrane	-0.11	Tony Pena	-1.29
Gabby Hartnett	-0.13	Manny Sanguillen	-1.34
Ted Simmons	-0.16	Rick Ferrell	-1.46
Roy Campanella	-0.52	Del Crandall	-1.50
Roger Bresnahan	-0.87	Bob Boone	-1.59
Bill Freehan	-0.91	Jim Sundberg	-1.61
Thurman Munson	-0.98	Wally Schang	-1.86

Joe Torre, Ted Simmons, Carlton Fisk, and Gary Carter ranked high among catchers. Torre and Simmons were heavy hitters, but neither was considered a strong catcher and each spent a lot of time playing other positions. How much this will reduce their support for the Hall of Fame remains to be seen. Fisk and Carter, on the other hand, have been fine all-around catchers, entirely deserving of election to the Hall. There don't seem to be any flagrant omissions among eligible catchers.

First Base

Lou Gehrig	0.71	George Sisler	0.29
Jimmie Foxx	0.55		
Eddie Murray	-0.05	Lee May	-0.68
Bill Terry	-0.14	Charlie Grimm	-0.77
Hank Greenberg	-0.18	Joe Kuhel	-0.78
Keith Hernandez	-0.26	Jake Daubert	-0.78
Johnny Mize	-0.30	Vic Power	-0.79
Bill Buckner	-0.31	Ed Konetchy	-0.80
Steve Garvey	-0.32	Willie McCovey	-0.83
Orlando Cepeda	-0.35	Ted Kluszewski	-0.84
Don Mattingly	-0.48	George Kelly	-0.85
Joe Judge	-0.49	Joe Adcock	-0.85
Stuffy McInnis	-0.51	Kent Hrbek	-0.89
Mickey Vernon	-0.56	Chris Chambliss	-0.96
Gil Hodges	-0.60	Fred Tenney	-0.98

First Base (cont.)

Tony Perez	-0.63	Frank Chance	-1.07
Frank McCormick	-0.65	Hal Chase	-1.20
Jim Bottomley	-0.66		

It took a long time for Johnny Mize to be elected. Why? It looks like Eddie Murray, Keith Hernandez, Steve Garvey, and Bill Buckner have had Hall-of-Fame careers. Will Orlando Cepeda's baseball pluses outweigh his criminal minuses? Joe Judge, Stuffy McInnis, Tony Perez, Mickey Vernon, Frank McCormick, and Gil Hodges may not have ranked very high but they out-ranked four Hall of Famers. Willie McCovey ranked surprisingly low. Frank Chance is the first of the Tinker-to-Evers-to-Chance infield to rank at the bottom of the rankings.

Second Base

Rogers Hornsby	0.69	Frankie Frisch	0.35
Charlie Gehringer	0.45	Eddie Collins	0.29
Nap Lajoie	0.44	Bobby Doerr	0.03
Joe Morgan	-0.05	Nellie Fox	-0.63
Ryne Sandberg	-0.16	Red Schoendienst	-0.63
Tony Lazzeri	-0.34	Bill Mazeroski	-0.72
Jackie Robinson	-0.36	Del Pratt	-0.75
Bobby Grich	-0.43	Lou Whitaker	-0.77
Billy Herman	-0.44	Uillie Randolph	-0.84
Rod Carew	-0.45	Frank White	-0.90
Joe Gordon	-0.45	Larry Doyle	-1.21
Buddy Myer	-0.53	Johnny Evers	-1.38

The difference in the ranking of Bobby Doerr and Joe Gordon is a surprise. Doerr has been underrated. Tony Lazzeri was not overlooked by the voters, but with Schoendienst in, Nellie Fox seems to have been. Notwithstanding his outstanding defense, Bill Mazeroski seems to be completely out of the running, beating out only one Hall of Famer—Johnny Evers.

Shortstop

Honus Wagner	1.13	Luke Appling	0.17
Ernie Banks	0.28	Arky Vaughan	0.11
Joe Cronin	0.17		
Joe Sewell	-0.01	PeeWee Reese	-0.37
Travis Jackson	-0.03	Maury Wills	-0.38
Vern Stephens	-0.09	Dave Concepcion	-0.41
Luis Aparicio	-0.12	Alvin Dark	-0.44

Shortstop (cont.)

Rabbit Maranville	-0.15	Bert Campaneris	-0.50
Lou Boudreau	-0.19	Joe Tinker	-0.50
Dick Bartell	-0.21	Art Fletcher	-0.52
Dave Bancroft	-0.22	Dick Groat	-0.53
Cal Ripken Jr.	-0.25	Garry Templeton	-0.54
Bobby Wallace	-0.26	Cecil Travis	-0.62
Ozzie Smith	-0.28	Johnny Pesky	-0.64
Alan Trammell	-0.31	Phil Rizzuto	-0.83

The biggest surprise here is Vern Stephens, never given much credit as a potential Hall of Famer. But there he is, around the mean for Hall-of-Fame shortstops. Seven were higher, seven lower.

Let's give Rowdy Dick Bartell some credit for being a top shortstop. It was extremely hard to accept Phil Rizzuto's low ranking. His career offensive stats were low but he would be expected to rise in the ranks when fielding stats and seasonal offense were included. But that was not the case. Subjectively, he was one of the top shortstops of his era, but the numbers don't show that. Tinker, Evers, and Chance still make one ask, Why?

Third Base

George Brett	0.36	Mike Schmidt	0.33
Frank Baker	-0.01	Stan Hack	-0.66
Pie Traynor	-0.04	Freddie Lindstrom	-0.66
Eddie Mathews	-0.05	Harlond Clift	-0.67
Brooks Robinson	-0.16	Larry Gardner	-0.71
Ron Santo	-0.19	Tommy Leach	-0.75
Jimmy Collins	-0.26	Al Rosen	-0.77
Buddy Bell	-0.27	Heinie Groh	-0.81
Ken Boyer	-0.41	Pinky Higgins	-0.88
Bob Elliot	-0.48	Harmon Killebrew	-0.89
George Kell	-0.51	Jimmy Dykes	-0.90
Wade Boggs	-0.57	Bill Madlock	-1.00
Dick Allen	-0.62	Eddie Yost	-1.31
Graig Nettles	-0.60		

Wow! George Brett and Mike Schmidt ahead of the great Pie Traynor. Well, get used to it. Ron Santo has certainly been overlooked, as well as Ken Boyer. Wonder what the odds are that Buddy Bell will be elected to the Hall of Fame?

Outfield

Ty Cobb	1.16	Ted Williams	0.41
Tris Speaker	0.83	Stan Musial	0.37
Babe Ruth	0.74	Joe DiMaggio	0.34
Willie Mays	0.58	Mel Ott	0.22
Hank Aaron	0.56	Paul Waner	0.03
Al Simmons	0.45	Frank Robinson	0.03
Mickey Mantle	-0.02	Al Oliver	-0.48
Goose Goslin	-0.06	Bobby Veach	-0.49
Al Kaline	-0.07	Dave Parker	-0.49
Roberto Clemente	-0.08	Dwight Evans	-0.49
Max Carey	-0.09	Bobby Bonds	-0.50
Carl Yastrzemski	-0.11	Lou Brock	-0.51
Joe Medwick	-0.12	Sherry Magee	-0.51
Harry Heilmann	-0.13	Willie Davis	-0.51
Kiki Cuyler	-0.15	Doc Cramer	-0.51
Sam Rice	-0.17	Cy Williams	-0.51
Edd Roush	-0.17	Enos Slaughter	-0.55
Pete Rose	-0.19	Reggie Jackson	-0.56
Rickey Henderson	-0.20	Dale Murphy	-0.56
Zack Wheat	-0.20	Earl Combs	-0.58
Joe Jackson	-0.22	Reggie Smith	-0.59
Willie Keeler	-0.22	Hack Wilson	-0.59
Jim Rice	-0.22	Willie Wilson	-0.60
Richie Ashburn	-0.23	Minnie Minoso	-0.61
Earl Averill	-0.23	Harry Hooper	-0.62
Fred Clarke	-0.24	Larry Doby	-0.62
Sam Crawford	-0.24	Babe Herman	-0.63
Andre Dawson	-0.24	Del Ennis	-0.64
Dave Winfield	-0.26	Carl Furillo	-0.67
Bob Johnson	-0.27	Jimmy Sheckard	-0.68
Chuck Klein	-0.28	Dixie Walker	-0.70
Heinie Manush	-0.29	Ralph Kiner	-0.71
Vada Pinson	-0.32	Bing Miller	-0.73
Duke Snider	-0.32	Tony Oliva	-0.74
Amos Otis	-0.40	Elmer Flick	-0.76
Billy Williams	-0.43	Gee Walker	-0.82
Lloyd Waner	-0.44	Rusty Staub	-0.82
Fred Lynn	-0.44	Willie Stargell	-0.87
Tim Raines	-0.45	Roy Thomas	-0.91
Ken Williams	-0.48	Charlie Keller	-0.97

Well, the traditional favorites still come out on top: Cobb, Ruth, Speaker, Aaron, Mays, Williams, Musial, DiMaggio. Rickey Henderson looks like a shoo-in. Why not Indian Bob Johnson, Richie Ashburn, and my old favorite, Vada Pinson? Jim Rice has slipped a little but Andre Dawson and Dave Winfield are moving up.

Pitchers

Walter Johnson	1.61	Addie Joss	0.43
Cy Young	1.36	Whitey Ford	0.40
Christy Mathewson	1.34	Bob Gibson	0.40
Pete Alexander	1.09	Warren Spahn	0.37
Lefty Grove	0.77	Jim Palmer	0.32
Tom Seaver	0.73	Rube Waddell	0.26
Ed Walsh	0.58	Steve Carlton	0.21
Sandy Koufax	0.53	Bob Feller	0.14
Juan Marichal	0.51	Carl Hubbell	0.13
Eddie Plank	0.50	Nolan Ryan	0.13
Three Finger Brown	0.49	Fergie Jenkins	0.10
Dizzy Dean	-0.02	Billy Pierce	-0.63
Gaylord Perry	-0.02	Tommy John	-0.65
Chief Bender	-0.03	Early Wynn	-0.66
Bert Blyleven	-0.08	Wilbur Cooper	-0.68
Dazzy Vance	-0.08	Red Ruffing	-0.69
Sam Leever	-0.12	Milt Pappas	-0.70
Joe McGinnity	-0.12	Wes Ferrell	-0.70
Don Sutton	-0.13	Mel Stottlemyre	-0.71
Jesse Tannehill	-0.19	Jack Coombs	-0.74
Ed Reulbach	-0.20	Red Faber	-0.76
Don Drysdale	-0.21	Virgil Trucks	-0.76
Deacon Phillipe	-0.23	Bob Shawkey	-0.77
Jack Chesbro	-0.26	Bucky Walters	-0.78
Robin Roberts	-0.27	Jerry Koosman	-0.79
Lefty Gomez	-0.27	Burleigh Grimes	-0.82
Luis Tiant	-0.28	Schoolboy Rowe	-0.83
Phil Niekro	-0.29	Jim Kaat	-0.83
Hal Newhouser	-0.30	Art Nehf	-0.83
Hippo Vaughn	-0.31	Slim Sallee	-0.84
Jim Bunning	-0.33	Ted Lyons	-0.88
Catfish Hunter	-0.33	Herb Pennock	-0.90
Vic Willis	-0.35	Dolf Luque	-0.91
Urban Shocker	-0.40	Rube Marquard	-0.93
Stan Coveleski	-0.41	Freddie Fitzsimmons	-0.93
Babe Adams	-0.42	Eppa Rixey	-0.95
Mort Cooper	-0.45	Jim Perry	-0.96
Bob Lemon	-0.45	Eddie Rommel	-0.97
Carl Mays	-0.45	Jack Powell	-0.99
Tommy Bridges	-0.49	Hooks Dauss	-1.01
Vida Blue	-0.50	Paul Derringer	-1.06

Pitchers (cont.)

Bill Donovan	-0.53	Lew Burdette	-1.08
Dave McNally	-0.54	Waite Hoyt	-1.12
Doc White	-0.55	Pop Haines	-1.15
Harry Brecheen	-0.57	Dizzy Trout	-1.18
Allie Reynolds	-0.58	Larry French	-1.22
Mickey Lolich	-0.63		

Walter Johnson's +1.61 SDs was the highest of any player at any position. There seems to be a good mixture of older and more modern players throughout the list. Someone must have forgotten about Ed Reulbach, Sam Leever, Deacon Phillipe, and Jesse Tannehill.

Then you look at the bottom of the list and wonder what Pop Haines, Ted Lyons, Waite Hoyt, Eppa Rixey, Herb Pennock, Red Ruffing, Rube Marquard, Burleigh Grimes, and Red Faber are doing down there.

THE GREATEST SEASON A PITCHER EVER HAD

Bob Gibson in 1968

PETER M. GORDON

◆ ◆ ◆

We remember 1968 as The Year of the Pitcher. The National and American Leagues combined for a .237 batting average. Twenty-one percent of all games played that year were shutouts. Only five National League players batted over .300, and Carl Yastrzemski won the AL batting title with a whopping .301 average.

The pitching achievements that year, on the other hand, were prodigious. Gaylord Perry of the Giants and Ray Washburn of the Cardinals pitched consecutive no-hit games in Candlestick Park in September. Jerry Koosman, then a rookie pitcher, won 19 games for the ninth-place Mets. Don Drysdale set the record by hurling 58⅔ consecutive scoreless innings for the Dodgers in May, and Denny McLain won an astounding 31 games for the pennant-winning Tigers—the highest total since Lefty Grove won the same number in 1931.

Cardinal ace Bob Gibson had the best year of all, going 22–9 and allowing a microscopic 1.12 earned runs per game. Beating the previous marks set by demigods Walter Johnson and Grover Cleveland Alexander during the dead-ball era, Gibson set the record for lowest ERA in a season by any pitcher with more than 300 innings pitched. Gibson's 1.12 ERA appears, in the words of Roger Angell, one of "baseball's Everests like DiMaggio's 56-consecutive-game hitting streak."

At the time, Drysdale's and McLain's achievements received more attention than Gibson's. The image of Gibson as one of the dominant pitchers of his time seems to have faded from memory more than that of his contemporaries Sandy Koufax and Tom Seaver. However, Gibson's

1968 season, despite his relatively modest won-lost record, may have been the greatest season a pitcher ever had.

Bob Gibson overcame a fatherless, disease-ridden childhood (he suffered from ricketts, asthma, pneumonia, and a rheumatic heart) in Omaha's black ghetto to star in baseball and basketball in high school and win a basketball scholarship to Creighton University. He signed with the Cardinals in 1957 but first played basketball for the Harlem Globetrotters. Gibson said that he disliked the clowning around the 'Trotters did because he burned to win all the time. Once Johnny Keane placed him in the Cardinals' rotation in 1961, he increased his win total each year—from 13 in 1961, to 15, 18, 19, 20, and 21 in 1966. He was on track for 22 wins in 1967 when a Roberto Clemente line drive struck him on the leg in a June game, cracking his ankle. After being sprayed with pain killer Gibson stayed in the game. He walked Willie Stargell, got Bill Mazeroski to pop up, and worked Donn Clendenon to a 3–2 count before coming down hard following through on a fastball and snapping his already cracked bone. Gibson recovered in time to win a couple of games at the end of the season and 3 games in the 1967 World Series.

The Cardinals were favored to repeat as National League pennant winners in 1968. A healthy Gibson was expected to win at least 20 games. Most National League batters that year considered Gibson the best pitcher and hardest thrower in the league. On Opening Day, Felipe Alou said, "A guy like Gibson makes us worry two months ahead of time because we know he'll open the season against us . . . he's always challenging the batter and never lets up. He can reach back anytime and burn your bat."

Gibson threw a fastball that appeared to rise through the strike zone from right to left and jump so sharply at the last minute that many batters mistook it for a slider. Gibson's slider arrived at about three-quarters the speed of the fastball, usually at the extreme corners of the plate. His curve broke down sharply and could freeze the most menacing batters. These pitches were delivered with a hard-driving lunge off the mound that made Gibson look as if he were leaping at the hitter. He would often finish his delivery falling off the mound to his left, but still fielded his position well enough to earn the Gold Glove for pitchers from 1965 to 1973. Many people considered him the best athlete in the game.

Gibson's scowling, intense demeanor intimidated batters. He worked rapidly, wasting no time between pitches. As Tim McCarver, the Cardinals catcher, recalls, Bob would get mad if the catcher came out to talk to him. A batter who tried to break Gibson's rhythm by stepping in and out of the batter's box often would usually find himself sprawled in the dirt.

Both the Cardinals and Gibson got off to slow starts in 1968. When Gibson lost a rain-delayed game to the Giants 3–1, his record dropped to 3–5 and the Cards fell to fourth. Gibson's ERA stood at 1.54; his teammates had scored a total of 4 runs in his 5 losses.

The Cardinals rallied, and Gibson pitched them into first place for good on June 2. Then he threw 5 straight shutouts. Clete Boyer, the Atlanta Braves third baseman and one of Gibson's frequent victims, called him "as great a competitor as I've ever seen. . . . Gibson has such a great arm, such great motion, and such complete command of his situation that all we opposing batters can do is admire him and maybe wait for him to hang a pitch." By July, Gibson was approaching Don Drysdale's consecutive-scoreless-innings record. After 47 scoreless innings he allowed a Dodger to score on a wild pitch that many observers felt John Edwards should have caught. Gibson won the game 5–1, then shut out the Giants and Juan Marichal in his next start. But for that wild pitch, Gibson would have set a new mark with 65 consecutive scoreless innings. From June 2 to August 4 he allowed 2 earned runs in 99 innings. After his victory over the Phillies on July 25 he had a 1.04 ERA for the season. The Cardinal bullpen had taken to playing checkers and cards during his starts.

Gibson won relentlessly throughout August as the Cards opened up a 14½-game lead. All in all, he won 15 straight games until Willie Stargell's home run beat him on August 24, 6–4. Three of the runs in that game were unearned. In fact, had the Cardinal fielders done their job Gibson might never have lost a game that summer. Typically, Bob won his 20th game on September 3 without a great deal of offensive support, beating the Reds 1–0. The clubhouse banter afterwards perfectly captured his frustration. "Maybe now you'll pass Marichal [the league leader in wins]," a teammate said. Gibby replied, "Not if you guys keep getting only one run a game."

With the Cardinals way out in front of the league and the pennant clinched in mid-September, Gibson may have unconsciously relaxed a little while going 2–3 for the month. His ERA increased from 0.99 at the end of his streak to the season-ending 1.12. He also, however, had more than his share of hard luck. On September 18 he lost 1–0 when Gaylord Perry pitched the first of the two consecutive no-hitters. Nonetheless, Gibson's skill and desire had already helped push his team to the top of the league; he eminently deserved the Cy Young and Most Valuable Player Awards he won for the season.

Tim McCarver, Gibson's catcher, attributed Gibson's great season to his "amazing control" and great strength. Phil Niekro talked about Gibson's strength after losing to him 1–0. "That Gibson is such a great

Bob Gibson

competitor that when he makes his first pitch of the game he figures that it's the ninth inning and he's ahead by one run." McCarver told *The New Yorker*'s Roger Angell that Gibson first became a great pitcher in the summer of 1966, when he learned to hit the corners consistently. That skill, combined with his ability to throw hard for nine innings, made him unhittable in 1968. An amazing 92 percent of his starts (32 of 34) were "quality" starts; only once did he allow as many as four earned runs in a game. That year, Gibson was never relieved during an inning. Although he was at times removed for a pinch hitter while trailing, no opposing team ever knocked him out of the box. He completed 28 of his 34 starts, leading the NL with 268 strikeouts and 13 shutouts. There were other great pitchers in the league at that time—Drysdale, Marichal, and Seaver, to name a few—but Gibson stood head and shoulders above all of them.

Many fans looked forward to the '68 World Series because of the pitching matchup between 31-game-winner Denny McLain and Gibson. McLain received the lion's share of the press attention. In 1968, proud, aloof black men like Gibson who forcefully spoke their minds were not often treated kindly by the press. Also, while it was easy to appreciate McLain's number of wins, Gibson's ERA seemed only slightly better than that of his fellow hurlers.

The attention lavished on McLain may have spurred Gibson's already fierce competitive instincts. In the first game of the Series, Gibson turned the Tiger batters into Little Leaguers, striking out 17 of them in one of the greatest individual performances of all time. Gibson concentrated so intently on the game that in the ninth inning, after fanning Al Kaline, he shouted impatiently at catcher Tim McCarver to throw the ball back. McCarver pointed instead to the scoreboard behind Gibson in center field. Gibson yelled, "Come on, let's go!" but McCarver didn't yield. Finally Gibson turned and saw the announcement that he had tied Sandy Koufax's record for most strikeouts in a World Series game. Gibson kicked impatiently at the mound while the applause from the crowd swelled, got the ball, and quickly struck out Norm Cash and Willie Horton to end the game.

Afterwards, a reporter asked Gibson if he was surprised by his performance. "I'm never surprised at anything I do," he said. The Tigers certainly were. "I've never seen such overpowering pitching," said Al Kaline.

Gibson won the fourth game, too, beating McLain 10–1 and setting a record for most consecutive wins in World Series games with seven. Gibson and Lolich were deadlocked 0–0 into the seventh inning of the final game, when Card center fielder Curt Flood misjudged a two-out, two-on fly ball hit by Jim Northrup. Northrup ended up with a triple, driving in the game-winning runs. Bob Broeg of the St. Louis *Post-Dispatch* put it well when he said, "If Flood didn't misjudge that fly ball, they might still be out there pitching."

By any standards, Gibson's 1968 season ranks among the greatest of all time. Gibson's comparatively low total of 22 wins should not hide the fact of his absolute dominance of the league. In his 34 starts, the Cardinals averaged a mere 2.8 runs per game—.8 runs less than they averaged overall. (This is a minuscule total for a pennant winner, but National League teams that year averaged only 3.4 rains per game.) It's impossible to calculate with certainty just how many games Gibson would have won had the Cardinals scored a normal amount of runs; I attempted to estimate it two different ways.

First, I calculated that if the Cardinals scored their average amount of runs during Gibson's starts, they should have scored 112 runs. Their actual total was 87. Thus, the Cardinals scored 29 percent fewer runs in Gibson's starts than they would have if they were able to maintain their average performance. It's reasonable to assume that these additional runs would result in additional wins. Increasing Gibson's wins by 29 percent and decreasing his losses subsequently, we arrive at a record of 28–3, more in line with his ERA.

Secondly, I studied the box scores for each of his starts. Manager Red Schoendienst took Gibson out of a game only if he was behind, so I assumed he would remain in the game with a lead. Also, since no one ever scores precisely 3.6 runs per game, I calculated the outcome for each game had the Cardinals scored at least 3 runs and then at least 4 runs while Gibson was pitching. Had the Cardinals scored at least 4 runs for each of Gibson's starts, the record would have been 31–2, with one no-decision, all other things being equal. Had they scored at least three runs, his record would have been 27–5, with two no-decisions. It's certainly reasonable to conclude that decent offensive support would have resulted in a much higher win total and brought Gibson the attention he deserved.

How does Gibson's 1968 rank against other spectacular seasons? Once I established a study group of forty famous seasons, I decided to compare each pitcher's performance to that of his team and his league. I calculated the percentage of team games won by each pitcher and the differences between the pitcher's winning percentage and that of his team to determine how much the pitcher's performance rose above that of his team. To measure a pitcher's performance versus the rest of his league I decided to use a statistic developed by Bill James in his *Historical Baseball Abstract.* James measured a pitcher's effectiveness versus his league by dividing the pitcher's runs allowed by the average league runs allowed. A result of 1.00 meant that the pitcher performed at the league average; the lower the number the better the performance. James said that only the greats went as low as .50. Gibson's percentage for 1968 was .42, by far the lowest post-war figure. I did not have access to the runs-allowed data for the hurlers in my study, so I compared ERA to league ERA, which resulted in slightly lower numbers than James obtained.

I gave the most weight to a pitcher's ERA vs. league because single-season won-lost records do not reliably reflect a pitcher's worth. Evaluating a pitcher's ERA against the rest of his league substantially removes any illusion caused by playing conditions (i.e., poor batting averages) that year; 1968 may have been The Year of the Pitcher, but only Bob Gibson had a 1.12 ERA. Chart One sorts the forty seasons I selected by pitcher's ERA vs. league, with the lowest, or best, numbers, first. Surprisingly, Rollie Fingers' 1981 season is first and Bob Gibson's 1968 season is second. Walter Johnson's 1913 season is third, followed by Brown in 1906 and Mathewson in 1905. This measurement places Gibson in the company of some of the greatest pitchers of all time. Note that McLain's 1968 season ranks fourth from last.

In 1981, Fingers's ERA vs. league was the lowest by .09; as a relief pitcher he won or saved 54 percent of his team's games. He pitched during a strike-shortened season, however, and worked only 78 innings. Even if he sustained this level of performance over the season, his total innings pitched would have been much fewer than Gibson's. I rate Gibson's season higher since he sustained a high level of performance over many more innings.

The choice between Johnson in 1913 and Gibson in 1968 is much tougher. The Big Train is only .02 behind Gibson in ERA vs. league, and he won 14 more games for a team with a slightly worse record. However, Johnson pitched during the dead-ball era, where home runs were not a factor. Despite the low batting averages in 1968, the home run was a constant threat. Willie McCovey led the NL with 36, followed by Dick Allen with 33 and Ernie Banks with 32. In 1913 Frank Baker led the American League with 12, followed by Sam Crawford with 9. So I rate Gibson's season a hair greater.

Despite the Cards' third-place finish in 1969, Gibson won 20 games that year with a 2.18 ERA. In 1971, he won 23 games and his second Cy Young Award, while batting .303. An arthritic elbow and sore knees began to take a toll, but when he retired after the 1975 season Gibson had 251 wins and was second to Walter Johnson with 3117 career strikeouts. Bob Gibson should go down in history as one of the great pitchers of all time—and as the pitcher who had the greatest season of all time.

GREAT PITCHING PERFORMANCES 1892–1987 Pct. Pct. ERA v.

Player	Year	Wins	Losses	Pct.	ERA	Team Wins	Team Losses	Tm. Pct.	Lge. ERA	Team Wins	Abov. Tm.	Lg. Pct.
Rollie Fingers	1981	6	3	0.667	1.04	62	47	0.569	3.66	9.7	0.098	0.28
Bob Gibson	1968	22	9	0.709	1.12	97	65	0.598	2.99	22.7	0.111	0.37
Walter Johnson	1913	36	7	0.837	1.13	90	64	0.584	2.93	40.0	0.253	0.39
Three Finger Brown	1906	26	6	0.813	1.04	116	36	0.763	2.63	22.4	0.049	0.40
Christy Mathewson	1905	31	8	0.795	1.27	105	48	0.686	2.99	29.5	0.109	0.42
Dwight Gooden	1985	24	4	0.857	1.53	108	54	0.667	3.59	22.2	0.190	0.43
Cy Young	1901	33	10	0.767	1.62	79	57	0.581	3.66	41.8	0.187	0.44
Pete Alexander	1915	31	10	0.756	1.22	90	62	0.592	2.75	34.4	0.164	0.44
Ron Guidry	1978	25	3	0.893	1.74	100	63	0.613	3.77	25.0	0.280	0.46
Lefty Grove	1931	31	4	0.885	2.06	107	45	0.704	4.38	29.0	0.181	0.47
Sandy Koufax	1966	27	9	0.750	1.73	95	67	0.586	3.61	28.4	0.164	0.48
Willie Hernandez	1984	9	3	0.750	1.92	104	58	0.642	3.99	8.0	0.108	0.48
Warren Spahn	1953	23	7	0.767	2.10	92	62	0.597	4.29	25.0	0.170	0.49
Spud Chandler	1943	20	4	0.833	1.64	98	56	0.636	3.30	20.4	0.197	0.50
Carl Hubbell	1933	23	12	0.657	1.66	91	61	0.599	3.34	25.3	0.058	0.50
Lefty Gomez	1937	21	11	0.656	2.33	102	52	0.662	4.62	20.6	-0.006	0.50
Tom Seaver	1971	20	10	0.667	1.76	83	79	0.512	3.47	24.1	0.155	0.51
Jack Coombs	1910	31	9	0.775	1.30	102	48	0.680	2.53	30.4	0.095	0.51
Vida Blue	1971	24	8	0.750	1.82	101	60	0.627	3.47	23.8	0.123	0.52
Dazzy Vance	1930	17	15	0.531	2.61	86	68	0.558	4.97	19.8	-0.027	0.53
Mort Cooper	1942	22	7	0.758	1.78	106	48	0.688	3.31	20.8	0.070	0.54
Hal Newhouser	1945	25	9	0.735	1.81	88	65	0.575	3.36	28.4	0.160	0.54
Dazzy Vance	1924	28	6	0.824	2.16	92	62	0.597	3.87	30.4	0.227	0.56
Steve Carlton	1972	27	10	0.730	1.97	59	97	0.378	3.46	45.8	0.352	0.57
Sandy Koufax	1963	25	5	0.833	1.88	99	63	0.611	3.29	25.3	0.222	0.57
Smokey Joe Wood	1912	34	5	0.872	1.91	105	47	0.691	3.34	32.4	0.181	0.57
Carl Hubbell	1936	26	6	0.812	2.31	92	62	0.597	4.02	28.3	0.215	0.57
Sandy Koufax	1965	26	8	0.765	2.04	97	65	0.599	3.54	26.8	0.166	0.58
Bucky Walters	1939	27	11	0.710	2.29	97	57	0.630	3.92	27.8	0.080	0.58
Cy Young	1892	36	11	0.766	1.93	93	56	0.624	3.28	38.7	0.142	0.59
Bob Feller	1940	27	11	0.711	2.61	89	65	0.578	4.38	30.3	0.133	0.60
Roger Clemens	1986	24	4	0.857	2.48	95	66	0.590	4.08	25.0	0.267	0.61
Babe Ruth	1916	23	12	0.657	1.75	91	63	0.591	2.81	25.3	0.066	0.62
Jim Konstanty	1950	16	7	0.696	2.66	91	63	0.591	4.14	17.6	0.105	0.64
Walter Johnson	1924	23	7	0.767	2.72	92	62	0.597	4.23	25.0	0.170	0.64
Hal Newhouser	1944	29	9	0.763	2.22	88	66	0.571	3.43	33.0	0.192	0.65
Dizzy Dean	1934	30	7	0.811	2.66	95	58	0.621	4.06	31.6	0.190	0.66
Denny McLain	1968	31	6	0.837	1.96	103	59	0.636	2.98	30.1	0.201	0.66
Bobby Shantz	1952	24	7	0.774	2.48	79	75	0.513	3.67	30.4	0.261	0.68
Don Newcombe	1956	27	7	0.794	3.06	93	61	0.604	3.77	29.0	0.190	0.81

BOOKS NO SERIOUS FAN SHOULD BE WITHOUT

The Essential Baseball Library

COMPILED BY PAUL D. ADOMITES

♦ ♦ ♦

(Contributors: Dick Beverage, Bill Borst, Jon Daniels, Cappy Cagnon, Bob Hoie, Tom Jozwik, Phil Lowry, John Pardon, Larry Ritter, Leverett T. Smith, Jules Tygiel, Alan Blumkin, Jack Carlson, Jay Feldman, Mark Gallagher, Lloyd Johnson, Jack Kavanaugh, Vern Luse, Frank Phelps, Louis Rubin, Adie Suehsdorf, David Voigt)

Recently we performed a quick phone survey of selected members, asking each "What baseball book can you return to most often?" In other words, "Which is your favorite?"

One of the first things we noticed was that most SABR members had trouble keeping that answer to fewer than six or eight books. The average SABR member is a genuine reader who has a baseball library, not just a book or two. The next logical question, then, becomes: What books make up the essential baseball library?

We arrived at a request for fifty books, because it seemed to be both sufficient and manageable. Around fifty members were asked to participate; twenty-three did. (This wasn't meant to be a purely quantitative scientific survey; the members asked to participate are a true blue-ribbon panel of serious baseball writers and researchers. In fact, five of those who responded wrote or edited books on the list.) The result was over sixty type- or hand-written pages. More than 200 books were mentioned.

Yet of all that, the amount of agreement was remarkable. The "library" created has fifty-seven entries. (Some are multiple-volume sets.) To be listed, a work had to be recommended by more than three participants.

Not surprisingly, the two works mentioned most often were the Macmillan *Baseball Encyclopedia* and Lawrence Ritter's *The Glory of Their Times*.

In addition to mere lists, the participants provided their comments—some a few words, some rather extensive. Some even engaged in a little stream-of-consciousness pondering in their replies. ("I liked this one better than that one, but if I mention his one book, I really should mention. . . .") Alan Blumkins's last comment was "I did not overlook Ball Four." Vern Luse's list is appended separately; he created an essential library for researchers who, like he, specialize in the minor leagues. Jay Feldman was careful to point out the difference between "essential" works and "favorites," and so didn't include Roger Angell, *Shoeless Joe,* or *Hoopla.* Tom Jozwik looked at it from this angle: "Suppose my wife decreed that my library had to be reduced to fifty books for whatever reason. What would I keep?"

The categorization here was not developed before the titles were counted; in other words, we didn't go looking for books to fill a category—the fifty-seven books selected had more mentions than the others. They've put them in categories to make for easier analysis. As always, there is blurring between some categories.

The biggest surprise is the author who appears most often: Donald Honig. Although almost no one would rank him with the great historians, his solid work on the American and National Leagues and his two interview books—*Baseball Between the Lines* and *Baseball When the Grass Was Real*—all made the list. Roger Angell, Thomas Boswell, Jim Brosnan, Robert Creamer, Pat Jordan, and John Thorn each placed more than one book in the library. Charles Einstein's *Fireside* trilogy and multi-volume histories by David Voigt and Harold Seymour were listed, too. (No one mentioned *The SABR Review of Books Volume 1;* although several other SABR publications, notably Lowry's *Green Cathedrals* and the two volumes of *Minor League Stars,* were listed.)

By categories, here are the books, with assorted comments from the contributors. A full list of the library is located at the end of this article.

Statistics

Neft, Cohen, Deutsch. *The Sports Encyclopedia—Baseball*
Reichler, Joseph L., ed. *The Baseball Encyclopedia*
The Sporting News Baseball Guides & Registers
Thorn and Palmer. *The Hidden Game of Baseball*

There was consistent agreement across this category. Few other statistical works were mentioned at all. Most contributors indicated that both the Neft/Cohen/Deutsch and Reichler works are necessary, although, typically, there were disagreements.

Alan Blumkin: "The Neft/Cohen work is better organized than _The Baseball Encyclopedia_. It is also easier to carry."

Jack Kavanagh: "The 1969 _Baseball Encyclopedia_ has more specific content for minor players, but the latest updating is, of course, necessary too."

Jack Carlson: "Neft and Cohen fill the few gaps left in _The Baseball Encyclopedia_, but don't include the 1800s."

Bob Hoie on _The Hidden Game:_ "If for nothing but the history of statistics and statistical analysis this would be essential."

Dick Beverage on the same: "This isn't really my area of interest, but the subjects this book raises are very thought-provoking and interesting."

History

Asinof, Eliot. _Eight Men Out_
Daguerreotypes. The Sporting News
Fleming, Gordon. _The Unforgettable Season_
Honig, Donald. _The American League_
   The National League
The Bill James Historical Baseball Abstract
Kahn, Roger. _The Boys of Summer_
Lieb, Fred. _Baseball as I Have Known It_
Okrent and Lewine, eds. _The Ultimate Baseball Book_
Seymour, Harold. _Baseball—The Early Years_

Baseball—The Golden Age

Spink, J.G. Taylor. _Judge Landis and Twenty-Five Years of Baseball_
Tygiel, Jules. _Baseball's Great Experiment: Jackie Robinson and His Legacy_
Voigt, David. _American Baseball_ (3 volumes)

Cappy Gagnon said of _The Bill James Baseball Historical Abstract:_ "Any words I use to praise this work will be insufficient." Frank Phelps noted that Bill dedicated the book to Bob Davids—"a perfect start!"

The two multi-volume scholarly baseball histories—by Harold Seymour and David Voigt—each had particular fans. Adie Suehsdorf on Seymour: "Impeccably researched, absolutely accurate, complete, and pleasingly written. All that's missing is the third volume on the modern era."

Frank Phelps on Voigt: "Outstanding scholarly history closely relating baseball to the mainstream of American history." On Professor Seymour, Frank noted, "Work of the highest quality." Bill Borst said simply of Seymour: "The best histories ever written." Alan Blumkin offered this perspective: "Seymour is more detailed (than Voigt) but also much more difficult to read."

Tom Jozwik on *The Boys of Summer*: "For some reason I haven't been able to get into Kahn's more recent works, but this one certainly belongs."

Jon Daniels clarified his feelings about two works. On *The Ultimate Baseball Book*: "The ultimate baseball *picture* book." And on Honig's *American League* and *National League*: "The pictures are what makes these two books worthwhile."

Dick Beverage had this to say about *Judge Landis*: "A good account of the impact the Judge had on the game during his term as commissioner." But Lawrence Ritter points out of the same book: "Actually Fred Lieb wrote this."

Our favorite comment on the category was Jack Carlson's note on *The Unforgettable Season*: "The AL race was close, too."

Team Histories

Mead, William B. *Even the Browns*
Putnam team histories

Dick Beverage on *Even the Browns*: "A most readable book with lots of good information about the wartime era."

Adie Suehsdorf on the Putnam series: "Pedestrian as some of them were, Harold Kaese's *Boston Braves* and Lee Allen's *Cincinnati Reds* are particularly good."

Dick Beverage has read all the Putnams. Here are his particular recommendations: *"The Yankees, The Dodgers,* and *The Giants,* all written by the legendary Frank Graham; Lee Allen's *The Reds; The Indians* has a complete discussion of the Cry Baby Indians of 1940 and the 1948 pennant; *The Senators* is valuable for its discussion of Walter Johnson; Lieb's *The Red Sox* and *The Tigers* and Lieb and Baumgartner's *The Phillies;* Kaese and Lynch's *The Milwaukee Braves* is an updated version of *The Boston Braves* through the first Milwaukee season."

In Their Own League

Coffin, Tristram. *The Old Ball Game*
Gerlach, Larry. *Men in Blue*
Kerrane, Kevin. *Dollar Sign on the Muscle*
Lowenfish and Lupien. *The Imperfect Diamond*
Ritter, Lawrence S. *The Glory of Their Times*

This category consists of works that truly are one of a kind (the best in an area, if not the *only*.) The biggest surprise to the compiler was the Coffin work. I stumbled across it in a New York secondhand bookstore, and it was only one of a fistful of baseball books I brought home that day. What a find. But I had since figured that no one else had ever seen it. I was glad to find out I was wrong. Apparently a similar thing happened to Tom Jozwik. His wife bought him the book for his birthday. He calls it "the best birthday present I ever received—from anybody." Frank Phelps is less emotional: Coffin is "must reading for those who would understand the public image of baseball."

Dick Beverage on *The Imperfect Diamond:* "A history of baseball labor relations, it's an extremely thoughtful book that makes one much more sympathetic to the players' position."

Dick Beverage on *Dollar Sign on the Muscle:* "A pity, but I see this book frequently on remainder tables."

Lawrence Ritter on *The Men in Blue:* "Interview-type books depend on the interviewer's skills as an interviewer and as a writer. Gerlach is tops on both counts."

Naturally, the praise was universal for Lawrence Ritter's *The Glory of Their Times.* Perhaps Louis Rubin said it best: "Simply the greatest baseball book ever written—the distilled essence of the game. I can read this one over and over."

Adie Suehsdorf adds a more thoughtful note on why Ritter's imitators didn't always compare. "This book opened the way for a number of oral histories and is still the best of the bunch. The tape recorder endows these books with vivid authenticity, and the best interviews are warmly human. Unfortunately, these are the exceptions. Many old-time ballplayers have no real perspective on themselves or the great men they played with or against. They have no talent for autobiography. For every Edd Roush, still sputtering vigorously and profanely about McGraw half a century after the fact, there are all too many Willie Kamms talking as though his career were someone else's."

Biography/Auto- and Other

Alexander, Charles. *Ty Cobb*
Bouton, Jim. *Ball Four*
Brosnan, Jim. *The Long Season*
    Pennant Race
Creamer, Robert L. *Babe*
    Stengel—His Life and Times
Durocher, Leo. *Nice Guys Finish Last*

Honig, Donald. *Baseball Between the Lines*
  Baseball When the Grass Was Real
Jordan, Pat. *A False Spring*
  The Suitors of Spring
Murdock, Eugene. *Ban Johnson, Czar of Baseball*
Smelser, Marshall. *The Life that Ruth Built*
Veeck, Bill. *Veeck as in Wreck*

The only subject that approached controversy in this survey concerned the two famous biographies of Babe Ruth. Only four books in the entire survey received more mentions than Robert Creamer's *Babe: The Legend Comes to Life*. Yet more than a few people felt strongly that Marshall Smelser's *The Life that Ruth Built* surpasses it. Both Bill Borst and Cappy Gagnon rated Smelser ahead of Creamer. Jon Daniels feels that *Babe* "isn't as provocative as Sobol's or as scholarly as Smelser's but definitely the most complete." Louis Rubin says, "Creamer's is very good. Smelser's is better."

Frank Phelps says that the Smelser work is "extremely detailed, exhaustively researched." Dick Beverage takes the other side: *"Babe* is the best baseball biography ever." Alan Blumkin goes one step further; he feels that both Creamer's *Stengel* and *Babe* are "probably the best baseball biographies ever written." But Frank Phelps called Murdock's book on Ban Johnson "the best baseball bio yet!"

Many people found *A False Spring* a book that was bigger than baseball. Tom Jozwik: "Beyond a surface story, it's a loss of innocence/coming-of-age tale, a diary of small-town life that'll make the city reader feel blessed with his postage stamp yard and high taxes." Jules Tygiel: "Perhaps the best book about life in the minor leagues and failure, rather than success, in baseball." Lawrence Ritter says that Pat Jordan is "another writer in the Angell-Boswell class." Jon Daniels remembers of *The Suitors of Spring:* "This is where I learned about Steve Dalkowski."

Two writers whom not only history, position, first names, and syllabification inevitably link are Jim Brosnan and Jim Bouton. Each seems to have a place in the hearts of SABR readers. Lawrence Ritter said of Brosnan's ground-breaking *The Long Season:* "As far ahead of its time as Galileo." Cappy Gagnon recalls a special treat from *The Long Season:* "His inclusion of Twain's critique of Fenimore Cooper's literary Indians is priceless."

And Dick Beverage asks the sensible question: "Why hasn't Brosnan written more books?"

On *Ball Four,* Jon Daniels comments, "The original 'kiss-and-tell' baseball book seems tame now." While Tom Jozwik cautions, "Never forget that before there was a Bouton, there was a Brosnan."

Fiction
Kinsella, W.P. *Shoeless Joe*
Malamud, Bernard. *The Natural*

It was frankly a surprise to the compiler that so many SABR members were unable to arrive at a consensus on more baseball fiction. Several were mentioned (Robert Coover's *The Universal Baseball Association Inc., J. Henry Waugh, Prop.* and Philip Roth's *The Great American Novel),* and some were praised highly. But not by more than a couple folks.

Jules Tygiel commented on *Shoeless Joe:* "I read this one aloud to my wife." Bill Borst mentioned Eric Rolfe Greenberg's *The Celebrant,* Philip J. O'Connor's *Stealing Home,* Mark Harris's *Bang the Drum Slowly,* Harry Stein's *Hoopla, Shoeless Joe,* and Coover. But of *The Natural,* he said, "The movie was better."

The Minors
Obojski, Robert. *Bush League*
Society for American Baseball Research. *Minor League Stars I and II*

Dick Beverage on *Bush League:* "The standard general history. You can't find as much information about all of the leagues under one cover any place else."

Anthologies and Collections
Allen, Lee. *The Hot Stove League*
Angell, Roger. *Five Seasons*
   Late Innings
   The Summer Game
Boswell, Thomas. *How Life Imitates the World Series*
   Why Time Begins on Opening Day
David, L. Robert, ed. *Insider's Baseball*
Einstein, Charles, ed. *The Fireside Books of Baseball* (3 volumes)
   The Baseball Reader (a one-volume compilation from the three)
Thorn, John, ed. *The Armchair Book of Baseball*

Bob Hoie on *Hot Stove League:* "One of the first serious baseball histories I read and it blew me away. I couldn't believe all that information was available. I've never been the same since." Cappy Gagnon agrees: "If he wrote the Yellow Pages, I'd read them. *Hot Stove League* is the only baseball book I've ever read with the word 'oleaginous' in it."

Lawrence Ritter on Einstein: "It's hard to understand how the publisher could let these classics go out of print."

Most of the people who mentioned Roger Angell or Thomas Boswell listed all their books. Except for Mark Gallagher on *Five Seasons:* "I never read *The Summer Game,* but it can't be any better than this one." Jack Carlson on Angell: "He excels as he spellbinds."

Alan Blumkin says, *"Five Seasons* contains one of the two most sensitive pieces of baseball writing I've ever read: the piece on the demise of Steve Blass' pitching effectiveness."

Bill Borst on Boswell: "The most penetrating baseball writer today, by far."

Negro Leagues

Holway, John. *Voices from the Great Negro Baseball Leagues*
Peterson, Robert. *Only the Ball Was White*

Universal agreement here, too. These two works, along with Jules Tygiel's *Baseball's Great Experiment* (listed in the "History" category) most people agree cover the subject pretty well.

Ballparks

Lowry, Phil. *Green Cathedrals*
Reidenbaugh and Carter, eds. *Take Me Out to the Ball Park*
Shannon, Bill. *Ballparks*

Tom Jozwik on *Take Me Out to the Ball Park:* "The most impressive book I've seen on the subject of stadia. By relating the history of what goes on inside the parks, this is something of a baseball history of many cities."

Adie Suehsdorf on *Green Cathedrals:* "A unique compilation of basic material not available elsewhere."

Vern Luse's Special Minor League Essential List

1. *Baseball—The Early Years* and *Baseball—The Golden Age* by Harold Seymour. The former has the best bibliography on baseball history; the latter is especially valuable for the tracing of the birth and early years of the National Association (Minor Leagues).
2. *Microfilm Index of Minor League Baseball Cities* by Jerry Jackson. Although this was not a published book, it has been one of the most frequently consulted of all my possessions.

3. *Guide to Ohio Newspapers 1793–1973*. Steven Gutgesell, printed by the Ohio Historical Society. Would that other states had such books!

4. *Texas League Record Book*, William Ruggles. Originally published in 1930, various editions of greater or lesser quality have been issued by the league.

5. *Baseball in California* and *Pacific Coast Leagues,* Fred Lange. Good data in first-person anecdotes ranging back to the 1880s.

6, 7, and 8. *Southern League Record Book, South Atlantic League Record Book,* and *American Association Record Book.*

9. *Who's Who,* reprints from Ag Press, dating back to 1913. Especially good in the '20s and '30s.

10. *Reach Guides* and *Spalding Guides:* of some use in the pre-WWI era, deteriorated heavily in 1919–1940 era, disappeared in 1946.

11. *Sporting News Guides:* quite reliable beginning in 1946, deteriorating in accuracy beginning about 1960.

12. *Sporting Life,* on microfilm. I have the complete run. This is without question the single most important research tool I own. For study in the 1883–1916 era, an unparalleled asset.

13. *The Sporting News,* on microfilm. Two shootings of early TSN exist— one is very bad, picture quality poor, and the other is negative (SABR copy).

My Turn at Bat
Great at the Bat
The High Hard One
Pitching in a Pinch
other Durocher book

The Greatest Batting Eye in History

CAPPY GAGNON

♦ ♦ ♦

The concept of "batting eye" has fascinated me ever since the early '50s, when I began playing Ethan Allen's "All Star Baseball" table game. It was easy to visualize a player's relative offensive capabilities as you lay his card on the spinner. I favored players who drew a lot of walks but who didn't strike out much.

What do you call a player who fits this category? In his *Baseball Abstract* each year, Bill James refers to a player's walk/strikeout ratio. My formula is a method to put a number on this ability. The batting eye index is determined by subtracting strikeouts from walks and dividing the result by games played.

What is a "good eye"? It is not just drawing walks, because Reggie Jackson did that. Nor is it merely avoiding strikeouts, because Yogi Berra did that. The "B.E.I." combines those two attributes.

Who is the all-time best? Ted Williams. Hands down. No contest. I'm glad, because he would be the consensus choice if baseball experts were asked the question. Therefore, the B.E.I. validates conventional wisdom.

I am even happier because the career top fifty of the B.E.I. also uncovers some favorite players of mine and introduces as many lesser-known players as Hall of Famers. How can you not like a stat that includes Ferris Fain with Lou Gehrig, Johnny Bassler with Mickey Cochrane, and Elmer Valo with Ty Cobb?

Ted Williams and his strike zone

On the all-time B.E.I. list are players from the nineteenth century, dead-ball, lively-ball, World War II, modern, and expansion eras. There are large and small players. Every defensive position and spot in the batting order is covered. The only missing ingredient is a Latin player (refer to my list of "leading Latin walkers" to see why).

In case anyone questions whether Teddy Ballgame had the greatest "eye" in history, the B.E.I. removes all doubt. The Splendid Splinter produced the five highest ratings of all time, eight of the top 11, and 11 of the top 23. In 1954 he drew 136 walks in only 117 games, while fanning 32 times, for an astounding .889 figure. During his monster 1941 season he reached .825 with 145 free passes and only 27 whiffs. Ted didn't get these big numbers by playing patty cake at the plate, either, since his 521 career home runs exceed the total of the next ten men on the B.E.I. list.

Many of the players on this list had nicknames which suggest their B.E.I. prowess: Brat, Camera Eye, Crab, Devil, etc. Johnny Pesky even had an apt surname; Stan Hack did not. It's too bad that Bris Lord, "The Human Eyeball," didn't make it.

Five of the top eight on the career list played for Connie Mack (Fain, Bishop, Collins, Cochrane, and Speaker). Was he the first manager to recognize the value of a good batting eye? His 1927 second-base platoon paired two of the top six "eyes" of all time. Twenty-six-year-old Bishop and forty-year-old Collins walked 165 times and scored 130 runs, while hitting an even .300. In Cochrane's worst season for strikeouts, he had 26.

Catcher Rick Ferrell is an interesting contrast to his brother Wes. Rick is in the Hall of Fame. But Wes outslugged him by an astounding 83 points.

Joe Sewell's strikeout column looks like a misprint. From 1925 through 1933, he struck out only 48 times. (A single month's swinging for Dave Kingman.) Joe's big brother Luke, a catcher, was also a tough guy to fan.

Elmer Valo was the only player who accompanied three different franchises to new homes (the Philadelphia Athletics, the Brooklyn Dodgers, and the Washington Senators). Players like Valo, with little power and average batting skill, truly had great "eyes," since it is unlikely they were being pitched around. Those who led off, like Stanky and Yost, were especially valuable for setting up the heart of the lineups that followed.

Just under the minimum career figure of .250 were Zeke Bonura, Willie Kamm, Joe DiMaggio, Andy High, Joe Judge, and Nellie Fox. An 800-game career minimum lopped off Johnny Lipon and ·Topper Rigney. Because of incomplete strikeout figures, some of the dead-ball players have only part of their careers included, and incomplete data kept others from being considered.

Generally, the highest figures were in the '20s and the lowest were in the '60s. The 1949 Red Sox had a very good team B.E.I. with 835 walks and only 510 strikeouts. The 1935 Phillies had no single player with more walks than strikeouts, including Ethan Allen.

Lifetime B.E.I. Leaders

Name	Games	BB	K	Margin	Index
Ted Williams	2292	2019	709	1310	.572
Ferris Fain	1151	903	261	642	.558
Max Bishop	1338	1153	452	701	.524
Eddie Stanky	1259	996	374	622	.494
Johnny Bassler	811	437	81	356	.439
Eddie Collins	2113	1213	286	927	.439
Mickey Cochrane	1482	857	217	640	.432
Tris Speaker	2173	1145	220	925	.426
Johnny Evers	824	488	142	346	.420
Lu Blue	1615	1092	436	656	.406
Joe Sewell	1902	844	114	730	.384
Roy Cullenbine	1181	852	399	453	.384
Elmer Valo	1806	943	284	659	.365
Arky Vaughan	1817	937	276	661	.364
Johnny Pesky	1270	663	218	445	.350
Charlie Gehringer	2323	1185	372	813	.350
Rick Ferrell	1884	931	277	654	.347
Augie Galan	1742	979	393	586	.336
Lou Gehrig	2164	1508	789	719	.332
Eddie Yost	2109	1614	920	694	.329
Stan Hack	1938	1092	466	626	.329
Jackie Robinson	1382	740	291	449	.325
Joe Morgan	2650	1865	1015	850	.321
Luke Appling	2422	1302	528	774	.320
Jim Gilliam	1956	1036	416	620	.317
Wade Boggs	848	522	254	268	.316
Ossie Vitt	989	437	131	306	.309

Lifetime B.E.I. Leaders (cont.)

Name	Games	BB	K	Margin	Index
Ty Cobb	2013	963	357	606	.301
Nick Etten	937	480	199	281	.300
Stan Musial	3026	1599	696	903	.298
Mel Ott	2732	1708	896	812	.297
Willie Randolph	1614	957	479	478	.296
Lou Boudreau	1646	796	309	487	.296
Babe Ruth	2503	2056	1330	726	.290
Richie Ashburn	2189	1198	571	627	.286
Albie Pearson	988	477	195	282	.285
Harry Hooper	1795	919	412	507	.283
Paul Waner	2549	1091	376	715	.281
Eddie Lake	835	546	312	234	.280
Buddy Myer	1923	965	428	537	.279
Cap Anson	2162	892	294	598	.277
Tommy Holmes	1320	480	122	358	.271
Earl Combs	1454	670	278	392	.270
Billy Werber	1295	701	363	338	.261
Mike Hargrove	1559	26	521	405	.260
Tommy Henrich	1284	712	383	329	.256
Sid Gordon	1475	731	356	375	.254
Muddy Ruel	1461	606	238	368	.252
Elbie Fletcher	1415	851	495	356	.251

B.E.I. Single Season Records

1.	Ted Williams	1954	.889
2.	Ted Williams	1941	.825
3.	Ted Williams	1946	.747
4.	Ted Williams	1947	.737
5.	Ted Williams	1949	.736
6.	Johnny Evers	1910	.720
7.	Mickey Cochrane	1935	.704
8.	Eddie Stanky	1945	.693
9.	Ted Williams	1958	.689
10.	Ted Williams	1950	.685
11.	Ted Williams	1955	.684
12.	Luke Appling	1949	.683
13.	Arky Vaughan	1936	.672
14.	Eddie Collins	1925	.670
15.	Ted Williams	1951	.662
16.	Elmer Valo	1952	.659
17.	Max Bishop	1927	.658
18.	Max Bishop	1929	.651
19.	Lou Gehrig	1935	.631

B.E.I. Single Season Records (cont.)

20. Ted Williams	1942	.627
21. Ferris Fain	1953	.625
22. Lu Blue	1929	.623
23. Ted Williams	1948	.620
24. Eddie Collins	1918	.619
25. Eddie Stanky	1950	.618
26. Augie Galan	1947	.605
27. Charlie Gehringer	1940	.604

Most Times Leading League In B.E.I.

Ted Williams	13	Arky Vaughan	4
Joe Morgan	12	Eddie Stanky	4
Jim Gilliam	8	Albie Pearson	4
Max Bishop	5	Carl Yastrzemski	4
Eddie Collins	5	Mike Hargrove	4
Willie Randolph	5	Johnny Evers	3
Tris Speaker	4	Lou Gehrig	3
Paul Waner	4	George Burns	3
Mel Ott	4	Augie Galan	3

Second basemen have fared well with this stat. The first leader in B.E.I. was Johnny Evers. His .720 mark in 1910 was not equalled for 31 years. In 1923, keystoner Eddie Collins struck out only 8 times to go with 84 free passes. His .524 edged out Speaker (who outhomered his 15 strikeouts by 2) and the Babe (who drew a Ruthian number of 170 walks and hit .393). Lu Blue put up a .651 B.E.I. in 1929, only to finish second to Max Bishop. Max did the same thing to four Hall of Famers in '32, when his .588 annihilated Cochrane, Ruth, Gehrig, and Sewell.

Year By Year B.E.I. Leaders

Year	Name	Games	BB	K	Margin	B.E.I.
1910	Johnny Evers	125	108	18	90	.720
1911	Jimmy Sheckard	156	147	58	89	.571
1912	Miller Huggins	120	87	31	56	.467
1913	Joe Jackson	148	80	26	54	.365
1913	Al Bridwell	135	74	28	46	.343
1914	Eddie Collins	152	97	31	66	.434
1914	Johnny Evers	139	87	26	61	.439
1915	Eddie Collins	155	119	27	92	.594
1915	Johnny Evers	83	50	16	34	.410
1916	Tris Speaker	151	82	20	62	.411
1916	Heinie Groh	149	84	34	50	.336
1917	Eddie Collins	156	89	16	73	.468

Year By Year B.E.I. Leaders (cont.)

Year		Name	Games	BB	K	Margin	B.E.I.
1917		Heinie Groh	156	71	30	41	.281
1918		Eddie Collins	97	73	13	60	.619
1918		Max Flack	123	56	19	37	.301
1919		Jack Graney	128	105	39	66	.516
1919		George Burns	139	82	37	45	.324
1920		Tris Speaker	150	97	13	84	.560
1920		Charlie Hollocher	80	41	15	26	.325
1921		Babe Ruth	152	144	81	63	.438
1921		George Burns	149	80	24	56	.376
1922		Tris Speaker	131	77	11	66	.504
1922		Charlie Hollocher	152	58	5	53	.349
1923		Eddie Collins	145	84	8	76	.524
1923		George Burns	154	101	46	55	.357
1924		Ken Williams	114	69	17	52	.456
1924		Rogers Hornsby	143	89	32	57	.399
1925		Eddie Collins	118	87	8	79	.670
1925		Max Carey	133	66	19	47	.353
1926		Tris Speaker	150	94	15	79	.527
1926		Paul Waner	144	66	19	47	.326
1927		Max Bishop	117	105	28	77	.658
1927		George Harper	145	84	27	57	.393
1928		Max Bishop	126	97	36	61	.484
1928		Paul Waner	152	77	16	61	.401
1929		Max Bishop	129	128	44	84	.651
1929	T	George Grantham	110	93	38	55	.500
1929	T	Mel Ott	150	113	38	75	.500
1930		Max Bishop	130	128	60	68	.523
1930		Mel Ott	148	103	35	68	.460
1931		Babe Ruth	145	128	51	77	.531
1931		Paul Waner	150	73	21	52	.347
1932		Max Bishop	114	110	43	67	.588
1932		Mel Ott	154	100	39	61	.396
1933		Mickey Cochrane	130	106	22	84	.646
1933		Paul Waner	154	60	20	40	.260
1934		Lou Gehrig	154	109	31	78	.507
1934		Arky Vaughan	149	94	38	56	.376
1935		Mickey Cochrane	115	96	15	81	.704
1935		Arky Vaughan	137	97	18	79	.577
1936		Lou Gehrig	155	130	46	84	.542
1936		Arky Vaughan	156	118	21	97	.672
1937		Lou Gehrig	157	127	49	78	.497
1937		Gus Suhr	151	83	42	41	.272
1938		Charlie Gehringer	152	112	21	91	.599

Year By Year B.E.I. Leaders (cont.)

Year	Name	Games	BB	K	Margin	B.E.I.
1938	Arky Vaughan	148	104	21	83	.561
1939	Luke Appling	148	105	37	68	.460
1939	Mel Ott	125	100	50	50	.400
1940	Charlie Gehringer	139	101	17	84	.604
1940	Elbie Fletcher	147	119	54	65	.442
1941	Ted Williams	143	145	27	118	.825
1941	Cookie Lavagetto	132	80	21	59	.447
1942	Ted Williams	150	145	51	94	.627
1942	Stan Hack	140	94	40	54	.386
1943	Luke Appling	155	90	29	61	.394
1943	Augie Galan	139	103	39	64	.460
1944	Nick Etten	154	97	29	68	.442
1944	Augie Galan	151	101	23	78	.517
1945	Eddie Lake	133	106	37	69	.519
1945	Eddie Stanky	153	148	42	106	.693
1946	Ted Williams	150	156	44	112	.747
1946	Eddie Stanky	144	137	56	81	.563
1947	Ted Williams	156	162	47	115	.737
1947	Augie Galan	124	94	19	75	.605
1948	Ted Williams	137	126	41	85	.620
1948	Bob Elliott	151	131	57	74	.490
1949	Ted Williams	155	162	48	114	.736
1949	Eddie Stanky	138	113	41	72	.522
1950	Ted Williams	89	82	21	61	.685
1950	Eddie Stanky	152	144	50	94	.618
1951	Ted Williams	148	143	45	98	.662
1951	Ralph Kiner	151	137	57	80	.530
1952	Elmer Valo	129	101	16	85	.659
1952	Jackie Robinson	149	106	40	66	.443
1953	Ferris Fain	128	108	28	80	.625
1953	Stan Musial	157	105	32	73	.465
1954	Ted Williams	117	136	32	104	.889
1954	Richie Ashburn	153	125	46	79	.516
1955	Ted Williams	98	91	24	67	.684
1955	Richie Ashburn	140	105	36	69	.493
1956	Ted Williams	136	102	39	69	.463
1956	Jim Gilliam	153	95	39	56	.336
1957	Ted Williams	132	119	43	76	.576
1957	Johnny Temple	145	94	34	60	.414
1958	Ted Williams	129	98	49	49	.380
1958	Johnny Temple	141	91	41	50	.355
1959	Eddie Yost	148	135	77	58	.392
1959	Jim Gilliam	145	96	25	71	.490

Year By Year B.E.I. Leaders (cont.)

Year	Name	Games	BB	K	Margin	B.E.I.
1960	Eddie Yost	143	125	69	56	.392
1960	Jim Gilliam	151	96	28	68	.450
1961	Albie Pearson	144	96	40	56	.389
1961	Jim Gilliam	144	79	34	45	.313
1961	Albie Pearson	160	95	36	59	.369
1962	Jim Gilliam	160	93	35	58	.363
1963	Albie Pearson	154	92	37	55	.344
1963	Jim Gilliam	148	60	28	32	.216
1964	Dick Howser	162	76	39	37	.228
1964	Jim Gilliam	116	42	21	21	.181
1965	Albie Pearson	122	51	17	34	.224
1965	Jim Gilliam	111	53	31	22	.198
1966	Curt Blefary	131	73	56	17	.130
1966	Joe Morgan	122	89	43	46	.377
1967	Al Kaline	131	83	47	36	.275
1967	Joe Morgan	133	81	51	30	.226
1968	Carl Yastrzemski	157	119	90	29	.185
1968	Rusty Staub	161	73	57	16	.099
1969	Harmon Killebrew	162	145	84	61	.377
1969	Willie McCovey	149	121	66	55	.369
1970	Carl Yastrzemski	161	128	66	62	.385
1970	Willie McCovey	152	137	75	62	.408
1971	Paul Schaal	161	103	51	52	.323
1971	Joe Morgan	160	88	52	36	.225
1972	Roy White	155	99	59	40	.258
1972	Joe Morgan	149	115	44	71	.476
1973	Carl Yastrzemski	152	105	58	47	.309
1973	Joe Morgan	157	111	61	50	.319
1974	Carl Yastrzemski	148	104	48	56	.378
1974	Joe Morgan	149	120	69	51	.342
1975	John Mayberry	156	119	73	46	.315
1975	Joe Morgan	146	132	52	80	.548
1976	Mike Hargrove	151	97	64	33	.219
1976	Joe Morgan	141	114	41	73	.518
1977	Mike Hargrove	153	117	58	59	.386
1977	Joe Morgan	153	117	58	59	.386
1978	Mike Hargrove	148	107	47	60	.405
1978	Joe Morgan	132	79	40	39	.296
1979	Willie Randolph	153	95	39	56	.366
1979	Pete Rose	163	95	32	63	.387
1980	Willie Randolph	138	119	45	73	.529
1980	Joe Morgan	141	93	47	46	.326
1981	Mike Hargrove	94	60	16	44	.468

Year By Year B.E.I. Leaders (cont.)

Year	Name	Games	BB	K	Margin	B.E.I.
1981	Joe Morgan	90	66	37	29	.322
1982	Willie Randolph	144	75	35	40	.278
1982	Bill Russell	153	63	30	33	.216
1983	Wade Boggs	153	92	36	56	.366
1983	Joe Morgan	123	89	54	35	.285
1984	Willie Randolph	142	86	42	44	.310
1984	Ozzie Smith	124	56	17	39	.315
1985	Toby Harrah	126	113	60	53	.421
1985	Pete Rose	119	86	35	51	.429
1986	Wade Boggs	149	105	41	64	.430
1986	Ozzie Smith	153	79	27	52	.340
1987	Willie Randolph	120	82	25	57	.475
1987	Ozzie Smith	158	89	36	53	.335

Second basemen Jackie Robinson, Jim Gilliam, Joe Morgan, and Willie Randolph have all proved they have the "necessities" to make this exclusive group. In fact, since 1957, only Joe Morgan (twice) and Willie Randolph have bettered .500.

The two highest second-place scores were achieved by Gehrig in 1935 and Appling in 1949. Lou's .631 was a nice figure, but he was easily outdistanced by Cochrane's .704. In '49 Old Aches and Pains had a mighty .683, but the Splinter was 53 points ahead.

Because of the free-swinging approach now in vogue, current players do not fare well under B.E.I. scrutiny, although Boggs seems destined for the top 20 and Randolph ranks only a fraction behind Ott, Musial, and Cobb.

As further proof, in 1987 only eleven players had B.E.I.'s greater than .200!

Leading Latin-Born Walkers

Name	Home	BB	Year
1. Martinez	Puerto Rico	87	1985
2. Minoso	Cuba	86	1956
3. Carrasquel	Venezuela	85	1954
4. Estallela	Puerto Rico	85	1942
5. Guerrero	Dominican Republic	83	1985
5. Perez	Cuba	83	1970
7. Avila	Mexico	82	1955
8. Moreno	Panama	81	1978
9. Phillips	Panama	80	1967
10. Mantilla	Puerto Rico	79	1965
10. Minoso	Cuba	79	1957

Leading Latin-Born Walkers (cont.)

Name	Home	BB	Year
10. Tartabull	Puerto Rico	79	1987
13. Carew	Panama	78	1978
13. Lezcano	Puerto Rico	78	1982
13. Cardenal	Cuba	77	1975
15. Carty	Dominican Republic	77	1970
15. Lezcano	Puerto Rico	77	1979
15. Minoso	Cuba	77	1954
19. Chacon	Venezuela	76	1962
19. Minoso	Cuba	76	1955
21. Carew	Panama	74	1974
21. DeJesus	Puerto Rico	74	1978
21. Estallela	Puerto Rico	74	1945
21. Guerrero	Dominican Republic	74	1987
21. Mangual	Puerto Rico	74	1975
21. Minoso	Cuba	74	1953
21. Perez	Cuba	74	1973
28. Carew	Panama	73	1979
28. Cruz	Puerto Rico	73	1984
30. Cruz	Puerto Rico	72	1979
30. Guerrero	Dominican Republic	72	1983
30. Minoso	Cuba	72	1951
33. Minoso	Cuba	71	1952
33. Orta	Mexico	71	1980
35. Martinez	Puerto Rico	70	1987
35. Ogilvie	Panama	70	1982
37. Carew	Panama	69	1977
37. Cruz	Puerto Rico	69	1977
37. Rodriguez	Puerto Rico	69	1974
40. Bernazard	Puerto Rico	68	1985
40. Martinez	Puerto Rico	68	1984
40. Taylor	Cuba	68	1962
43. Bernazard	Puerto Rico	67	1982
43. Carew	Panama	67	1976
43. Carew	Panama	67	1982
43. Carty	Dominican Republic	67	1976
43. Minoso	Cuba	67	1961
43. Montanez	Puerto Rico	67	1971
49. Aparicio	Venezuela	66	1969
49. Cardenas	Cuba	66	1969
49. Cedeno	Dominican Republic	66	1980

BASEBALL'S FIRST GREAT PROFESSIONAL TEAM WENT UNDEFEATED. BUT HOW MANY GAMES DID THEY WIN?

The 1869 Red Stockings

DARRYL BROCK

♦ ♦ ♦

On October 18, 1869, the Cincinnati Red Stockings defeated the Philadelphia Athletics, 17–12, in a hard-fought game at the Union Grounds in Cincinnati. The next morning the Cincinnati *Enquirer* reported the result as the fifty-eighth consecutive season victory for the undefeated home team. The rival *Commercial,* whose baseball writer had covered the Red Stockings throughout the long season and accompanied them on tours to both coasts, listed it as the team's 57th win in 57 games played.

Two weeks later the Red Stockings journeyed to Louisville. Playing on November 3 with only eight players (pitcher Asa Brainard had missed the train), they soundly thumped the Kentucky Base Ball Club, 58–8, before darkness ended the six-inning contest. Captain Harry Wright entered the victory in his team's scorebook as number 56.

The next day, with Brainard on hand, the Red Stockings took on a "picked nine" of top players from Louisville's various clubs. They won again, 40–10. On this occasion, however, Wright did not give the contest a number—nor did he count it among the team's victories.

The next game—the Red Stockings' season finale—took place on November 6. It was played in Cincinnati, against New York's powerful Mutuals. The Red Stockings won, 17–8. Wright counted the final victory as 57. From that point on, all "official" 1869 Red Stocking season totals, including statistics compiled by Wright and released to newspapers, would be based upon his core list of 57 games.

The *Commercial,* having evidently attuned itself to prevailing orthodoxy, echoed Wright's total of 57 wins in 57 games, even though that was the number it had printed three games previously. The *Enquirer,* also repeating an earlier figure, numbered the final victory as 58. The New York *Tribune* reported 61 wins in 61 games.

How many games did the Red Stockings win in pro baseball's inaugural season? Confusion has not diminished with passing years. While individual player stats—particularly those of star shortstop George Wright— continue to be taken directly or extrapolated from Harry Wright's totals, the number of victories in 1869 (and, by extension, the historic two-season win streak snapped by the Brooklyn Atlantics on June 14, 1870) varies.

The problem is two-pronged. First, the Red Stockings played and won more than 57 games that year. But how many more? Of those contests, which should be counted? And second, Cincinnati was involved in some protested games that were not counted as wins on every list.

Some papers printed lists of Red Stocking victories containing certain rain- or otherwise-shortened contests in which the Red Stockings were headed for sure victory. Leading the Baltics of Wheeling, West Virginia 52–8 on June 30, the Red Stockings departed in the top of the fifth inning to catch a boat. On July 28, Cincinnati led the St. Louis Empires 17– 0 when rain stopped play in the fourth.

Strictly speaking, those contests should not have been included. The rulebook required a minimum of five complete innings for a decision; Harry Wright scrupulously observed that.

There were also preseason games against "field" nines. Nobody has ever suggested that they be counted—even though at least one of those contests was relatively close. The Red Stockings defeated the "field" by only nine runs, 24–15, in their first warm-up game, April 17, 1869.

The "field" on that particular day included the best players from local amateur clubs, together with a few Red Stocking Juniors. The Junior players, mostly of high-school age, wore uniforms identical to those of the famous First Nine. They too went undefeated that year, winning all 17 of their games. Harry Wright used them as a sort of farm club from which he drew substitutes in emergencies.

Conversely, nobody has suggested omitting any of the victories officially registered by the Red Stockings—with one possible exception, which will be discussed—even though some came against pathetically weak opponents. The Red Stockings blasted their archrivals, the Cincinnati Buckeyes, 103–8 and 72–15 (the latter in five innings). They beat the Fort Wayne Kekiongas, 86–8; the Cream Citys of Milwaukee, 85–7; the Riversides of Portsmouth, Ohio, 40–0; the New Orleans Southerns, 35–3; the

The 1869 Cincinnati Red Stockings. Standing: Cal McVey, Charles Gould, Harry Wright, George Wright, Fred Waterman. Seated: Andy Leonard, Doug Allison, Asa Brainard, Charles Sweasy

Mutuals of Springfield, Massachusetts, 80–5; the Pittsburgh Olympics, 54–2; the Unions of St. Louis, 70–9; the Pacifics of San Francisco, 66–4 (six innings); the San Francisco Atlantics, 76–5 (five innings); Omaha City, 65–1; and the Marions of Indiana, 63–4.

Most of those clearly didn't belong on the field with the Red Stockings. What they shared in common, however, was that they were established organized ballclubs and as such recognized by the governing National Association of Base Ball Players. Member clubs could send representatives to the annual winter meeting to vote on matters of rules and procedures. They could also participate in formal matches—hence Harry Wright considered them legitimate opponents.

A *match* was a best-of-three series between two teams during the course of a season. Contenders were supposed to agree in advance whether a game was to be a "match contest." If so, the challenger (not necessarily the visitor) had certain rights—such as selecting the type of ball to be used. The loser of the first game had the right to demand a rematch within a specified length of time. The team that won two games formally bested the other that season. In New York, a reigning champion kept the symbolic "whip pennant" until losing to a match challenger.

In Harry Wright's view—for the most part traditional and legalistic—an opponent therefore "counted" if capable of playing a match contest. Since "picked nines" did not exist as recognized entities and were incapable of engaging in matches, Wright did not count them.

By his lights he was undeniably correct. Yet the Association had relatively little authority. And the match system was rife with controversy. When facing strong inter-sectional opponents—most notably Philadelphia's Athletics—New York used to claim that their losses had not come in match games. That way they could keep the championship streamer among themselves. That ploy was used against the Red Stockings in 1869 by the pennant-holding Brooklyn Eckfords, who maintained that the first of their two solid losses to the Cincinnati club had not been within the match framework. Wright quite properly counted the win.

In short, a case could have been made—as the *Tribune* evidently did—for stretching the list of Red Stocking victories beyond the boundaries of the match system. From today's standpoint it makes little sense that Wright counted the Red Stockings' victory over the weak Kentuckys of Louisville, while ignoring the victory over the stronger Louisville picked nine. And how about two uncounted wins against a group of San Francisco all-stars? In the wake of "Waterloo defeats" suffered by that city's leading teams (in five contests they had averaged only 4 runs to the Red Stockings' 58), a select squad of the losers' best players, calling themselves the "California Nine," combined to "hold" the Red Stockings to a 46–14 win. Three days later the same players met the Red Stockings in Sacramento and again were defeated, 50–6. Decisive losses, true, yet those two contests, like the one in Louisville, were not counted among the Red Stockings' victories.

The other prong of the problem involves protest. Consider a famous game against the Troy Haymakers (a club seldom referred to by its official name, the Union of Lansingburgh). The Red Stockings had narrowly defeated the Haymakers in Troy, 37–31, in June. When the Haymakers journeyed to Cincinnati for a rematch two months later, the city overflowed with sporting fanatics from around the country. Gamblers bet huge amounts. The early "line" had the Red Stockings by a margin of 10 runs, and Haymaker bettors enjoyed the long end of two- or even three-to-one odds. It was rumored that Troy's John Morrissey, former U.S. boxing champion and current congressman from New York, had upwards of $20,000 riding on the Haymakers.

Playing before a boisterous capacity crowd some twelve thousand strong, the Red Stockings lost the coin flip and went to bat first. They were ignominiously "whitewashed" in the first inning, a development that provoked another wave of betting. The Haymakers scored 6 runs in their half of the first. But the Red Stockings came back with 10 in the second to 7 for the Haymakers, then 3 in the next two innings while shutting out their opponents to tie the score at 13–13. In the fifth each team scored four times, making it 17–17.

Leading off the top of the sixth, Cincinnati right fielder Cal McVey hit a foul tip that Haymaker catcher William Craver failed to hold. McVey swung at the next pitch, and a second foul ball landed between Craver's feet. The Rules stated that a "foul bound," a foul caught on one bounce, constituted an out. Craver snatched the ball up—with a handful of gravel, according to one account—and demanded of the umpire, "How's that?"

Observers at the press table, located behind the first base line, could not tell whether Craver had grabbed the ball in the air or on the ground. The umpire, J.R. Brockway of the Great Western Club of Cincinnati, a respected local player, judged with no hesitation that Craver had not caught the ball on the bounce and that McVey was therefore not out.

At that point the Haymakers' president abruptly ordered his players from the field. To a crescendo of jeers and groans—and a few rocks from a gang of boys—they packed up their bats, boarded a waiting horse-drawn omnibus, and departed through the carriage gate. McVey held his position at the plate during the confusion that followed. Brockway finally mounted a chair and announced that the victory was awarded to Cincinnati because the Unions had refused to proceed with the game—a statement he reiterated and signed in the Red Stockings' scorebook.

For weeks, charges and counter-charges were hurled in the sporting press. The Haymakers claimed they had been victimized by a partisan umpire, and that they had taken the only honorable course in departing. Red Stocking supporters charged that the Haymakers had been ordered to pull out of the game in order to protect the stakes of big-money interests in the east, who had been getting inning-by-inning accounts via telegraph. Majority opinions tended to support the Red Stockings; the Troy club had been involved in too many questionable games in the past.

In any case, both teams had agreed to the choice of umpire at the game's outset. His decision was final. The requisite five innings had been completed; he was perfectly within his rights to award a victory.

In later years, writers scanning the list of Red Stockings game scores have called the contest a tie. But in 1869 virtually nobody except the

Haymakers did so. The Cincinnati team won by forfeit—simple as that. Had the Red Stockings quit the diamond in Troy (or several other cities) where the umpiring had been questionable at best, they could have counted on an identical decision being rendered against them.

The Red Stockings had been involved in a strangely similar occurrence only three weeks earlier, on August 5, against the Central Citys of Syracuse. On the previous day, the Red Stockings had easily defeated the Syracuse visitors 37–9. But in the rematch, with Brainard mysteriously missing and catcher Allison unable to play his usual position because of badly cut and bruised hands, the two teams were tied 22–22 after seven innings.

In the top of the eighth, the Red Stockings broke loose for 14 runs before making an out. As dusk approached, it became evident to the Cincinnati press that the Syracuse players, particularly the pitcher, were stalling in hopes of the game being called and the result reverting to a tie. When Harry Wright went down swinging for the first out, the Central Citys charged that he had done so deliberately. Wright hotly objected, but the argument continued during the next three batters' turns. Finally—with McVey coming up to bat—the Syracuse team was ordered from the field by its president. Not all of the players immediately responded, but play stopped. McVey stood at the plate for five full minutes. Finally umpire Joe Doyle of the Cincinnati Buckeye Club awarded the victory to the Red Stockings, citing the Central Citys' refusal to continue. The game was called with two out in the top of the eighth, the score remaining as it stood—36–22 for the Red Stockings. Nobody except the Central Citys ever considered it anything but a Cincinnati victory.

In sum, while several of the Red Stockings' wins might be considered equivalent to modern-day protested contests, they were counted as full-fledged victories at the time. There is no reason now to change that practice. But there is substantial reason to add the three victories against those relatively strong "picked nines" from San Francisco and Louisville to Harry Wright's total, making the 1869 record 60–0 and the 1869–70 victory streak 84 consecutive games before the loss to the Brooklyn Atlantics.

Sixty victories without a loss: a memorable total, one representing, I think, the most accurate present-day measure of the Red Stockings' unparalleled dominance.

Single-Season Wonders

JAMIE SELKO

♦ ♦ ♦

I was always struck by Sparky Anderson's major league playing career: one year, 152 games. If you look through any record book that shows career stats, you quickly see that there are basically two types of short-career players: those whose careers consist of the proverbial "cup of coffee" in the bigs, and those who got a real chance and just didn't cut it. But you don't see many who played a single, full season, then vanished. Of more than 13,000 men who have played ball, I wondered, how many more Sparkys were there?

The answer: precious few. In the entire history of major league baseball, fewer than forty players appeared in at least half of their team's games one year and never played again. Concentrated in the three-league season of 1890 and the war years, one-year regulars surrendered to changing times and better-qualified teammates. What follows is a position-by-position review (with games played at the position indicated) of the top three one-year players and notable others.

1B

1. **146 games**—Dutch Schiebner. Dutch, who was born in Charlottenburg, Germany, was the fill-in for the Browns during the year George Sisler was out. He hit .275 with 4 home runs, which was not that good in the 1920s, and certainly not good enough to replace Mr. Sisler.

2. **145 games**—Art Mahan, 1940 Phillies. Art hit .244 with only 2 home runs and 39 RBIs for the futile Phils. He also pitched in one game.

3. **124 games**—Johnny Sturm, 1941 Yankees. He fell between Babe Dahlgren and Buddy Hassett in the Yankee search for a replacement for

Lou Gehrig. Had only 23 extra-base hits and 36 RBIs to go with his .239 average.

Others:

Monk Sherlock. He hit .324 in 92 games—70 at first—as a 1930 Phillies replacement for injured Don Hurst.

Jim Hart—a .311 hitter in 58 games for the 1901 Orioles.

Skyrocket Smith—was only twenty when he got his shot with Louisville in 1888. He hit .238 in 58 games.

2B

1. **152 games**—Sparky Anderson. An outstanding fielder for many years in the Dodger minor-league chain, he finally got his shot with the '59 Phillies. He held the record for fewest total bases and lowest slugging percentage, 150-plus games, and hit only .218.

2. **114 games**—Moon Mullen. He had only 13 extra-base hits for the 1944 Phils while batting .267.

3. **97 games**—Ace Stewart, 1895 Chicago. Hit .241 with 8 home runs, fielded .911.

Others:

Skeeter Kell—George's brother. Hit .221 in 75 games for the 1952 Philadelphia A's.

John Sipin—went on to long-time stardom in Japan after hitting .223 in 68 games for the 1969 Padres.

3B

1. **147 games**—Al Boucher, 1914 St Louis Feds. Hit .231 before disappearing.

2. **126 games**—Buddy Blair, 1942 A's. Hit a respectable .279 with 66 RBIs and 26 doubles.

3. **124 games**—Bob Maier. Third baseman for the champion Tigers in 1945, lost his spot to George Kell. Hit .263 with 1 home run.

Others:

Johnny Tobin, brother of good-hitting pitcher Jim. Hit .252 for '45 Red Sox in 84 games.

SS

1. **95 games**—Gair Allie, who played in 121 games for the '54 Pirates. Hit .199 and has one-year-career strikeout record of 84.

2. **94 games**—Harvey Aubrey. Hit .212 for the 1903 Boston National League entry.

3. **74 games**—Ben Conroy. In 117 games for Philadelphia's 1890 AA team, he hit a pathetic .171.

OF

1. **117 games**—Goat Anderson. He hit a lowly .206 for the 1907 Pirates. Although he scored 73 runs and had 27 steals, he managed only 12 RBIs and five extra-base hits.

2. **105 games**—Ernie Sulik, who hit a respectable .287 for the 1936 Phillies.

3t. **101 games**—Larry Murphy, .265 hitter for the 1891 AA Washington team.

3t. **101 games**—Rasty Wright, who split the 1890 season between the Cleveland NL and the Syracuse AA teams. He hit .282 and set two one-year records with 89 runs and 81 walks.

Others:

Buzz Arlett—had the best one-season career of all time: 26 doubles, 7 triples, and 18 home runs to go with a .313 average and a .538 slugging percentage for the 1931 Phils. Alas, the minor-league legend couldn't field.

Tex Vache—Hit .313 in 110 games (53 as an outfielder) for the 1925 Red Sox. He hit .340 in non-pinch-hitting roles.

Carlos Bernier—8 triples and 15 stolen bases with a .213 average in 105 games for the '53 Pirates.

Pete Gray—probably the most famous one-year ever. For the St. Louis Browns in 1944, this one-armed outfielder batted .218 in 77 games.

C

1. **80 games**—Harry Sage. Anemic hitting (.149) for Toledo in 1890.

2. **76 games**—Paul Florence, 1926 Giants. Hit .229.

3. **62 games**—Bill Ludwig, 1908 Cards. Hit .182.

P

1. **62 games**—Bill Wakefield, best pitcher on the '64 Mets; he was 3–5 with a team-leading 3.61 ERA.

57 games—Rich Thompson. 3–8 reliever for the 1985 Indians. He had a 6.30 ERA.

48 games—Parke Swartzel. He was 19–27 with 45 complete games and 410 innings pitched for Kansas City's 1889 AA team. He holds one-year records with 117 walks and 147 strikeouts.

47 games—Henry Schmidt, a 21-game winner for the 1903 Dodgers. He had 29 complete games, 301 innings pitched, and a 3.83 ERA.

Among other one-year players who played over 100 games but not predominantly at one position are Scotty Ingerton of the 1911 Boston Braves, who hit .250 in 521 at bats. He played 58 games at third, 43 in the outfield, 12 at first, 11 at second, and 4 at short. There was also Tom Cahill, who batted .256 for the American Association Louisville club in 1891. In addition to 2 games at third, 6 at second, and 12 in the outfield, he also played 49 at short and 56 behind the plate.

Little-Known Facts

The New York Yankees won the 1923 pennant by refusing to play the Chicago White Sox and the Detroit Tigers; as a result, Washington lost the pennant by one game. . . . Hank Greenberg, who hit 58 home runs for Detroit in 1938, could have broken Babe Ruth's single-season record of 60; Greenberg hit three homers in one game on July 12, but nobody was watching. . . . Wiley Fox, player-manager for the old Bare Legs in 1886, once ordered himself to bunt, and refused. Even though he subsequently hit a home run, he fined himself and was later fired for punching himself in the nose.

Conrad Horn

The Punch-and-Judy All-Star Team

LARRY THOMPSON

◆ ◆ ◆

Baseball fans have a habit of making up all manner of teams: All-Joneses, All-Polish, All-Funny-Nicknames. To these exercises in trivia, I add my own contributions: a team and an alternate team of the worst hitters ever to play regularly in the major leagues.

I hasten to add that my "all-star" team of bad hitters consists of good baseball players. The requirements for selection were a minimum of 3000 plate appearances during a major league career. Any player whom management considers competent enough to send to the plate at least 3000 times is one of the game's elite. Consequently, selection for the teams is recognition of a sort for a group of mostly forgotten, flea-flicking hitters who enjoyed long and notable careers.

I used essentially the same hitting formulas as Pete Palmer did to come up with a list of the *best* hitters in the book he and John Thorn co-authored, *The Hidden Game of Baseball*. I also tossed in a selection of baseball's worst hitting pitchers, although I created that list using a formula based solely on lowest batting averages over at least ten seasons and 250 at bats.

An important point to emphasize is that hitting skills have to be evaluated in the context of their times. My first choice as weakest-hitting first baseman is Klondike Douglas. Douglas's hitting statistics actually look better than second-place Tom Jones's but Klondike spent most of his career in the hard-hitting 1890s, while Jones spent his entire career during the pitcher-dominated first decade of this century. Likewise, batting averages are not the best determinant of a hitter's value at the plate. On-base percentage and slugging average are better measures of the offensive talents and contributions of a player.

Who was the worst hitter ever to play regularly in the major leagues? Even among quarrelsome statisticians the choice seems clear: Bill Bergen, a catcher for Cincinnati and Brooklyn during the early years of the century. Bergen hit over .200 only one year, had no power or speed, and hardly ever walked. Yet for seven of his eleven years in the National League he was the number-one catcher on his team.

The second-worst hitter was probably Hal Lanier, a shortstop for the Giants and Yankees in the 1960s and 1970s. At first glance, Lanier's batting stats don't look any worse than those of a couple dozen other weak-hitting shortstops. In addition to compiling low batting averages, however, Lanier didn't walk much or steal bases. Therefore, he comes out well below such notoriously weak-hitting shortstops as Mark Belanger.

In presenting the "all-star" and alternate "all-star" teams of baseball's worst hitters, I have elected to present their statistics on a "seasonal" basis, that is, by taking their career totals and dividing by seasons, to create hypothetical single season using 600 plate appearances as the standard. Career totals for each hitter can easily be found in standard reference books; my feeling was that a presentation of an average season would be more meaningful.

So here they are, baseball's worst hitters, an agreeably obscure team of good-field, no-hit players from the past.

The All-Star Team

	AB	R	H	2B	3B	HR	RBI	BB	SB	BA	OBA	SLG	OPS
1B													
Klondike Douglas (1896–1904)	555	73	152	17	6	2	55	45	17	.274	.328	.336	.664
2B													
Eddie Miksis (1944–1958)	560	70	132	17	3	8	42	40	10	.236	.287	.322	.609
3B													
Lee Tannehill (1903–1912)	566	50	125	20	4	0	52	34	9	.220	.265	.273	.538
SS													
Hal Lanier (1964–1973)	579	46	132	17	3	1	43	21	2	.228	.255	.275	.530
OF													
Mickey Doolan (1905–1918)	565	48	130	23	8	1	52	35	16	.230	.275	.306	.581
Dick Harley (1897–1903)	557	75	146	11	5	2	46	43	27	.262	.315	.312	.627
Mike Hershberger (1961–1971)	551	61	139	23	3	4	53	49	11	.252	.313	.328	.641

The All-Star Team (cont.)

	AB	R	H	2B	3B	HR	RBI	BB	SB	BA	OBA	SLG	OPS
C Bill Bergen (1901–1911)	583	27	99	9	4	0	37	17	4	.170	.193	.201	.394
RHP Dean Chance (1961–1971)										.066	—		—
LHP Dick Ellsworth (1958–1971)										.088	—		—

The Alternate All-Star Team

	AB	R	H	2B	3B	HR	RBI	BB	SB	BA	OBA	SLG	OPS
1B Tom Jones (1902–1910)	571	51	143	18	5	0	50	29	20	.251	.287	.303	.590
2B Gary Sutherland (1966–1978)	563	55	137	20	3	4	43	37	2	.243	.290	.311	.601
3B Frank O'Rourke (1912–1931)	557	75	141	27	6	2	59	43	14	.254	.307	.333	.640
OF Johnny Cooney (1921–1944)	565	68	162	22	4	0	37	35	5	.286	.328	.342	.670
Jim Busby (1950–1962)	559	71	146	21	5	6	58	41	13	.262	.312	.350	.672
Gil Coan (1946–1956)	555	74	141	19	8	8	54	45	16	.254	.310	.359	.669
C Malachi Kittredge (1890–1906)	557	52	122	15	4	2	54	43	9	.219	.275	.274	.549
RHP Bill Hands (1965–1975)										.078	—		—
LHP George Brunet (1956–1971)										.089	—		—

HOW TO MAKE FRIENDS, INFLUENCE PEOPLE, SUFFER NO BORES, AND LEARN IMPORTANT BASEBALL FACTS WITHOUT EVER HAVING TO LOOK THEM UP

The Great American Trivia Sting

ROBERT E. SHIPLEY

♦ ♦ ♦

The Objective: To set up and execute a well-deserved sting operation against the perfectly obnoxious baseball trivia bore of your choice.

The Mark: Any insufferable acquaintance who insists on torturing the entire world with constant, meaningless baseball minutiae. I am not talking about the average enthusiastic baseball fan, but about the person who seems to gain feelings of superiority by learning and then expounding on every boring and trivial detail of the game. You know the type well. His/her last conversation with you probably began with "What was the highest fielding average ever achieved by a third baseman using a Wilson glove?" For the purposes of this demonstration we will refer to the deserving mark as "Insufferable." We will also assume that the individual is male, even though this is not a prerequisite.

The Set-Up: You approach Insufferable with a sporting proposition to prove that, contrary to his own opinion, anyone can learn to become a baseball trivia expert with a minimum amount of effort. After deciding on an appropriate wager—perhaps for Insufferable to avoid all talk of trivia for a month—you suggest the following rules:

1. Only one question will be used to decide the bet. (As you will see, you can liberalize this rule later to your own advantage.)

2. The subject of the question will be limited to guessing the pennant winner for any major league pennant race since 1876.

3. Insufferable gets to select the contestant.

4. You will be allowed one minute before the contest to pass your secret formula for trivia success along to the contestant.

5. The contestant will be allowed to ask two questions (clues) and will be given two chances to guess the pennant winner based on the answers to the clues. Obviously, the clues cannot be any variation of: "Which teams were in the World Series that year?" or "Which team had the best won-lost record?" etc.

The Sting: You arrive at the appointed time to discover that Insufferable has selected his cousin Larchmont as the contestant. Although you fully expected Insufferable to choose, perhaps, a five-year-old child or someone in a coma, the selection of Larchmont does appear to go beyond the bounds of fair play. Insufferable is justifiably smug—secure in the knowledge that Larchmont once thought the Bronx Bombers were a group of terrorists from New York City. Your work is cut out for you.

Larchmont sits as if in a trance, preoccupied with adjusting his favorite red paisley bow tie and picking dried spaghetti sauce off his Madras shirt. With great trepidation you take him aside to whisper your secret instructions. He seems to understand, but who knows?

The game begins. Opening his *Total Baseball* with a Cheshire grin, Insufferable decides to go for a merciless kill. "Larchmont, old buddy, name the pennant winner in the Union Association in 1884."

Eyes rolling toward the ceiling, Larchmont slowly forms the first question that you imparted to him. "Which team led the league in runs scored that year?"

The grin quickly disappears from Insufferable's face. In barely audible tones he replies, "St. Louis."

"Then St. Louis was the pennant winner," Larchmont says matter-of-factly.

Insufferable's silence tells the whole story. Larchmont claps his hands in glee, knocking his glass of iced tea into his shoe. He seems not to notice.

With growing rage, Insufferable demands another chance—double or nothing. Graciously, you consent.

No fool, Insufferable searches for a pennant winner that did not lead the league in runs scored. The silence is broken only by the sound of flipping pages and of Larchmont absentmindedly squishing iced tea in and out of his toes.

Finally: "Which team won the National League pennant in 1966?"

Without hesitation Larchmont counters, "Which team led the league in runs scored?"

"Atlanta."

"Then Atlanta was the winner."

"Wrong! Wrong! Wrong!" Insufferable shouts in triumph.

"He gets another clue," you remind.

"No problem," Insufferable replies, his confidence restored.

Larchmont pauses to remember the second question. Finally he blurts out, "Which team gave up the fewest runs in the league that year?"

Insufferable answers by slamming the book shut and storming from the room.

Opening the discarded volume to officially confirm the outcome, you tell the confused cousin, "Los Angeles, Larchmont. Los Angeles gave up the fewest runs."

"Then, Los Angeles was the pennant winner."

"Precisely."

Why The Sting Works: While not 100 percent foolproof, the league leaders in runs scored and least runs allowed (opponent runs) are the two most powerful historical predictors of pennant success. Between 1876 and 1987, 50.2 percent of all pennant races were won by the team that led the league in runs scored. Thus the contestant has a one-in-two chance of deriving the right answer after the first clue. In 79 percent of the pennant races during the same period, the pennant winner either was first in runs scored or in least runs allowed. Hence, in eight out of ten contests, the contestant will be able to guess the pennant winner after two clues.

As shown in the table below, your chances for success improve the more unscrupulous Insufferable is. For example, he is more likely to pick pennant races in the more distant past to avoid lucky guesses based on general knowledge of current events. Unfortunately for him, these two predictors were even more powerful before 1980. (While not shown, these predictors succeed only 37.5 percent of the time from 1980–1987.) Or, if Insufferable tries to confuse the issue by turning to one of the past major leagues other than the National and American Leagues (i.e., Union Association, American Association, Players' League, or the Federal League) your chances for success are improved to no worse than 86 percent (92 percent for the nineteenth century).

Percentage of Pennant Races in Which Winners Led Their League in Runs Scored or Least Runs Allowed
1876–1987

	NL	AL	Other	Composite
1876–1987	77	82	86	79
1876–1900	79	—	92	83
1876–1910	82	100	92	87
1876–1920	82	95	86	86
1876–1930	83	97	86	88
1876–1940	81	95	86	86
1876–1950	82	92	86	86
1876–1960	82	88	86	85
1876–1970	81	86	86	83
1876–1980	80	86	86	83

This table also suggests refinements to the sting which you may want to attempt to improve your chances of success. For example, if Insufferable is agreeable, you could limit your universe to pre-1940 American League pennants, thus giving yourself no less than a 95 percent chance of success.

Of course, you could even try to limit the contest to pre-1910 American League pennants, where the chance of success is 100 percent. But I am sure you would not want to take advantage—good sport that you are!

The Rise and Fall of Louis Sockalexis

JAY FELDMAN

♦ ♦ ♦

> This is bounding Sockalexis,
> Fielder of the mighty Cleveland.
> Like the catapult in action,
> For the plate he throws the baseball,
> Till the rooter, blithely rooting,
> Shouts until he shakes the bleachers.
> "Sockalexis, Sockalexis,
> Sock it to them Sockalexis."
> —*1897 poem, author unknown*

Every year the *Cleveland Indians Media Guide* contains a short item called "History of Cleveland Names," which traces the titles of Cleveland's professional baseball clubs, beginning with the Forest Citys (1869) and continuing through the Spiders (1889), Blues (1900), Bronchos (1902), and Naps (1903).

The last—and longest—entry on the list reads: "1915—INDIANS. (A local newspaper ran a contest and the name Indians was suggested by a fan who said he was doing it in honor of an Indian player named Luis [sic] Francis Sockalexis, who was known as the Chief—the first American Indian to play in the major leagues. He was born in Old Towne [sic],

Maine in 1873 and played three seasons in a Cleveland uniform. In 1897 he hit .331, which was his best in the three seasons. The Chief died in 1913.)"

As interesting and informative as this brief history may be, it doesn't begin to tell the remarkable and poignant story of Sockalexis' meteoric big league career. Nor does it give any hint of the intriguing process by which, in the three-quarters of a century since his death, his life and deeds have taken on near-mythic proportions. Stories with little or no factual basis get repeated and embellished in a sort of historical folk-process version of the old party game of "Telephone" until Sockalexis takes on a Paul Bunyanesque aspect. In the legend of Louis Sockalexis, the threads of fact and fiction are intricately woven together into a tapestry of heroic dimensions, and while separating those threads is often difficult and sometimes impossible, one thing remains absolutely clear: Without question, Louis Francis Sockalexis ranks among the truly tragic figures in baseball history, a man of immense talent and unlimited potential whose "tragic flaw" led inevitably and inexorably to his downfall.

A Penobscot whose grandfather had been a tribal chief, Sockalexis was born on October 24, 1871 (not 1873 as indicated in the *Indians Media Guide*). He starred in track, football, and baseball in high school and prep school, but it was on the diamond, where he batted left and threw right, that Sockalexis really shone. Possessed of a cannon arm, a powerful swing, and blazing foot speed, "Sock" tore up the summer leagues around Maine in the early 1890s, and his reported feats from this period quickly took on a legendary quality: hitting a baseball the length of the Penobscot reservation (600 feet); throwing a baseball (1) over the top of a hotel tower, (2) over a ballpark grandstand and two rows of houses, and (3) across the Penobscot River.

It was in these summer leagues, supposedly, that an opposing manager named Gilbert Patten was so inspired by the Indian's play that he used Sockalexis as the model for his enormously popular Frank Merriwell stories for boys, written under the pen name of Burt L. Standish.

Sock's summer-league exploits also attracted the attention of fellow player Mike "Doc" Powers. Powers, who would later play with the Philadelphia Athletics, was then captain of the baseball team at Holy Cross, and he recruited Sockalexis for the college's nine. Turning down an offer to play professionally in the New England League, Sock entered the Worcester, Massachusetts school in the fall of 1894 as a "special student."

During his two-season college career, the bigger-than-life Sockalexis image continued to grow. In one game against Brown, he stole six bases (two for himself and four as a designated runner for an injured Holy Cross player).

Louis Sockalexis

In another game he went 4-for-5 at the plate, including a home run that cleared the fence and broke a fourth-story window in the Brown University chapel. Against Williams College Sockalexis is reputed to have hit a ball over the center fielder's head and scored standing up before the outfielder had even caught up with the ball. His overall batting average at Holy Cross was .444.

The stories of his Herculean throws from the outfield abound. One is described in the Worcester Telegram account of '96 Holy Cross-Georgetown game: "The crowd went into ecstasies over many plays, but there was one which raised their hair. It was a throw by Sockalexis from center field which cut off a run at the plate. It was a magnificent liner from the shoulder passing through the air like a cannon ball and reaching home plate in plenty of time." Another oft-repeated tale tells how, in a game against Harvard, a batter hit a ball well over the Indian's head. The playing field had no fence, and the ball rolled beyond some trees into a tennis court. Sockalexis, so the story goes, chased the ball down and threw a frozen rope to the pitcher, thereby holding the batter to a triple. After the game, two Harvard professors who were at the game measured the distance of the throw at 414 feet.

In 1897 Sockalexis followed Doc Powers to Notre Dame, where he was observed by Cleveland Spiders star and future Hall of Famer Jesse Burkett, who arranged a tryout with the National League club. Manager Patsy Tebeau signed Sock on sight for $1500 a year.

Sockalexis was an instantaneous success. Before the season even began, he was a hero. The March 27, 1897 issue of *Sporting Life* contained this report: "SOCKALEXIS, THE INDIAN, came to town Friday, and in 24 hours was the most popular man about the Kennard House, where he is stopping. He is a massive man, with gigantic bones and bulging muscles, and looks a ball player from the ground up to the top of his five feet, 11 inches of solid frame work. In a letter to [Spiders] President Robison, Mr.

John Ward says: 'I congratulate you on securing Sockalexis. I have seen him play perhaps a dozen games, and I unhesitatingly pronounce him a wonder. Why he has not been snapped up before by some League club looking for a sensational player is beyond my comprehension. . . . THEY'RE INDIANS NOW. There is no feature of the signing Sockalexis more gratifying than the fact that his presence on the team will result in relegating to obscurity the title of 'Spiders' by which the team has been handicapped for several reasons, to give place to the more significant name 'Indians.'"

On the field Sockalexis was equally sensational. For the first two and one-half months of the season his name was in the headlines on a daily basis for his spectacular hitting and fielding, and he became the hottest gate attraction in baseball.

On June 16 the Cleveland club came to the Polo Grounds for the first time, and the park was packed with New York fans eager to see pitcher Amos Rusie even the score with Sockalexis. In their first meeting Sock had tagged the Giants' ace for two hits. Rusie, who would later be elected to the Hall of Fame, owned the best curveball of the day, and the New York press had hyped the showdown for weeks. When Sockalexis came to bat in the first inning, a group in the bleachers rose to their feet and split the air with derisive war whoops. Undeterred, Sock smacked a Rusie curveball over the right fielder's head for a home run, bringing the war whoops to an abrupt end.

On July 3 Sockalexis was hitting .328 (81-for-247), with 40 runs scored, 39 RBIs, and 16 stolen bases. And then, suddenly the bottom fell out. He did not appear in the lineup again until July 8; he played on July 11 and 12, not again until July 24–25 and after that only three more times the remainder of the season.

Hughie Jennings, another future Hall of Famer, would later describe our hero's precipitous downfall in a series of syndicated reminiscences called *Rounding Third* (1926). "The turning point in his career came in Chicago," wrote Jennings. "It happened as a result of a play in the opening game of the series. When Cleveland came to bat in the ninth, the score was 3–0 in favor of Chicago. Cleveland filled the bases with two out, and Sockalexis came to bat. He hit a home run. Then, in the home half of the inning, Chicago got two men on bases with as many out.

"The batter smashed a long drive to the outfield. It looked like a home run, but Sockalexis made an almost impossible one-handed catch of the ball. His home run and his catch enabled Cleveland to win, 4–3.

"After the game the Spiders celebrated their unusual victory. Sockalexis, the hero of the occasion, was finally induced to take a drink by the jibes of his more or less intoxicated teammates. It was the first taste he ever had of liquor, and he liked it. He liked the effects even better, and from that time on Sockalexis was a slave to whiskey."

Great tale that it is, there are only two small problems with Jennings' story: (1) Except for a single grain of truth, it's a total fabrication; (2) from 1926 on, everyone who wrote about Sockalexis took the Jennings fable as gospel, and with subsequent embellishments became one of the cornerstones of the Sockalexis legend—the unquestioned beginning of his swift and irreversible slide—and in this form it has survived to the present day.

To begin with, none of the three home runs Sock hit in '97 came against Chicago. The one shred of veracity in the story is traceable to three consecutive games played in St. Louis at the beginning of the season. The following game accounts from the May 8, 1897 issue of *Sporting Life* not only indicate where Jennings found his inspiration, but also show how outstanding Sockalexis' play was.

ST. LOUIS vs. CLEVELAND at ST. LOUIS, APRIL 29. The Browns pulled an apparently lost game out of the fire in the ninth inning. With the score 6–4 against them, they went in, and singles by Dowd, Turner, Hartman and Bierbauer tied the score. With the bases full and two out, Sockalexis made a great catch of McFarland's long fly, which saved the game for his side. [The game ended in a 6–6 tie.]

ST. LOUIS vs. CLEVELAND at ST. LOUIS, APRIL 30. The Clevelands won their first game this season, defeating the Browns by a score of 12–4. . . . Sockalexis knocked the ball over the center field fence, one of the longest hits ever made on the grounds. [Since Cleveland never scored more than two runs in inning of the game, Sockalexis' round-tripper couldn't possibly have been a grand slam.]

ST. LOUIS vs. CLEVELAND at ST. LOUIS, MAY 1. Sockalexis covered himself with glory. In five times at bat made four hits, one a three-bagger when the bases were full. [Cleveland won the game, 8–3.]

Obviously, Jennings rolled these three games into one and came up with his neat little fiction. Equally untrue, and much more to the point, is the notion that Sockalexis had never touched a drop of whiskey in his life. In fact, he had once been reprimanded by the Jesuit fathers at Holy Cross for imbibing, and his Notre Dame career had come to an unceremonious end when he was dismissed from the school after having been arrested for public drunkenness. And when Cleveland owner Robison finally reached the point of fining and suspending Sockalexis at the beginning of August '97, he was quoted in the August 7, 1897 edition of *The Sporting News* as saying, "It was reported to me quite early in the season, soon after Sockalexis had been secured by the Cleveland club, that he had been intoxicated, and I found on investigation and by authority which I could not doubt that the story was correct. I spoke to the Indian about it, and he admitted that he had been in such a condition but pleaded extenuating circumstances and promised to abstain from then on. For a time I heard no more stories, but lately it has come to my ears that he has been drinking a good deal, and I received indisputable evidence today that he had been intoxicated two nights this week."

So, rather than fitting the convenient racial stereotype of the red man who takes one drink and becomes an incurable, overnight drunkard, it is clear that Sockalexis was no stranger to alcohol. It seems, moreover, particularly when confronted by Robison, that Sock was able to keep his drinking under control, for until July 3 he was playing every day and doing a more than adequate job. What happened, then, to cause such a dramatic reversal in Sockalexis' fortunes?

According to a story later told by manager Tebeau, Sock had "celebrated the Fourth of July by an all-night carousal in a red light joint" and had either jumped or fallen from a second-story window. (Larry Rutenbeck of Wichita, Kansas, who has done extensive research on Native Americans in baseball, points out that Sock was known as "The Red Romeo" and further notes that he may have been attempting to elude the said establishment's bouncer when he went out the window.) In the process, he hurt his foot, and the *Cleveland Plain Dealer* of July 6, 1897 mentioned the injury in noting his absence from the lineup the previous day.

In its July 13 edition under the headline, "A WOODEN INDIAN," the *Plain Dealer* account of the prior day's 8–2 loss to Boston reported that Sockalexis "acted as if [he] had disposed of too many mint juleps previous to the game. . . . Sockalexis . . . was directly responsible for all but one of Boston's runs. . . . A lame foot is the Indian's excuse, but a Turkish bath and a good rest might be an excellent remedy."

The foot injury, then, which forced him out of the lineup, was in all probability the catalyst for Sockalexis' hitting the skids. When he was playing every day, he was able to hold his drinking to a manageable level, but sitting on the bench, he could no longer keep it together. He played once in August and twice in September and finished the year with a .338 average.

In 1898 he played in 21 games and hit .224, and the next year made only seven appearances before being released. He bounced around the

New England minor leagues for a time, being picked up and released by one club after another. On August 24, 1900, the *Holyoke* (Massachusetts) *Times* told how "Louis Sockalexis, the once famous National League baseball player, appeared in court this morning on a charge of vagrancy and was given 30 days in the county jail. . . . Sockalexis presented a sorry appearance. His clothing indicated that it had been worn for weeks without change. His hair was unkempt, his face gaunt and bristly with several weeks' growth of beard, and his shoes so badly broken that his toes were protruding . . . he attributed his downfall to firewater. He said, 'They liked me on the baseball field, and I liked firewater.'"

   Sockalexis eventually returned to the anonymity of the Penobscot community, where he played some recreational ball with local clubs. He died on December 24, 1913 at the age of forty-two, while working as a woodcutter on a logging operation.

   In 1915 Cleveland's new American League team adopted the name "Indians." In 1934 the State of Maine honored Sockalexis with a formal ceremony to unveil a monument at his grave in the Penobscot tribal cemetery. In 1956 he became the first inductee into the Holy Cross Athletic Hall of Fame.

   In *Rounding Third,* Jennings wrote, "Yes, he might have been the greatest player of all time. He had a wonderful instinct and no man seemed to have so many natural gifts as Sockalexis." Given Jennings' track record for accuracy, this may well be hyperbole. Even if it is a bit of an exaggeration, though, it says something essential about Sockalexis: The man had some ineffable quality that caused people to idealize and romanticize him and his exploits—he thoroughly captured the popular imagination. Louis Sockalexis was the stuff that legends are made on.

Little-Known Facts

Babe Ruth once hit a ball that landed on a train passing outside the ballpark and was delivered two months later by parcel post to the home of Ty Cobb, who brought the ball to Yankee Stadium and handed it to the umpire when Ruth appeared at the plate for the second time in the first game of a doubleheader. Ruth was declared out, and the Yankees lost the pennant by one game. . . . Mordecai Rhodes, left-handed pitcher for Boston, played for seventeen years in the major leagues without a nickname.

Conrad Horn

**KNOWN AS HOT-BLOODED, ILL-TEMPERED, AND
WHO KNOWS HOW MANY OTHER ETHNIC
INSULTS, THE CUBAN RIGHTY WAS A
PIONEER, A PERFORMER, AND,
POSSIBLY, A HALL OF FAMER**

Dolf Luque, Baseball's First Hispanic Star

PETER C. BJARKMAN

♦ ♦ ♦

Perhaps the most spurious of apocryphal tales within the ample cata-
logue of legends that often substitute for serious baseball history is the
one surrounding the fiery-tempered Cuban hurler Adolfo Luque, who
pitched a dozen seasons for the Cincinnati Reds. Legend has it that
Luque, after taking a severe riding from the New York Giants bench,
stopped in mid-windup, placed the ball and glove gingerly alongside the
mound, then charged straight into the New York dugout to thrash flaky
Giants outfielder Casey Stengel to within an inch of his life.

This tale always manages to portray Luque within the strict perimeters
of a familiar Latin American stereotype—the quick-to-anger, hot-blooded,
and addle-brained Latino who knows little of North American idiom or
customs of fair play and can respond to the heat of combat only with
flashing temper and flailing fists. The image has, of course, been rein-
forced over the long summers of baseball's history by the unfortunate (if
largely uncharacteristic) real-life baseball events surrounding Latin hurlers.
Juan Marichal once brained Dodger catcher John Roseboro with his Louisville slugger when the Los Angeles receiver threw the ball to his pitcher
too close to Marichal's head. The Giants' Ruben Gomez was infamous for

memorable brushback incidents involving Carl Furillo and Frank Robinson. He once plunked heavy-hitting Joe Adcock on the wrist, released a second beanball as the enraged Brave first sacker charged toward the mound, then retreated to the safety of the dugout only to return moments later wielding an unsheathed switchblade.

The oft-told story involving Luque's kamikaze mission against the Giant bench seems, in its most popular version, either a distortion or an abstraction of real-time events. Neither the year (it had to be between 1921 and 1923, during Stengel's brief tenure with McGraw's club) nor circumstances are often mentioned when the legend is related, and specific events are never detailed with any care. This story always seems to receive far more press than those devoted to the facts and figures surrounding Luque's otherwise proud and productive twenty-year big-league career. He was a premier pitcher of the lively-ball era, a winner of nearly 200 major league contests, the first great Latin American ballplayer ever, and the first among his countrymen to pitch in a World Series, win 20 games in a single summer or 100 in a career, or lead a major league circuit in victories, winning percentage, and ERA. Dolf Luque was—indeed!—far more than simply the hot-tempered Latino who once, in a fit of temper, silenced the loquacious Charles Dillon Stengel.

For the record, the much ballyhooed incident involving Luque and Stengel does have its basis in raw fact. And like the Marichal-Roseboro affair four decades later, it appears to have contained events and details infrequently if ever properly reported. The setting was actually Cincinnati's Redland Field (later Crosley Field) on the day of a rare packed house in midsummer of 1922. The overflow crowd—allowed to stand along the sidelines, thus forcing players of both teams to take up bench seats outside the normal dugout area—added to the tensions of the afternoon. While the Giant bench, as was their normal practice, spent the early innings of the afternoon disparaging Cincinnati hurler Luque's Latin heritage, these taunts were more audible than usual on this particular day, because of the close proximity of the visiting team bench, only yards from the third-base line. Future Hall-of-Famer Ross Youngs was reportedly at the plate when the Cuban pitcher decided he had heard about enough from offending Giant outfielder Bill Cunningham, a particularly vociferous heckler seated boldly on McGraw's bench. Luque did, in fairness of fact, at this point leave both ball and glove at the center of the playing field while he suddenly charged after Cunningham, unleashing a fierce blow that missed the startled loudmouth and landed squarely on Stengel's jaw instead. The unreported details are that Luque was at least in part a justified aggressor, while Stengel remained a totally accidental and unwitting victim.

The infamous attack, it turns out, was something of a humorous misadventure and more the stuff of comic relief than the product of sinister provocation. While the inevitable free-for-all that ensued quickly led to Dolf Luque's banishment from the field of play, the now enraged Cuban soon returned to the battle scene, again screaming for Cunningham and brandishing an ash bat like an ancient lethal warclub. It subsequently took four policemen and assorted teammates to escort Luque from the ballpark yet a second time. The colorful Cincinnati pitcher managed to foreshadow both Marichal and Gomez all within this single moment of intemperate action. Yet what passed for comic interlude had dire consequences as well. Luque had suddenly and predictably played an unfortunate role in fueling the very stereotype that has since dogged his own career and that of so many of his countrymen. Yet like Marichal, he was in reality a fierce competitor who almost always manifested his will to win with a blazing fastball and some of the cleverest pitching of his age. He was, as well, a usually quiet and iron-willed man whose huge contributions to the game are unfortunately remembered today only by a diminished handful of his aging Cuban countrymen. So buried by circumstance are Luque's considerable and pioneering pitching achievements that reputable baseball historian Lonnie Wheeler fully reports the infamous Luque-Stengel brawl in his marvelous pictorial history of Cincinnati baseball, *The Cincinnati Game,* with John Baskin, (Orange Frazer Press, 1988)—then devotes an entire chapter of the same landmark book to "The Latin Connection" in Reds history without so much as a single mention of Dolf Luque or his unmatchable 1923 National League campaign in Cincinnati.

It is a fact now easily forgotten in view of the near tidal wave invasion of Latin players during the '80s—especially the seeming explosion of talent flooding the majors from the tiny island nation of the Dominican Republic—that before Castro shut down the supply lines in the early '60s, Cuba had dispatched a steady stream of talented players to the big leagues. The first and perhaps least notable was Esteban Bellan, an altogether average infielder with the Troy Haymakers and New York Mutuals of the National Association in the early 1870s; the first National Leaguers were Armando Marsans and Rafael Almeida, who both toiled over a few brief seasons with the Cincinnati club beginning in 1911. After the color barrier was bashed in 1947, the '50s ushered in quality players from Cuba as widely known for their baseball abilities as for their unique pioneer status—Sandy Amoros of the Dodgers, Camilo Pascual, Pete Ramos, Connie Marrero, and Julio Becquer with the Senators, Minnie Minoso, Mike Fornieles, and Sandy Consuegra of the White Sox, Chico Fernandez of the Phillies, Roman Mejias with the Pirates, Willie Miranda of the Orioles, and stellar lefty Mike Cuellar, who launched his illustrious pitching career with Cincinnati in 1959.

The best of the early Cubans, beyond the least shadow of a doubt, was Luque, a man who was clearly both fortunate beneficiary and ill-starred victim of racial and ethnic prejudices that ruled major league baseball of his era. While dark-skinned Cuban legend Martin Dihigo was barred from the majors, the light-skinned Luque was welcomed by management, if not always warmly accepted by the full complement of southern boys who staffed most big-league rosters. Ironically, Havana-born Luque had been raised only a decade and a half earlier and less than fifty miles from Dihigo, who himself hailed from the rural village of Matanzas. Yet while Luque labored at times brilliantly in the big leagues during the second, third, and fourth decades of the century, his achievements were always diminished in part because he pitched the bulk of his career in the hinterlands that were Cincinnati, in part because his nearly 200 big-league victories were spread thinly over twenty years rather than clustered in a handful of 20-game seasons (he had only one such year). And in the current Revisionist Age of baseball history writing—when Negro leaguers have at long last received not only their rightful due, but a huge nostalgic sympathy vote as well—Martin Dihigo is now widely revered as a cult figure and enshrined in Cooperstown for his Cuban and Mexican League play, while Luque himself lies obscured in the dust and chaff of baseball history.

The memorable pitching career of Dolf Luque might best be capsulized in three distinct stages. First were his early years of pitching in two different countries. Beginning professional play in Cuba in 1912 as both a pitcher and hard-hitting infielder, Luque displayed considerable talent at third base as well as on the mound. A mere six months later the talented youngster was promptly recruited by Dr. Hernandez Henriquez, a Cuban entrepreneur residing in New Jersey and operating the Long Branch franchise of the New Jersey-New York State League. A sterling 22–5 record that first New Jersey summer, along with a strange twist of baseball fate, soon provided the hotshot Cuban pitcher with a quick ticket to big-league fame. Professional baseball was not played in New York City on the Sabbath, and visiting major league clubs often supplemented sparse travel money by scheduling exhibition contests with the conveniently located Long Branch team on the available Sunday afternoon dates. It was this circumstance that allowed Luque to impress Boston Braves manager George Stallings sufficiently to earn a big-league contract late in the 1914 season, the very year in which Boston surprisingly charged from the rear of the pack in late summer to earn lasting reputation as the "Miracle Braves." In his debut with Boston, Dolf Luque became the first Latin American pitcher to appear in either the American or National League, preceding Emilio Palmero of the Giants by a single season and Oscar Tuero of the Cardinals by four campaigns.

Dolf Luque

Brief appearances with Boston in 1914 and 1915 provided little immediate success for the Cuban import, who soon found himself toiling with Jersey City and Toronto of the International League and Louisville of the American Association. A fast start (11 wins in 13 appearances) in the 1918 campaign, however, brought on stage two for Luque: a trip to Cincinnati. Luque was an immediate success in the Queen City, winning 16 games in the combined 1918–1919 seasons, throwing the first shutout by a Latin player, and playing a major role out of the bullpen when the Reds copped their first-ever National League flag in 1919. Luque himself made history in that fall as the first Latin to appear in World Series play. He threw five scoreless innings in two Series relief appearances, while the underdog Reds beat Charles Comiskey's Chicagoans in the infamous Black Sox Series.

It was Luque's 1923 campaign that provided his career hallmark. It was, indeed, one of the finest single campaigns ever enjoyed by a National League hurler. Luque went 27–8 and led the league in wins, winning percentage (.771), ERA (1.93), and shutouts (6). The six shutouts could well have been ten: he had four scoreless efforts erased in the ninth inning. His 1.93 ERA was not matched by a Latin hurler until Luis Tiant registered an almost unapproachable standard of 1.60 in the aberrant 1968 season. That same summer Luque also became the first pitcher among his countrymen to sock a major league homer, while himself allowing only two opposition homers in 322 innings, the second-stingiest home run allowance in the NL and close on the heels of the 1921 standard of one in 301 innings, recorded by Cincinnati Reds teammate and Hall-of-Famer Eppa Rixey.

Dolf Luque would never again enjoy a 20-win season. He did come close with a 16–18 mark (and league-leading 2.63 ERA) during the 1925 campaign. He did win consistently in double figures, however, over a ten-year span extending through his first of two brief seasons with Brooklyn at the outset of the next decade. It is one of the final ironies of Luque's career that while he was not technically the first Latin ballplayer with the Cincinnati Reds (following Marsans and Almeida in that role), he did actually hold this distinction with the Brooklyn Dodgers team he joined in 1930. And while he made his historic first World Series appearance with the Reds he made a truly significant Series contribution for the Giants by winning the critical fifth and final game of the 1933 Series with a four-inning relief stint against the Washington Senators.

The third and final dimension of Luque's lengthy career is the one almost totally unknown to North American fans, his brilliant three decades of seasons as player and manager in the winter-league play of his Caribbean homeland. As a pitcher in Cuba, Luque was legendary, compiling a 93–62 career mark spread over twenty-two short seasons of wintertime play, ranking as the Cuban League's leading pitcher (9–2) in 1928–29. In 1917 he was the league's leading hitter (.355), and he also managed league championship teams on eight different occasions.

Perhaps Luque's most significant contribution to the national pastime was his proven talent for developing big-league potential in the players he coached and managed over several decades of winter-league play. One of Luque's brightest and most accomplished students was future New York and Brooklyn star hurler Sal (the Barber) Maglie, who learned his tough style of "shaving" hitters close from his famed Cuban mentor. Luque was Maglie's pitching coach with the Giants during his 1945 rookie season, as well as his manager with Cienfuegos in the Cuban League that same winter, and at Puebla in the Mexican League in the summer seasons of 1946 and 1947. Maglie has often credited Luque above all others for preparing him for the major leagues. So did Latin America's first big-league batting champion, Bobby Avila, who played for Luque in Puebla during the Mexican League campaigns of 1946 and 1947. It was this very talent for player development, in the end, that perhaps spoke most eloquently about the falseness of Luque's popular image as an emotional, quick-tempered, and untutored ballplayer during his own big-league playing days.

When it comes to selecting a descriptive term to summarize Luque's career, "explosive" has often been the popular choice. For many commentators, this is the proper phrase to describe his reputed temperamental behavior, exaggerated onfield outbursts, infrequent yet widely reported pugilistic endeavors (Luque never shied away from knocking down his share of plate-hugging hitters, of course, but then neither did most successful moundsmen of his era). For these others, it characterizes a career that seemed to burst across the horizon with a single exceptional year, then fade into the obscurity of a forgotten journeyman big-leaguer. But both notions are wide-of-the-mark distortions, especially the one that sees Luque as a momentary flash on the baseball scene. "Durable" would be the far more accurate description. Luque was a tireless warrior whose pitching career seemed to stretch on almost without end. His glorious 1923 season came at the already considerable age of thirty-three; he again led the Senior Circuit in ERA (2.63) two summers later at age thirty-five; he recorded 14 victories and a .636 winning percentage in 1930 while pitching for the Dodgers at the advanced age of forty; his two shutouts that season advanced his career total to 26, a mark that was unsurpassed among Latin pitchers until the arrival of Marichal, Pascual, Tiant, and Cuellar in the decade of the Sixties. Referred to widely as the rejuvenated "Papa Montero" by 1933, he recorded eight crucial wins that summer and the clinching World Series victory at age forty-three. His big-league career did not end until he was forty-five and had registered twenty full seasons, only one short of the National League longevity standard for hurlers held jointly by Warren Spahn and Eppa Rixey.

Luque's unique claim on durability and longevity is even further strengthened when one takes into consideration his remarkable winter-league career played out over an incredible thirty-four summers in Cuba. Debuting with Club Fe of Havana in 1912 at age twenty-two, the indefatigable right-hander registered his final winter-season triumph at age forty-six in 1936, then returned a full decade later to pitch several innings of stellar relief work in the 1945–46 season at the unimaginable age of fifty-five. Luque's combined totals for major league and winter-league baseball—stretching over almost thirty-five years—total 284 wins, a figure still unrivaled among all his Latin countrymen. And for those critics who would hasten to establish that longevity alone is not sufficient merit for baseball immortality, it should also be established that Luque's twenty-year ERA of 3.24 outstrips such notable Hall of Famers as Bob Feller, Early Wynn, and Robin Roberts. Perhaps the greatest irony surrounding Luque's big-league career is the misconception that he was a cold, laconic, and hot-tempered man, either on the field or off. When he died of a heart attack in July 1957 at age sixty-six, legendary sportswriter Frank Graham provided the final and perhaps most eloquent tribute: "It's hard to believe. Adolfo Luque was much too strong, too tough, too determined to die at this age of sixty-six . . . he died of a heart attack. Did he? It sounds absurd. Luque's heart failed him in the clutch? It never did before. How many close ball games did he pitch? How many did he win . . . or lose? When he won, it was sometimes on his heart. When he lost, it was never because his heart missed a beat. Some enemy hitter got lucky or some idiot playing behind Luque fumbled a ground ball or dropped a sinking liner or was out of position so that he did not make the catch that should have been so easy for him."

New focus on Latin players has also brought Luque's name (if not full memory of his career) back into our collective baseball consciousness. Any proper list of all-time Latin American hurlers reveals him as surpassed in accomplishment only by Marichal and by his own modern-day alter-ego and fellow countryman, Tiant. Even today Luque still far outdistances all other Latin hurlers, including such memorable figures as Mike Cuellar, Camilo Pascual, Juan Pizarro, Dennis Martinez, and Fernando Valenzuela. In the now-forgotten category of hitting by pitchers, Dolf Luque led the Cuban winter circuit in batting, posting a career .252 average in winter-league play, and batting over .227 during twenty major league seasons. For the educated fan who has pored religiously over the game's rich archives, Dolf Luque is a presence unmatched by all other Hispanic heroes of sport's golden decades between the two great wars.

It would surely be an exaggeration to argue for Luque's enshrinement in Cooperstown solely on the basis of his substantial yet hardly unparalleled big-league numbers, though some have grabbed immortality with far less impressive credentials. It would be equally absurd to dismiss him as a journeyman pitcher of average talent and few remarkable achievements. Few other hurlers have enjoyed his dominance over a short span of seasons. Fewer still have proved as durable or maintained their dominance over big-league hitters at so hoary an age. Almost none have contributed to the national pastime so richly after the door slammed shut upon an active big-league playing career. Almost no other major league pitcher did so much with so little fanfare.

Luque's Winterball Statistics

The following Cuban winter league statistics for Adolfo Luque are provided with the assistance of reputable Cuban baseball scholar and journalist Angel Torres and have previously appeared in their most complete form (including yearly batting statistics omitted here) in Torres' own self-published, heavily illustrated, and little-circulated book entitled *La Historia del Beisbol Cubano, 1878–1976* (Los Angeles, 1976).

Year	Team	G	CG	W–L	Pct.
1912	Club Fe	7	2	0–3	.000
1913	Club Fe	2	0	0–2	.000
1913–14	Habana	6	3	2–3	.400
1914–15	Almendares	16	6	7–4	.636
1915–16	Almendares	20	11	12–5	.706
1917	Orientales	9	6	4–4	.500
1918–19	None		Did not play		
1919–20	Almendares	15	9	10–4	.714
1920–21	Almendares	10	6	4–2	.667
1921	Almendares		Did not play due to injury		
1922–23	Habana	23	12	11–9	.550
1923–24	Habana	11	5	7–2	.778
1924–25	Almendares	3	3	3–0	1.000
1925–26	None		Did not play		
1926–27	Alacranes	16	13	10–6	.625
1927–28	Almendares	13	6	6–4	.600
1928–29	Cuba-Habana	17	9	9–2	.818
1929–30	Habana	15	7	4–8	.333
1930–31	None		Did not play		
1931–32	None		Did not play		
1932–33	Almendares	6	2	2–2	.500
1933–34	Season cancelled				
1934–35	Almendares	10	6	6–2	.750
1935–36	Almendares	7	5	4–2	.667
1936–37	Almendares	7	1	2–2	.500
1937–38	Almendares	1	0	0–1	.000
1938–39	Almendares	1	0	0–1	.000
1945–46	Cienfuegos	1	0	0–0	.000
Totals	22 years	210	99	93–62	.600

During approximately the same period (the 19 seasons he pitched between 1923 and 1947) Negro League Hall-of-Famer Martin Dihigo compiled a comparable pitching record in the same Cuban Professional Baseball League, recording 262 game appearances, 120 complete games, and a slightly superior won-lost record of 106–59.

Latin-American Big-League Pitchers

Eleven pitchers below comprise a select list of Latin American-born hurlers who have won a minimum of 100 big-league games through 1989. This listing of all-time greats among Latin pitchers is arranged on the basis of total wins, with career leaders in other statistical categories indicated by boldface. While the all-time leader in career losses, Luque ranks well up in all other statistical categories, standing third in victories, fourth in ERA, and third all-time in innings pitched.

Pitcher	W–L	Pct.	ERA	IP	SO	BB
Juan Marichal (Dominican) 1960–75	243–142	.631	2.89	3509	2303	709
Luis Tiant Jr. (Cuba) 1964–82	229–172	.571	3.30	3486	2416	1104
Dolf Luque (Cuba) 1914–35	194–179	.519	3.24	3220	1130	918
Dennis Martinez (Nicaragua) 1976–92	193–156	.563	3.62	3160	1693	926
Mike Cuellar (Cuba) 1959–77	185–130	.587	3.14	2808	1632	822
Camilo Pascual (Cuba) 1954–71	175–170	.506	3.63	2930	2167	1069
Fernando Valenzuela (Mexico) 1980–91	141–118	.544	3.34	2356	1764	918
Juan Pizarro (Puerto Rico) 1957–74	131–105	.555	3.43	2034	1522	888
Joaquin Andujar (Dominican) 1977–88	127–118	.518	3.58	2154	1032	731
Pedro Ramos (Cuba) 1955–70	117–160	.422	4.08	1643	1415	629
Mario Soto (Dominican) 1977–88	100–92	.521	3.47	1731	1449	657

Latin Pitchers as Hitters

Among hard-hitting Hispanic pitchers, Luque led in almost all lifetime batting categories, including runs scored, hits, triples, RBIs, and batting average. Luque also won a Cuban League batting title in 1917 (.355 during a 25-game season) and compiled a lifetime .252 average over 22 seasons of Cuban winter-league play (in 671 career at bats).

Pitcher	AB	Runs	Hits	2B	3B	HR	RBI	BA
Dolf Luque (1914–35)	1043	96	237	31	10	5	90	.227
Camilo Pascual (1954–71)	977	71	198	32	5	5	81	.203
Juan Pizarro (1957–74)	658	72	133	18	2	8	66	.202
Ruben Gomez (1953–67)	477	58	95	11	1	3	22	.199
Fernando Valenzuela (1980–91)	672	37	130	15	1	7	55	.193
Jesse Flores (1942–50)	304	18	55	7	2	0	22	.181
Sandy Consuegra (1950–57)	218	15	37	2	0	0	18	.170
Mike Fornieles (1952–63)	308	25	52	7	1	1	16	.169

ONE OF BASEBALL'S GREAT HISTORIANS RECALLS THE GAME'S FLAVORFUL NONCONFORMISTS

Thank God for Nuts!

DAVID Q. VOIGT

♦ ♦ ♦

America's enduring flirtation with major league baseball still challenges students of national character to try to explain the phenomenon. After all, a typical game offers as little as ten minutes of action during its two-and-one-half-hour course. Obviously other factors must invigorate the spectacle. Not the least of these are the antics of the ubiquitous nuts who are counted among the few constants in the known universe. Indeed, baseball is fortunate to be surfeited with perennial crops of nuts who sprout in all the game's constituencies. By their antics they enrich the game and contribute mightily to the dynamic flow of American humor.

Like the populace that wallows in it, American humor resembles a crazy quilt of diversity which shows little signs of merging into a singular form. Ever mixing and growing, the flood of American humor gains strength from media revolutions which have augmented spoken discourse with publications and broadcasts, thus lending credence to the late Marshall McLuhan's punning observation that the medium provides the massage!

And ever roiling in the flood of American humor is a whirlpool of nutty behavior. Indeed, nuts are almost as old as American society. Until 1800, according to Eric Partridge's *Dictionary of American Slang*, the word "nuts" designated commendable zealous behavior on the part of targeted individuals. But by 1858 the term had come to denote wrongheaded behavior. And so with other shadings the same meaning applies.

Major league baseball owes much to its plentiful nuts. This was a point well grasped by the late baseball historian Lee Allen, whose loving recollections of the game's nutty characters included the benediction, "Thank God for Nuts."

Baseball's history is dotted with memorable nutty episodes that have found their place in the humorous folklore of America. What aficionado has not heard of the Cleveland Wanderers of 1899, losers of 134 games? Or of the 239 errors committed by the 1930 Phillies? Or bonehead Fred Merkle's failure to touch second base that contributed to the Giants' narrow defeat in the 1908 pennant race? Or Babe Ruth's still-debated called-shot homer in the 1932 World Series? Or the miracle Giant victory of 1951, an event that triggered joyous rioting at the Polo Grounds with one loving couple shucking off taboos and copulating in one of the box seats! And in 1983 the Yankees-Royals "Pine Tar" incident unleashed emotions that spilled into a New York appellate court, threatened counteraction from organized umpires and saddled the Yankee owner with a hefty fine for importunate remarks.

In its time each such incident seemed portentous and calamitous, but soon each was perceived as but another of the "silly season" episodes that dot baseball history. As such they become humorous sagas to be told and retold before gatherings of fans.

While designated nuts crop up among the game's heroes and villains, their natural habitat is in the ranks of the fools. As engagingly analyzed by sociologist Orrin E. Klapp, the fool is institutionalized in all major cultures, serving such useful functions as sublimating aggression, releasing tensions, maintaining social control, and binding people into communities of laughter. In our highly diverse American society, Klapp dredged up at least twenty-five subtypes of fools which he lumped into five major categories. These categories are incompetents or ludicrous rôle failures (like baseball's bonehead Merkle), discounting types who serve to deflate authoritarians (like notorious umpire baiters), nonconformist types (like Alex Johnson refusing to run out ground balls), over-conformers (like Ted Williams, who busted more than one hotel room mirror while practicing his swing), and comic butts or jesters (like Tug McGraw, who parried a prying reporter's question to how he spent his salary by quipping, "Ninety percent I spend on broads and Irish whiskey; the other ten percent I probably waste!").

Klapp's categories make a handy road map for chasing down and sampling baseball's nutty characters. While time and space limits insure notable omissions, the following "kook's tour" can provide a panoramic view of baseball nuts that could inspire more extensive foraging.

1. The Main Grove—the Player Nuts

In numbers and notoriety, nuts from the ranks of major league players lead all other constituencies of baseball. Among players branded as ludicrous role failures none tops the opprobrium heaped on "Bonehead" Fred Merkle for failing to touch second base in a crucial 1908 game. But Merkle's all-round first-base play was never questioned, which was not the case with latter-day first sackers like Zeke Bonura and Dick "Dr. Strangeglove" Stuart, who rank high in the annals of stone-fingered ineptitude. Recently another, "Marvelous Marv" Throneberry, cashed in on his dubious reputation with a lucrative pact for doing commercials for a beer company; Marv joined other ex-athletes turned barfly touts, including catcher Bob Uecker, who transcended a six-season .200 batting average.

Of course, any player is fated to perform ludicrously somewhere along the line. Indeed, awesome virtuosos like Warren Spahn and Joe DiMaggio had off-moments at the bargaining tables. Spahn once opted for a straight salary of $25,000 over a club offer of ten cents for each paying fan; that blunder cost him an estimated pay of $182,000 for 1953! A similar choice once cost DiMaggio an estimated $50,000 in extra pay.

In what was truly a far-out, ludicrous performance Braves pitcher Pascual Perez was dubbed "Wrong Way Pascual" in 1982. Slated to pitch at Atlanta Stadium, this Dominican rookie got lost on Atlanta's freeway system and circled the city three times before running out of gas. Yet Pascual's "lost patrol" performance was credited with jollying the slumping Braves out of a losing streak as the much-kidded Pascual, wearing "I-285" on his warmup jacket, later won four games in the team's stretch drive to a divisional championship.

A second Klapp category, that of discounting types, features the kind of nuts who grow in a society where sham, braggadocio, phony behavior, and false fronting abound. In his time "King" Kelly was a notorious braggart as in our time was Reggie ("I'm the straw that stirs the drink!") Jackson. However, both managed to match big mouths with big deeds. This was less true of Art Shires, the self-styled "Arthur the Great" who joined the 1928 White Sox saying: "So this is the great American League . . . I'll hit .400." For a time the posturing Shires did well enough, but he never played a full season. Even in his fourth and final season he brashly sent a telegram of acceptance to the Boston Braves which he signed, "Your latest sensation." Alas, in 82 games he hit .238.

Such effrontery was exceeded by Ken "Hawk" Harrelson, an overrated slugger of the 1960s and later a vice-president of the White Sox, who gained notoriety as a bucker of baseball's conservative dress code by affecting long hair, batting gloves, sweatbands, and flamboyant dress. Although denounced as a fop, Harrelson saw his reputation grow when he defied A's owner Charley Finley, who cut him loose. To Finley's discomfiture Harrelson sold his dubious services to the Red Sox in 1968 for a $75,000 bonus.

If player poseurs like these are themselves deflatable, Babe Ruth's ability to puncture the stuffed shirts of big wigs had fans laughing with him rather than at him. On meeting field Marshal Ferdinand Foch at Yankee Stadium, Ruth blithely quipped, "Hiya, Gen, I heard you were in the war!" On another occasion, on meeting President Calvin Coolidge at the Stadium he commented, "Hot as Hell, ain't it, Pres?" While such examples of *lese majeste* are Olympian, Pete Rose's flip response to the congratulatory phone call from President Jimmy Carter at the close of the 1980 World Series is worthy of the genre. But anyone out to top Ruth in the debunking department would have to go all the way; indeed, Ruth helped to debunk his own funeral. Surely he'd have loved this exchange between his pallbearing buddies Joe Dugan and Waite Hoyt. While serving at the funeral on the steamy day in 1948, Hoyt allowed that he could use a beer. "So could the Babe," quipped Dugan.

As a transgressor of societal norms, Ruth was a giant; his hearty appetite for wenching and carousing evokes astonishing gasps even in this hedonistic and revelatory age. In Ruth's time bowdlerizing reporters tidied up mention of many of his excesses, but enough seeped through to astonish even now.

If freer attitudes toward sex now lighten the onus placed on taboo violators, autobiographical revelations from the pens of players like Jim Bouton, Bo Belinsky, Kirby Higbe, and Joe Pepitone still scandalized; thus, for tattle-taling such muckrackers were shunned. Proof may be seen by the stormy reception that greeted Bouton's blockbusting *Ball Four*. To this day Bouton is *persona non grata* at Yankee old-timer games, but his celebrity status dates from the book's appearance.

The sorriest of all player deviants would probably be the accused game-fixers. In this shady enterprise the eight damned Black Sox stand alone, but baseball history is pock-marked with names of others like Jim Devlin, umpire Dick Higham, Hal Chase, and more recently Denny McLain and drug abusers.

The most memorable of nutty nonconformists may be those players who under game pressures express their frustration creatively. Thus, when outfielder Frenchy Bordagaray concluded an argument with an ump by spitting in the official's eye, he was fined $500 and suspended. As Frenchy ruefully lamented, "The penalty is a little more than I expectorated." But that spitter was outgobbed by Ted Williams, who on multiple occasions spat in the direction of heckling fans or the Fenway Park pressbox. In retaliation Boston writers hung the label of "'The Splendid Spitter" on Ted.

In a career-long feud with his critics, Williams refused to doff his cap when applauded and at times vented frustrations by signaling hecklers with obscene finger gestures. Once, he angrily flung his bat into the stands and it happened to hit owner Tom Yawkey's housekeeper. For that and other outbursts Ted was targeted as a towering nonconformist, despite his over-conformity in other areas.

Overconformers are, in fact, poles apart from nonconformists. In this category Ty Cobb loomed large. His mania to be best fueled both his greatness and his pathetic alienation. On and off the field he was driven; once, upon returning to his hotel room and finding that his roommate had beaten him to the bathtub, he flew into a rage. Later he explained, "Don't you see, I have to be first in everything." Nor did he mellow much when his career ended.

It would seem that hard-driving players risk being branded special sorts of nuts. Thus, Pete Rose's "Charley Hustle" exertions evoke admiration and jeers. To an extent so does Steve Carlton's stoical training which included stuffing his left arm in a vat of rice, sometimes choosing his own catcher, stuffing his ears with cotton when pitching, and refusing to communicate with the media. And nonconformists come in varied sorts. Rogers Hornsby eschewed movies lest they damage his batting eye, but steadfastly insisted on frequenting race tracks in defiance of Commissioner Landis' edict.

But some overconformers manage to enthrall fans. One, pitcher Mark Fidrych, became America's beloved "bird" (named after "Sesame Street's" Big Bird). In 1976 Fidrych's antics of talking to the ball, tidying up the mound, and darting about thanking teammates after each win charmed fans. When interviewed at the end of his great season, Fidrych gushed, "I'm just loving it . . . what a dream!" Of his charisma his manager said, "Babe Ruth didn't cause this much excitement in his brightest day." Although that is debatable, Fidrych's appeal stemmed from an artful blending of over- and non-conformity. Thus, on meeting President Gerald Ford, he requested that worthy to get his son to fix him up with a date.

Perhaps one of the keys to becoming a player hero is to avoid being branded as a singular kind of nut. If true, then for sheer variety the category of tricksters, jesters, and comics stands alone.

Today jesters and comic butts seem to get lumped together as "flakes," but baseball's broad historical landscape is dotted with unique zanies. Thus, who can forget Germany Schaefer, a turn-of-the-century speedster,

stealing second base and then stealing first and being credited with another steal? His ploy had legislators speedily passing a rule forbidding
such retreats. Or how about Gabby Street amazing a 1908 crowd by
catching a ball which fell 555 feet from the Washington Monument?
Ironically, Hank Helf of the 1940 Cleveland Indians caught one dropped
from 700 feet and earlier on another Indian, Joe Sprinz, suffered a fracture of the jaw trying to catch an 800-foot drop—but only Street's feat is
remembered. Or Lefty Gomez in a bases-loaded situation fielding a ball
and tossing it to second baseman Tony Lazzeri, who had no play? Asked
why, "Goofy" Gomez replied that he had been reading in the papers
about what a smart player Lazzeri was!

At any time practical jokers infest clubhouses, dugouts, and bullpens.
Among the more notorious was reliever Moe Drabowsky, who used the
bullpen phone to order pizzas and sometimes to falsely alert enemy relievers to get warmed up. In the Cardinal clubhouse Walker Cooper once
managed to tie a mate's sweatshirt into twenty-five knots and Del Rice
was the master at nailing shoes to floors. Elsewhere, there was Sparky
Lyle imprinting his buttocks on the icing of a birthday cake, and Doug
Rader picking his nose and planting the detritus on a nearby bare arm.

That such antics now are recorded in newspapers and magazines testi-
fies to changing norms in American society. But if present standards
admit grosser forms of behavior, the same standards appear less tolerant
toward rule breakers or hecklers. Indeed, some observers have noted a recent decline in bench jockeying, which they blame on the player union
movement; supposedly, brotherhood has added an environment of "leg-
islated courtesy."

Because ballplayers always have lived highly pressurized lives, it is not
surprising that some display symptoms of mental illness; indeed, it is a
tribute to human resilience that so many adapt to the major league pressure cooker. But woe betide one who displays symptoms of mental illness, as our civilization is not that far removed from the days when
inmates of Bedlam were objects of public gawking and ridicule.

Thus, the suicides of players like Marty Bergen, Chick Stahl, and Wil-
lard Hershberger loom darkly in baseball history and are still topics of
gossip. To a lesser extent gossip and ridicule are still heaped on players
with known or suspected symptoms of mental illness. In the case of outfielder Jimmy Piersall such antics as running the bases backwards and
climbing backstops were ridiculed and fans and enemy dugouts labeled
him "nutsy"; later, when his condition became known, his ordeal was received with mixed bad taste and understanding in a book and a movie.
Today the stigmatized Piersall is still viewed as a head case; his recent dis-

missal from an announcer's job dredged up past examples of his quirky behavior.

Other players with milder symptoms played under the same shadows. Included are pitchers like Steve Blass, whose inability to find the plate ended his career; Steve Dalkowski, whose awesome promise as a fireballer ended in the minors for similar reasons, and Kevin Saucier, who had a fear of hitting batters that made him fearful of going to the park and forced his recent retirement at age twenty-seven.

Undoubtedly there are others who conceal their symptoms. For this, blame the societal taboo on mental illness which has many Americans so fearful of exposure that they refuse to draw on medical policies to pay for symptom treatment. And even if ballclubs now provide paid therapy, the strains of exposure still pose formidable obstacles.

On the whole the brighter side eclipses the seamy side in the world of nutty behavior. Indeed, the word nut is such a generalized catchword that nearly everyone has been on its receiving end at some time. Mostly the term evokes laughter and therein it is a source of strength for baseball. Moreover, players are by no means the only designated nuts as the game's other constituencies provide enough cases to deflect attention toward fans, owners, umps, media people and other auxiliaries of major league baseball.

2. The Peripheral Groves

1. Shaking the Managerial Tree

Any fan out to gather nuts in May will find good pickings among baseball's managers. In the early years bluff Cap Anson was targeted by fans because of his size and his aggressive, umpire-baiting style. As Anson grew older fans dubbed him "Unk," "Pappy," and "Grandpa" among other hoary terms. In retaliation, Anson once donned a long white beard and wore it during a game, performing well despite the prop and accompanying jeers. Yet fans never ceased ragging the big man, and his passing from the baseball scene left a lonesome gap.

Early in this century a new target, burdened with an even greater Napoleonic complex, appeared in the person of John McGraw. Like Anson, McGraw was targeted by fans everywhere. Some of McGraw's shrewd ploys, like the time he pinched one of his players to authenticate a hit-by-pitch claim, had fans screaming "Muggsy," an epithet he despised. When he loudly berated his 1916 team for quitting, home fans joined the chorus. So did his one-time buddy, then the victorious Dodger manager Wilbert Robinson.

By then Robinson's own nutty credentials were well established. His excess poundage had writers and fans calling him the "Round Robin" and chortling over his earlier attempt to catch a ball dropped from an airplane. Circling under the missile, the roly-poly ex-catcher got the heel of his glove on the missile, which deflected it into his chest. The blow felled him, and as he beheld his spattered chest, Robinson screamed, "I'm dead! I'm covered with blood!" But then, to his chagrin, he learned that the "ball" was really a burst grapefruit!

Similar charges of nutty incompetence dogged Casey Stengel for years—charges Stengel deflected by playing the role of comic jester. One of his more famous capers had him tipping his cap toward fans and releasing a captive bird. Later, as a winning Yankee manager and as a horrendous loser with the 1962 Mets, his mastery of confusing rhetoric charmed fans, even if they knew they were being conned. "We're a fraud," Stengel admitted after a defeat, adding, "The attendance got trimmed again."

Fans responded to nutty jester types like Stengel and his successor Yogi Berra. As a player Berra was already a celebrated malaprop, one who when roused out of bed by a phone call responded to the apologetic caller by saying, "That's okay. I had to get up to answer the phone anyhow." In actuality, Berra is not a very funny character, but like the Hollywood starlet he, too, was made to fit the part.

Of course, it's tough being a manager. Whatever one's style the manager is a sure bet to be blamed for losses and targeted as some kind of nut. Knowing this, one can imagine ordinary managers thanking the gods that a towering nut like Billy Martin is (or was) around to take up much of the flak. His antics like feuding with players, sometimes punching them out, or kicking dust over umps are too well known to dredge up here.

2. The Owners

Unlike dumped-on managers, baseball owners are better shielded from accusing critics. Still, baseball history is dotted with owner nuts. Indeed, in the judgment of financiers, being a baseball owner is being a foolish investor; that so many opt to do so suggests that they are really seeking self-aggrandizement.

The list of nutty owners of baseball history is long. One could begin with Chris von der Ahe, the legendary owner of the St. Louis Browns who became the comic butt of so many funny Dutchman stories in the 1880s and '90s.

Echoes of von der Ahe's style characterized modern owners like Bill Veeck and Charley Finley. As a promoter Veeck's ability to charm fans was proved during four separate stints as a club owner. One of these included a hopeless stint with the St. Louis Browns which saw Veeck cut a legendary caper by signing and sending to bat midget (43" tall) Eddie Gaedel, armed with toy bat and wearing uniform No. ⅛. Such stunts, mingled with a solid knowledge of baseball, endeared the pixie-like Veeck to fans and cast him as a lovable folk character.

Not so with Charles Oscar Finley, whose erratic behavior cast him as a petulant nut. Although brilliantly successful at times, Finley lacked Veeck's comic genius touch. Such Finleyesque ploys as bribing his men to wear beards and mustaches, decking them in garishly colored uniforms, plumping for orange-colored bases and balls, designating a mule as the team totem, and coining corny nicknames were laboriously contrived; often as not they had fans laughing at the owner rather than with him.

Erratic behavior also characterizes incumbent owners Ted Turner and George Steinbrenner. Turner's nutty qualifications stem from his jousts with former Commissioner Bowie Kuhn, who fined Turner for tampering with other team's players and who sternly ended the Atlanta owner's quixotic attempt to function as field manager. And a Turner decision to evict the team totem, Chief Noc-A-Homa, from his wigwam in order to add more seats in 1982 and again in 1983 was followed each year by a serious losing streak. That caper cast Turner as the nut who brought down Noc-A-Homa's curse!

Happily for Turner, whose prowess as a yachtsman was redeeming, there was also the mighty presence of Steinbrenner to overshadow his foibles as a baseball owner. The Yankee boss has won his spurs as the terrible-tempered Mr. Bang among owners by virtue of his frenzied spending at player auctions and his penchant for meddling in team affairs, for firing underlings (including a secretary for getting a wrong kind of sandwich), and for dueling with officials. Indeed, a decade of this stormy petrel finally caused a *New York Times* scribe to explode with this advice: "Go away, please, and take your favorite manager with you."

Among owners vilified as meddling nuts Steinbrenner stands tall in baseball history, but at times nearly every owner has been targeted. Thus, reclusive Phil Wrigley's stubborn refusal to light up Wrigley Field, his team's woeful performance since 1945, and such abortive innovations as replacing the manager with a system of rotating coaches helped to certify this late owner. And the roll call of situational nuts among owners included cash-poor types like Gerry Nugent of the Phillies, who ran the club as a parasite team; Judge Emil Fuchs, whose pinchpenny practices at Boston extended to his personally chasing foul balls hit into the stands;

Clark Griffith of the Senators, who once sold son-in-law Joe Cronin to make money, and Cal Griffith, whose racist statements and his inability to match his big-spending colleagues cast him as a forlorn nut.

3. The Umpires

If being a clubowner facilitates one's nutty reputation, consider the lot of an umpire. From the moment these officials take the field to choruses of ritualized boos their competence is called into question. And once at work hardly a game is played without someone challenging their mental togetherness. Among the plenteous examples, umpire Red Jones used to bristle at being called "Meat"; to his surprise he was targeted by orchestrated jeers from the White Sox bench which sounded, "We can't call you 'Meat' today!" And the refrain quickly followed, "Because it's Friday!" Then there was Beans Reardon, who was asked by a catcher how he managed to get his square head into a round mask, and plate ump Bill McGowan asking Nick Altrock what happened to the woman who was being carried from the stands on a stretcher and getting in reply, "You called one right and she fainted."

As baseball's manufactured villains, umps have long been cast as comic butts. But occasionally they fight back, as when one visited the hospitalized Leo Durocher; asked why he came by to see that notorious umpire baiter, the ump replied, "I came to see if you were dying."

4. The Media

That so many yarns become part of baseball's folklore owes to the game's vital media constituency. While free publicity has always been a powerful support for baseball, media men have also titillated fans with exposés of baseball's madcap sides.

As myth-makers generations of sportswriters coined and tagged players with nicknames like "The Little Napoleon," "The Duke of Tralee," "The Colossus of Clout," and "The Georgia Peach." And always there were snide labels like "The Splendid Spitter" which could tag players as nuts. Routinely the daily copy of sportswriters bristled with colorful comments that collectively and individually identified nuts.

Among the great sportswriters' sallies the late Red Smith's are treasured by his fans. Because Smith believed that a writer's tongue should ever repose in its natural habitat, the left cheek, he never failed his readers. As a nut designator Smith could call Bowie Kuhn "the greatest commissioner since Spike Eckert" and with barbed sarcasm could pronounce the "free agent system . . . the greatest thing to happen to baseball since Candy Cummings invented the curve."

Alas, it would take volumes to exhaust the witticisms and witlesscisms of the media people. And along the way one would bump into deliriously nutty statisticians, dubbed "figure filberts" by one quipster. The original might have been Ernie Lanigan, a notorious flake who daily amazed historian Lee Allen by routinely ordering a breakfast of ham and eggs with a shot of whiskey. Usually he left the ham and eggs.

5. The Fans
Finally, any review of baseball's nutty characters must include the fans, that wellspring from which all other constituencies of the game arise. Like the term "kranks," which it replaced, the word "fans" is synonymous with nuts. Ubiquitous fans crop up as collectivities and as individu-

---

An All-Nut Team From Major League Baseball

Pitchers—Bugs Raymond, Pascual Perez, Bo Belinsky, Lefty Gomez, Dizzy and Daffy Dean, and relievers Al Hrabosky and Moe Drabowsky.
Catchers—Yogi Berra, Clyde Kluttz, and Earl Battey.
Infielders—Fred Merkle, Dick Stuart, Ed Bouchee, 1b; Billy Martin, 2b; Garry Templeton, ss; and Germany Schaefer, 3b.
Outfielders—Jim Piersall, Frenchy Bordagaray, Dizzy Nutter, Leon "Daddywags" Wagner, Babe Herman, and Peanuts Lowrey.
Owners—Bill Veeck, Charley Finley, Chris von der Ahe, George Steinbrenner, and Judge Emil Fuchs (consortium).
Manager—Casey Stengel.
Groundskeeper—Maury Wills.
Commissioner—Spike Eckert.
Chief Scout—Leon (John Dillinger) Hamilton.
Team Talisman—Charles "Victory" Faust.

---

als. Collectivities include the ballpark crowds, the newspaper fans, radio and TV fans, and the collectors and fetish freaks. Among the latter sort, some now shell out money to players for autographs and one of the collector freaks recently paid $25,000 for a 1910 Honus Wagner card.

As for the ballpark fans, their ranks have always shown madcap tendencies. The victorious pennant celebrations of fans have often been riotous; victory-sated fans tear up playing fields and sometimes trash cities as happened during the Big Buc Binge of 1970 and the Tigers' 1984 victory. Other notorious riots of recent vintage included the Cleveland Beer Riot of 1974 and Chicago's Disco Riot of 1979.

But in the annals of nutty ballpark fans it is the individual characters who stand out. Still remembered fondly in Brooklyn is Hilda Chester and her jangling cowbell and barbaric yawp; on one occasion she dispatched a note to manager Durocher telling him to pull his starting pitcher, and Durocher, thinking the note came from his boss, actually did. Another notorious individual was the curvaceous stripper, Morganna the Wild One, who on several occasions sallied onto the field at Cincinnati and confronted on-deck batters with her irresistible demand of "Kiss me."

Certainly baseball's penchant for inspiring tomfoolery and laughter goes far to explain the game's mythic hold on the American populace. This is a point that major league promoters ought never to forget. When cursing hefty salaries or thanking the god Mammon for hefty TV contracts, such worthies should take time to breathe another prayer, "Thank God For Nuts."

Little-Known Facts

The longest game in major league history took 14 days, 12 hours, and 36 minutes to play because New York, which beat Boston 1–0, allowed everyone in Boston a chance to hit at least once. . . . The shortest game in minor league history was played between two teams of midgets. . . . Ten years ago, Henry Wilson Welch was a broken-down, penniless bum wandering the streets of Chicago in search of a nickel for a glass of beer. Where is he now? Today, Henry—or Hank, as they used to call him—is the star center fielder for the Chicago Cubs.

Conrad Horn

THE REMARKABLE LIFE OF A MAN
CALLED "DUMMY"

William Ellsworth Hoy,
1862–1961

JOSEPH M. OVERFIELD

♦ ♦ ♦

Back in 1955, while searching the old newspaper files at the Buffalo Historical Society, I came across a photograph of the 1890 Buffalo Players' League team, from which I was able to have copies made. At the time, surprisingly, two members of the team, Connie Mack and Dummy Hoy, were still alive. I wrote to each of them, enclosed a picture, and asked some questions about that ill-starred Buffalo club, one of the most inept in baseball history, finishing in eighth place, twenty games out of seventh.

I received a short, rambling note from Mack, who was then ninety-two. The venerable one thanked me for the picture, answered none of my questions, and concluded by writing, "You must be very old to remember Deacon White." (I was thirty-nine at the time.) Properly humbled, I awaited with some trepidation a reply from Mr. Hoy, who was just three months younger than Mack.

When Hoy's letter came, it put all my fears to rest. Datelined, most appropriately, Mt. Healthy, Ohio, November 15, 1955, the letter was six pages in length and written in a bold, unquivering, and beautiful hand that completely belied the age of the writer. All of my questions were answered in sentences that were grammatically pure and perfectly punctuated.

Those of us who are inveterate letter writers sometimes gain rich rewards. This was such a time.

135

I was to exchange many letters with Hoy. The last one I received from him was dated January 3, 1961. He was ninety-eight then, and it was just eleven months before his death on December 15, 1961, five months and eight days short of his 100th birthday. He had lived longer than any other major league ballplayer.

I never met Hoy, other than through our letters, but I was fortunate enough to see him on television when he threw out the first ball at the 1961 World Series between Cincinnati and New York.

There was always some question about Hoy's true age. Some sources said he broke in with Oshkosh, Wisconsin at age twenty, while later accounts reported him to be twenty-four when he made his debut. His reply to my inquiry about this discrepancy follows:

> I will tell you how this happened [the discrepancy] and go bail on the correctness of my figures. They were copied from the family Bible!
>
> One rainy day in the spring of 1886, the Oshkosh players were assembled in the clubhouse getting ready for opening day. A newspaperman entered to take down the age, height, and weight of each player. When it came my turn to be interviewed, he omitted me because I was a deaf mute. Also, he had not the time to bother with the necessary use of pad and pencil. When I read his writeup the next day, I found he had me down for twenty years of age. He had made what he considered a good guess.
>
> Now in my school days, I had been taught to refrain from correcting my elders. Then too, he had *whiskers!* After thinking it over, I decided to let the figures stand. It was in this way that I became known as the twenty-year-old Oshkosh deaf-mute ballplayer. What would you have done if you were in my place?
>
> However, later on, I was pinned down by an alert Cincinnati insurance man at the Methodist book concern where I was employed at the time. He told me to write down my full baptismal name, together with the day, month and year of my birth. Nobody had ever asked me such a question before. If they had, I certainly would have written down 1862 and not 1866.

In the *Sporting News Record Book,* Hoy is listed as the first outfielder to be credited with three assists from outfield to catcher in a single game. In a letter I received from Hoy in 1959, he recalled this feat:

> The first putout was accomplished when a batter made a basehit to me in the outfield. The runner on second was put out by my throw to the catcher. The next out at the plate was made in the exact way as

the first. The third play was a basehit over shortstop in about the eighth inning. I picked up the ball, threw to the catcher and caught the runner attempting to score from second. I had no other fielding chances whatsoever during the entire game, the three assists being all the chances I had. The game took place on June 19, 1888, and was a regularly scheduled National League game between Washington (my club) and Indianapolis, then a member of the National League. Do you know of any other player who duplicated this feat? Bear in mind the three assists were on basehits to the outfield. If you know of any, who is he? I want to shake his hand.

(Note: Two other outfielders are credited with three assists to the catcher in one game. They are Jim Jones of the Giants on June 30, 1902, and John McCarthy of the Cubs on April 20, 1905.)

The box score of the game from *Sporting Life* substantiated Hoy's recall in every detail. It was truly a remarkable performance, but just as remarkable was his perfect recall of it seventy-one years later.

Hoy played eighteen seasons as a professional, remarkable in light of his late start, his deafness, and his muteness. He was one of two deaf mutes to gain fame in the majors. The other was pitcher Luther (Dummy) Taylor, who won 117 games, all but one for the New York Giants, for whom he won 27 games in 1904. According to *Daguerrotypes (The Sporting News)*, Paul Hines, famed outfielder of the last century, was deaf. His deafness, however, did not develop until he was thirty-four, after a beaning in 1886 by Jim (Grasshopper) Whitney of Kansas City; of course, he did not have the additional handicap of muteness. (Strangely, Hines and Whitney were teammates the next season at Washington.)

Hoy's late start in the game may be attributed partly to his infirmity—which, incidentally, followed an attack of meningitis when he was three—but to a greater extent to economics. In an interview with Art Kruger for a publication called *The Silent Worker* and later condensed in the May 1954 issue of *Baseball Digest,* Hoy recalled that his father gave his sister a cow and a piano when she was eighteen, and to each of his brothers, when they became twenty-one, a suit of clothes and a buggy, harness, and saddle. When William reached majority, his father gave him only the suit, but promised him free board until he was twenty-four. "Being handicapped by deafness, it was my thought that I would make better progress in life if I worked as a cobbler and lived at home, rather than to accept the buggy, harness and saddle and leave home." So, he recounted to Kruger, he opened a shoe shop in his native Houcktown, Ohio, after graduating from the State School for the Deaf at Columbus, where he had won highest honors and had been valedictorian of his class. Business was dull, especially in the summer when most everyone in Houcktown went around sans shoes, so there was plenty of time for William to play ball with the young men of the town. He told Kruger that a man from nearby Findlay noticed him one day and asked him to play a game in Kenton, which was a few miles away. He agreed and did so well against a former professional pitcher that he decided to give baseball a try.

Frank Selee, later to enjoy success as a major league manager, was the skipper at Oshkosh of the Northwest League in 1886 when Hoy signed his first contract. Selee was perspicacious enough to see Hoy's innate ability and stayed with him that first difficult year, despite his .219 batting average. He improved next year to .367, stole 67 bases, and led Oshkosh to a pennant. This performance earned him a promotion to Washington of the National League where he batted .274 and led the league in stolen bases with 82.

His career from that point on was peripatetic, to say the least. Besides Washington, he played for Buffalo of the Players' League, St. Louis of the then major league American Association, and for Cincinnati, where he starred from 1894 to 1897, only to be traded to Louisville. After two seasons with that National League club, he cast his lot with Ban Johnson's fledgling American League, playing for Chicago in 1900 and then again in 1901, the AL's first year of major league status. He returned to Cincinnati for a final major league fling in 1902, batting .259 in 72 games. He was one of twenty-nine men to play in four major leagues: National, Players', American Association, and American.

Hoy wound up his career in 1903 at Los Angeles in the Pacific Coast League where he played in every one of his team's 211 games. His average was a modest .261, but he totaled 210 hits and stole 46 bases, five more than his age.

At five feet, five inches and 150 pounds, Hoy, who batted left and threw right, did not have the heft to be a power hitter, but he did get his share of doubles and triples and was an excellent baserunner. In the field his speed was an asset and he was considered to be a reliable fielder with a strong and accurate arm. Detroit writer H.G. Salsinger, quoting an old-time St. Louis writer, Thomas Lonergan, wrote, "Hoy was the smartest player he had ever seen, swift as a panther and very fast in getting the ball in from the outfield." Of his throwing prowess there can be little question: witness his three assists to the plate previously described, and the fact that he was in double figures in assists every season except for 1902 at Cincinnati. His lifetime total (major and minor) was 389, including a league-leading 27 with Louisville in 1898 and an incredible 45 with the 1900 Chicago club.

Dummy Hoy

It has been widely written that it was because of Hoy that umpires began to raise their right hands to signify strikes. Paul Helms—wealthy West Coast businessman, founder of the Helms Foundation, and a nephew of Hoy's—states this unequivocally in the Kruger article above mentioned. On the other hand, the authoritative Lee Allen, in his *Hot Stove League,* tells us that Charles "Cy" Rigler of the National League was the first to follow this practice, and he did not come into the league until 1905, two years after Hoy's retirement. According to Allen, Cincinnati players used to signal strikes to Hoy in this manner.

How good a player was Hoy? It is the conclusion here that he should rank high, even meriting Hall-of-Fame consideration. Hall-of-Famer Tommy McCarthy, with whom Hoy is often compared, was a contemporary, playing from 1884 to 1896. The two were teammates at Oshkosh in 1887 and at St. Louis (AA) in 1891. A comparison of the two players' major league records seems to indicate that Hoy has been overlooked far too long.

	Hoy	**McCarthy**
Years	14	13
Games	1798	1275
At bats	7123	5128
Hits	2054	1496
Doubles	248	192
Triples	121	58
Home runs	40	44
Runs	1426	1069
RBIs	726	666
Stolen bases	597	467
Walks	1004	537
Average	.288	.292

	Fielding	
Putouts	3932	2034
Assists	286	301
Errors	384	261
Average	.917	.899

Note: Hoy played 1797 games as an outfielder and one game at second base. McCarthy played 1189 games in the outfield, 39 at second base, 37 at third base, 20 at shortstop, and 13 as a pitcher.

It is unlikely at this late date that Hoy will gain much Hall-of-Fame support, any more than will his teammate on the 1890 Bisons, Jim (Deacon) White, one of the truly great players of the game's early years. But there can be no doubt that Hoy was an outstanding player, whose accomplishments loom even larger, considering he could neither hear nor speak.

REJECTED ONCE AS BEING TOO SMALL,
HE BECAME A NEGRO LEAGUES STAR

Judy Johnson, a True Hot Corner Hotshot

JOHN B. HOLWAY

♦ ♦ ♦

William "Judy" Johnson was one of the slickest fielding third basemen in the history of black baseball—or any other baseball. Old-timers who saw him cavort with the old Philadelphia Hilldales or Pittsburgh Crawfords in the 1920s and '30s inevitably link his name with that of Brooks Robinson. Connie Mack, the sweet-natured owner of the Philadelphia A's, watched Judy dance around the bag at Shibe Park in the 1920s and sighed. If Johnson were only white, Mack said, "he could write his own price."

The old Negro leagues produced many great third basemen—Jud Wilson, Oliver (Ghost) Marcelle, and Ray Dandridge. But many authorities consider Johnson the finest of all.

Dandridge may have been flashier, but Johnson "was like a rock," commented ex-outfielder Jimmy Crutchfield, "a steadying influence on the club. Had a great brain, could anticipate a play, knew what his opponents were going to do."

"He had intelligence and finesse," explained Willie Wells, one of the game's great shortstops.

Judy was an excellent sign-stealer, too, Ted Page pointed out. "He and Josh Gibson—boy, they trapped more men off third base! Judy'd put a little whistle on to Josh, who was catching, and I'd say, 'Oh, oh, they got something cooking.'"

In Cincinnati in the 1930s the Crawfords were playing a team of white big league all-stars. Leo Durocher reached third base and began dancing

141

off the bag down the line to rattle the pitcher. Judy gave Gibson "the whistle."

"Durocher started in toward home," Johnson recalled, "and I moved up with him. Then I just backed up, put my foot about two feet in front of the base. Josh had the best snap, wouldn't move to throw, just snapped the ball. I caught it. Here comes Durocher sliding in and the umpire says "You're out."

Some twenty years later Johnson and his wife were leaving Milwaukee County Stadium, where their son-in-law, Bill Bruton, had just finished playing a World Series game against the New York Yankees. In the crowd they jostled against none other than Durocher. "Leo," Judy said, "do you remember playing a barnstorming game in Cincinnati back in 1934 or so?"

Durocher stepped back and blinked. "Yes," he responded, "I remember you, Judy, damn your soul. That's the day you tricked me." Johnson was born October 26, 1899 in Snow Hill on Maryland's eastern shore, not far from the birthplace of another famous Hall-of-Fame third baseman, Frank "Home Run" Baker.

Judy remembers frosty mornings in Snow Hill. He and his sister slept in a loft which they reached by climbing a ladder and awoke to the smell of country breakfast cooking. His father, a sailor, moved the family to Wilmington, Delaware, when Judy was about ten. Johnson recalls his first uniform vividly. His mother sewed a big "D" on the shirt for the team he played on. "I was strutting around at five a.m., even though we didn't play until two in the afternoon," he said.

After a game he always managed to hang around the team captain's house to talk baseball—and to steal glances at the captain's sister, Anita. Somehow he and Anita ended up sitting on the bench in front of the house until her father coughed. "That meant 'Get,'" Judy explained. "She'd walk me to the corner, and I'd give her a 'hit-and-run' kiss." The two were married for more than sixty years until her death in 1986.

Anita became a schoolteacher. In later years when Judy went to Cuba to play winter ball, she stayed home, adding her salary to the family income. Without her, Judy said emotionally, "I probably couldn't have been a ballplayer. She was a great, great woman."

Johnson received his first big break when many of the black league stars were summoned into service in World War I and he got a call to play with the Bacharach Giants, at the age of eighteen, for a salary of $5 a game.

In 1919 he tried out for the famous Philadelphia Hilldales but was rejected as being too small. Judy then joined the Madison Stars of Philadelphia, a training ground for the Hilldales, who were fast developing into the top black club in the East.

The Hilldales had been organized years some eight years earlier as a neighborhood amateur club in Darby, a suburb south of Philadelphia. Ed Bolden, a taciturn postal official, took over the club and began signing professional players. By 1920 he was ready to bring up young Johnson, paying the Madison Stars the munificent sum of $100. Judy understudied Bill "Brodie" Francis that season and the next spring took over the third-base job from Francis.

The Hilldales built up a rapid fan following. "We had our own park in Darby," Johnson explained, "and our crowds got so large we had to enlarge the park—not just for Negroes, but for white fans, too. Both the Athletics and Phillies were down in the standings and people were getting season tickets to see us. You couldn't buy a box seat."

Rookies were at the bottom of the pecking order in those days. "Here, Slacky, take my bats," catcher Louis Santop ordered Johnson one day after the team had played in New York. While the older players took the subway to Harlem for a little fun, they made Judy catch a train back to Philadelphia laden with Santop's uniform roll and bat bag plus his own equipment. "I looked like a porter," Johnson recalled. "I had to hire a taxi to carry those bats. But you had to do it."

In 1923 Bolden formed the Eastern Colored League with his own team plus the Bacharach Giants of Atlantic City, the Cuban Stars, Harrisburg Giants, Baltimore Black Sox, New York Lincoln Giants, and Brooklyn Royal Giants. He also raided Rube Foster's Negro National League, signing catcher Raleigh "Biz" Mackey, first baseman George "Tank" Carr, and second baseman Frank Warfield to give the Hilldales the strongest team in the East. Johnson's contribution was a modest .237 batting average, but he played a strong, steady game at third base.

Judy journeyed to Cuba that winter along with many black and white stars from the States. Against the stellar pitching of Dolf Luque, Jess Petty, Fred Fitzsimmons, and most of the two Negro leagues' top hurlers, Johnson raised his average to .345.

He hit a solid .327 during the summer of 1924 as the Hilldales repeated as champions. That fall, in black baseball's first World Series, the Hilldales faced the Kansas City Monarchs, champs of the western or Negro National League. Because of a tie, the best-of-nine series actually went ten games before the Monarchs emerged victorious. Judy led the hitters on both teams with a .364 average. His sixteen hits included six doubles, a triple, and a home run, the latter an inside-the-park job with two aboard in the ninth inning to win Game Six for the Hilldales.

The following year the Hilldales captured their third straight flag and grimly entrained for Kansas City for a chance at revenge against the

Monarchs. This time the Hilldales, after losing the first two games, bounced back to win the next three and gain the championship. Johnson hit an even .300 in the five-game series.

That winter Johnson joined many other black stars who were finding Palm Beach, Florida, to be a lucrative wintering spot. Two rival hotels, the Breakers and the Poinciana, signed the best black professional ballplayers to wait on tables and to entertain guests on the baseball diamond. The rivalry between the two hotels was intense, but it was the opportunity to make money that lured many of the players. The pay and tips were excellent. In addition, there were floating crap games and, for the really adventurous, rum running from nearby Cuba to the Prohibitionist but thirsty mainland.

Judy didn't participate in these off-the-field enterprises, but he observed them—the rum was sometimes stacked against the wall of the dormitories right up to the ceilings. He remembers being awakened one night when several white men burst into the dorm, shined flashlights in his eyes, and demanded to know where his "brother" was. They apparently meant outfielder George Johnson and assumed that Judy was related. Judy said he didn't know, and the men, presumably underworld figures in search of their cut, eventually left. It was a close call.

The Hilldales lost the 1926 pennant to the Bacharachs but Judy finished with a .302 average. There were compensations for missing out on the pennant, for it meant the Hilldales were free to barnstorm against white big leaguers again and to make a lot more money doing it. Later he sailed back to Cuba for the winter season, hitting .372. Johnson slumped to .228 with the Hilldales the following year and to .231 in 1928. But one year later he hit a robust .416, sixth best in the league. (There were no fewer than four .400 hitters that season.)

The Eastern Colored League folded in 1930 under the impact of the Depression, and Johnson jumped to the independent Homestead Grays, who may have been the best black team in the East if not in the country. That fall Cum Posey, the Grays' owner, challenged Pop Lloyd's Lincoln Giants for the mythical championship of black baseball. The Grays won, six games to four, with Johnson hitting .286.

He rejoined the Hilldales in 1931. With the Depression hitting hard, the players waived their salaries to enable teams to make ends meet and instead divided whatever money was left after expenses. They had to bounce from game to game by bus, playing anywhere and any time they could. "We used to play two games every Thursday, two on Saturday, and three on Sunday," Johnson remembered. "I recall times we'd go to New York to play a doubleheader and then a night game. We'd leave Coney Island at one o'clock at night, ride all night in the bus, and get into Pittsburgh for a twilight game on Monday. We used to get $1.50 a day eating money."

During that period an athlete played anywhere he could make a buck. In 1932 Judy jumped back to the Grays. In the middle of the season virtually the entire Grays team jumped to the Pittsburgh Crawfords, the Grays' bitter crosstown rivals owned by numbers king Gus Greenlee.

The '32 season was a long one. It began with ten days of spring training at Hot Springs, Arkansas, where the players took the mineral baths. By the end of March they would travel to New Orleans for a doubleheader and then start playing their way north. The season ended late in October when the last of the exhibitions against white major leaguers was over, and the players—the fortunate ones anyway—dispersed for a full season of winter ball. On their rare days off, Johnson and the Crawfords went to watch the white major leaguers play to see what they could learn. "We never had to pay to go to see the A's or Yankees," Johnson said. "The only park where we had to pay was St. Louis, and they put us in the Jim Crow section. Other than that, every big league park knew us."

Judy batted .333 for the Crawfords in 1934 and then improved his average in 1935 to .367, based on incomplete figures. That autumn he found himself in another World Series as the Crawfords tangled with the New York Cubans. Johnson was in a long slump when he came to bat in the ninth inning of the sixth game, the Craws one game down, the score tied 6–6, and the bases loaded. He drove a 3–2 pitch on the ground past first base, and the Crawfords had tied the series. The following day Gibson and manager Oscar Charleston slugged homers to wrap up the title for the Craws.

Johnson's average slipped to .282 in 1936, and he retired the following year. After Jackie Robinson broke the color line in the big leagues, Judy was hired by the Athletics as a scout. "I could have gotten Hank Aaron for them for $3500 when he was playing with the Indianapolis Clowns," he said. "I got my boss out of bed and told him that I had a good prospect and he wouldn't cost too much, but he cussed me out for waking him at one o'clock in the morning. He said, 'Thirty-five hundred! That's too much money.' Too much for a man like that! I could have gotten Larry Doby and Minnie Minoso, too, and the A's would still be playing in Philadelphia because that would have been all the outfield they'd have needed."

From the A's Judy switched to the Phillies and helped sign Richie Allen. "He lived in Wampum, Pennsylvania, about sixty or seventy miles out of Pittsburgh," Johnson commented. "The Pirates had him at their park I don't know how many times, but they wouldn't give a nickel to Babe Ruth if they could get him for nothing, so I told our general manager, 'That's the best-looking prospect I've ever seen; please don't lose him,' and he went out there and signed him."

Until his retirement from scouting in 1974, Judy went to Florida with the Phillies every spring. "Mr. [Bob] Carpenter, the owner, liked me because I can help the Negro boys, also the white boys. If a kid does something wrong, I've got to go through the motions and show him the right way. You can't just holler at him; you've got to show him how the ball is handled, and that's what my boss liked about me."

Next to his wife, Johnson's first love in recent years was teaching baseball. "I'd rather do it than anything," he often said. "I even coach a sandlot team in Wilmington."

The late Ted Page, another former Negro league standout, once said he believed the major leagues squandered one of their most valuable resources by not employing Johnson as a manager or at least as a coach. "He had the ability to see the qualities, the faults, of ballplayers and have the correction for them," Page remarked. "Several years ago Willie Stargell was continually popping the ball up. He was turning his head. Judy would see things like that. I bet he could have helped Stargell out of his slump. Some have it and some don't. Judy should have been in the major leagues fifteen or twenty years as a coach. He was a scout, but he would have done the major leagues a lot more good as someone who could help develop players."

A PIONEER BOTH AT BAT AND IN THE FIELD

Dickey Pearce: Baseball's First Great Shortstop

DUANE A. SMITH

♦ ♦ ♦

With the home team down 2–0 in the bottom of the first inning, partisan fans roared when their hero, Dickey Pearce, led off for the Brooklyn Atlantics with a soft fly ball just out of the reach of the shortstop, ". . . one of his peculiar hits—a ball flying in a tantalizing manner." Unfortunately, the next batter forced Pearce at second, and there the inning's promise died. The crowd, estimated at 20,000, groaned.

They knew and appreciated their favorite, Pearce; a century later he has been almost forgotten. Dickey, all 5 feet 3½ inches, 161 pounds of him, played the game as few others of his generation. He was one of baseball's most famous early stars. Although a pesky hitter and the inventor of the bunt, his lasting contribution came from his innovative creation of the modern position of shortstop. A sure-handed fielder (in this day before gloves), and blessed with relatively good speed (considering his pudgy physique), a competitive nature, "unflappable coolness," and a baseball sense, Pearce played shortstop with natural grace and developed strategies and techniques that revolutionized play at the position. Others would copy, but few would equal him during his lifetime.

Those developments, however, came on other days. On this day, June 14, 1870, the fans who crowded around the field only wanted Pearce to lead the home team to victory. He had done it many times since he started playing back in the 1850s, but even Pearce had never been in a game quite like this one. The man and his legend had literally come together.

In the fourth, his team now trailing 3–0, Pearce singled again, this time igniting a two-run rally. This was no run-of-the-mill baseball game. It was destined to become the most famous one in the early annals of baseball. The visiting Cincinnati Red Stockings had won eighty-nine games in a row over the past two years, the Atlantics outranked all others as the 1860s' most famous team. They had handed the Red Stockings their last defeat way back on October 1, 1868. At stake stood both prestige and money; the odds favored the visitors 5–1 before the game.

Odds such as those did not deter one of the game's "old timers." Dickey Pearce led off the sixth with a hit and scored the tying run. The two teams battled to a 5–5 draw at the end of nine innings, which satisfied the Atlantics. But Cincinnati insisted that the game be "played out." Not until the bottom of the eleventh did the Atlantics score three runs to snatch an 8–7 victory from what seemed certain defeat.

Never before had a game generated so much attention. One spectator likened it in "interest equal to that manifested" during the Civil War when people stood around newspaper offices by the hundreds awaiting war news. Now they wanted the baseball score. "The most exciting game on record" made the Atlantics the champion nine of the United States once again, cheered the Brooklyn *Union* the next day.

It was Brooklyn and New York's finest baseball moment to date. The state and its two neighboring cities were the birthplace of American baseball, which had started in the urban environment and spread throughout the state and west across the Mississippi River. The Atlantics and the city of Brooklyn had dominated baseball for most of the 1860s, but this game was justly called "the most brilliant victory known in the history of their organization."

Dickey Pearce had risen to the challenge once more, his efforts being instrumental in the victory. He had either two or three hits, depending on which account one reads. The fourth-inning infield roller was scored as an error by some reporters. Despite that little difference of opinion, they unanimously praised Dickey, who had just returned to the team after some now unknown disagreement, "Pearce's nerve and judgment, and his skillful, scientific play at bat was of valuable service to the Atlantics." "Pearce appeared again in the nine and contributed not a little to victory." "Pearce again played his old position, and greatly strengthened the Atlantics."

The day after the game, a reporter for the Brooklyn *Union* averred, "A fact made plainly apparent by the contest of yesterday is, that baseball has become permanently established as the most popular and exciting sport of the American people." Pearce had done a great deal to create that popularity.

This thirty-four-year-old veteran Brooklyn-born player, the son of English immigrants, had started playing baseball in 1856. Pearce told early baseball historian Henry Chadwick that his first game came on September 18 for the Atlantic nine, when they challenged and defeated the Baltics of Yorkville, then a New York suburb. Pearce played center field.

"That was Dick Pearce's advent in a match. Dick told me that when he first went out to play ball he knew nothing of the game."

The next year he played regularly for the Atlantics at shortstop, the position that gave him his fame and the one that he molded into its present form. Chadwick continued, "When a hit was made and the runner ran for a base the fielders nearby would try to hit the runner with the ball—that was the way base runners were then put out—and this Dick thought was the life of the game, and he soon learned to plunk the fellows real easy when he went to short field." He played in all eight match games that year and the next, and in 12 games out of 15 in 1859 for the "champion" Atlantics.

Baseball, almost exclusively an urban sport at birth, was centered in New York/Brooklyn, then known as the "base ball capital." Here it had grown rapidly, replacing cricket as the most popular sport. The "New York game" prevailed over various other versions played in different locales. Out of the amazing number of teams competing, the Atlantics won the Brooklyn championship in 1857 and the metropolitan championship the next year.

In this atmosphere Pearce gained fame, even though the reporter of the New York *Clipper* insisted for a while on spelling his name Pierce. "Among the more noticeable features of play by the Atlantics was the fielding of Pierce" [Sept. 12, 1857]. ". . . good catches on fly made by Pierce. Pierce's short quite up to his usual, effective style" [July 16, 1859].

The game was catching on, and Pearce was riding a crest of popularity. Feverish excitement reached its pre-war peak in 1858 in a series of three "all-star" games played between those arch rivals, New York and Brooklyn. New York won two of the three, the first time that admission was charged to watch a baseball game. Dickey played in only the last two games, totalling seven runs scored, a 29 to 8 victory and a 29 to 18 defeat. After both games, the players and their friends sat down to a "sumptuous collation" and were royally entertained. Although his team lost, Pearce maintained the outstanding caliber of his play in these games and for the next decade.

September 10, 1858

NEW YORK				BROOKLYN			
	Outs	**Runs**	**Left**		**Outs**	**Runs**	**Left**
Gelston, ss	2	5	0	Pidgeon, p	3	3	0
Wadsworth, 1b	5	2	0	Manolt, cf	4	1	1
Benson, cf	3	4	0	Grum, rf	2	2	2
Pinckney, 2b	3	3	1	M. O'Brien, 3b	4	1	0
Thorne, p	2	5	0	P. O'Brien, 1f	5	1	0
Tooker, 1f	2	3	1	Price, 1b	3	1	1
De Bost, c	5	2	1	Boerum, c	2	3	0
Burns, rf	2	3	1	Pearce, ss	2	3	0
McCosker, 3b	3	2	1	Oliver, 2b	2	3	0
	27	29	5		27	18	4

New York   7 0 0 3 3 2 5 3 6 = 29
Brooklyn   2 0 0 2 0 2 4 4 4 = 18

Passed Balls—Boerum 8, De Bost 3. Struck Out—M. O'Brien, P. O'Brien, Boerum. Run Out between Bases—M. O'Brien by Gelston. Fly Catches Missed—P. O'Brien, Price, Pearce, Burns 2, Gelston, Pinckney, Thorne 2. Umpire—Dr. Adams, Knickerbockers.

Pearce gave the Atlantics an aggressive hitter, who often led off, and an exceptional fielder regardless of what position he played. In 1869 a reporter for the Boston *Chronicle* praised his batting prowess: "I cannot better give you an idea of skillful batting than by describing the style of batting of Pearce and Chapman of the Atlantic nine, the former being what I consider one of the most 'scientific'—if I may use the term—batsmen in the country. Pearce in an important match comes to bat, views the position of the field and finds an open spot or weak point on the field and aims to send the ball there. . . . When he takes his bat in hand he has a special object in view . . . this is in fact, the great end of skillful batting."

He showed some flashes of power, but Pearce became legendary largely because of his "tricky hit," now known as the bunt. In his time, if a ball hit in fair territory it was fair no matter where it rolled and Dickey used this to advantage better than any of his contemporaries. Pearce counted on surprise and his speed to reach first base before a play could be made.

Of his fielding, it was said, "There are few who equal him, and in regard to coolness, nerve and judgment in critical positions of a game there are none to surpass him even in these days [1870] of skillful ball players.

[Last season] but few errors were charged to him while the good plays were numerous.

"A point of Dick's play is his deliberate style of throwing—it is a rare thing for him to overthrow a ball to a base. No man knows better when a throw to first is useless or not." Moreover, Pearce had "pluck in facing hot balls."

Baseball expanded throughout the 1860s, even with the loss of some of the star players to military duty during the war. Pearce, who did not serve in the Union army, continued to play for the Atlantics, a champion club during most of these years. From the 1855 season through 1869, it ran up a 225–34 record, with five ties. Dickey played in 211 of those games, scoring 907 runs while being put out 720 times.

The versatile Dickey not only played shortstop, he also caught, patrolled left field, and in emergencies could hold down second or even pitch. The only player to surpass him in popularity was James Creighton, the best pitcher of his generation. To circumvent strong reservations about paying players, Brooklyn sponsored a benefit game for both of these men on November 16, 1861. The lateness of the season and the "free contests" that were the "order of the day" kept the crowd small.

Creighton and Pearce led the charge as baseball passed from the amateurism of earlier years to professionalism. Eagerness for top-notch teams that could win with regularity meant that gentlemen and local players would be supplemented by the best athletes available. Evasion of the rule against paying players seems to have occurred at least as early as 1860, when "battling" fast-ball pitcher Creighton reportedly received money.

Some protests against "ringers" naturally surfaced, but team backers and spectators generally supported the idea of beating bitter rivals with whomever they could get. In order to keep the home team competitive, payments had to be made just to stay even with other nines who were doing the same thing. The skill of the local team also improved when players of the caliber of Pearce anchored the infield. Considering the materialistic character of America in this generation, it was not surprising that Pearce, Creighton, and others were willing and happy to be paid to play. Thus the sport evolved, and Dickey helped bring on the new era and the professionalism that soon came to be a baseball hallmark.

The game was not always fun. Cold weather in those late days of October and November often made "playing ball a very disagreeable task." A "sudden wind, dust and rain storm" complicated a June 23, 1860 game. On one occasion, when Pearce was catching, a "severe blow to the face from a foul ball nearly broke his jaw" and forced him to leave the game in the first inning.

His temper occasionally got the best of him. On August 26, 1865 a reporter felt compelled to reprimand him for "forgetting himself in one instance in a manner we trust never to see again." Chadwick remembered that temper and wrote in 1870, "Dick used to be a first class growler, and that, too, in the model growling nine of the country. But he has wisely seen the error of his ways in this respect, and since then he has got that temper of his under excellent control."

Pearce obviously could not maintain his high level of play all the time. When the Atlantics lost in early November 1860, the report of the game said Pearce "was not playing well." After a 40–14 victory in September 1868, a reporter expressed surprise, "Pearce indulged in a little loose play, something new for Dick by the way."

Pearce and four others temporarily "seceded" from the Atlantics in 1866 over a matter not fully understood publicly even then. He played briefly for the Excelsior club but rejoined the Atlantics in August in time to star in some of the year's best games. He remained with that team throughout the rest of the decade.

In June and July 1868, the "famous Atlantic Club of Brooklyn" took a western tour that started in Syracuse and went as far west as St. Louis. They had traveled before and each time they toured, the team members exported the game and their skills to the fans and younger teams.

On this particular 1868 tour, the Atlantics won 17 and lost 1. Their one loss came in Buffalo, 19–15, showing that upstate New Yorkers had learned their lessons well. The "Atlantics took the defeat good naturedly" and "fraternized" with the victors after the game. With the help of Pearce's fielding, they turned four double plays in defeat. Another hard-fought contest came in Rockford, Illinois, where they ran up against the Forest City nine with Albert Spalding pitching. Trailing 24–16, the Atlantics "got their backs up and showed their country cousins how to play an up-hill game." They rallied to win 31–29 with Pearce leading off and scoring three runs.

Most of the games ended in routs, with scores like 66–11, 31–7, and 103–8. The defeat of its best team notwithstanding, the *St. Louis Times* applauded the Atlantics' star: "Pearce has been noted as a superior shortstop for ten years, and to-day has no equal in the base ball field. He bats with great judgment and safety, and, place him anywhere in the field, he is equally reliable."

In addition to the regular games, Pearce also played in bizarre versions of baseball. Winter baseball on ice skates was popular for two decades. The February 4, 1861 contest between the Atlantics and Charter Oaks for a silver ball drew an estimated twelve to fifteen thousand people to Brooklyn's 8th Ward, where a ten-acre field had been flooded. "Of the

Atlantics, we noted fine play on the part of Pierce [sic], who proved himself as good a short stop on ice, as he is on a summer's day. He made several splendid fly catches, and for an inning or two caught capitally behind."

The popular Pearce warranted a longer write-up than any other player in his team's 36–27 victory. The only modifications to the game were that each team played with ten men, a second catcher being added, and skaters did not have to stop at the base. Although the winners received praise for "Atlantic play" (a great compliment in those days), both teams were "obliged to substitute" their second nine players who were more proficient skaters.

But it was the summer game that became the national pastime. And the Cincinnati Red Stockings of 1869 and 1870 pioneered the idea of hiring professional players to play for the glory of an entire city. Their success not only ended New York and Brooklyn's domination of the sport, it stimulated the launching of professional nines to represent many other cities.

This change helped bring about the demise of the mighty Atlantics. Pearce played for the team through the 1870 season, taking the mound in relief again in November, and baffling the opposition with his "slow pitching." His effort went for naught, as the Atlantics lost that contest. The 1870 season marked the last hurrah for this Brooklyn team, which disintegrated that winter over the question of professionalism vs. amateurism. Pearce and five others left, Dickey joining the New York Mutuals.

One more time that winter, Pearce played a game on ice skates, this time for the Capitoline nine. The "Caps" won a five-inning massacre 37–1, with Dickey getting four hits and scoring four runs. Pearce attracted more attention, though, when the pitcher failed to appear on time. "Pearce took his place, and it was really a treat to see how cleverly Dick played his points on the village batsmen. In the whole five innings but four first-base hits were made."

Now thirty-five years old, Pearce served as a bridge between the early days and the new decade. Only six of the professionals listed in *Beadle's Base-Ball Player* for 1871 were over thirty, and two of those had just barely reached that plateau.

Pearce played two years with the Mutuals, including being captain (field manager) in 1872. Managing took its toll, as evidenced by his batting average, which sank to .188. The Mutuals, meanwhile, went 17–18 in the professional championship season and 34–20 overall.

The next year Dickey returned to his old Atlantic team and played two more seasons with them. His hitting rebounded, and he was still capable of playing a great game. On October 21, 1874 he hit three singles against

Boston pitching star Al Spalding in leading his team to victory. "Veteran Dick Pearce bore off the palm in handling the ash."

Dickey Pearce went west to St. Louis in 1875 to captain and play for that city's first professional team. Fans perhaps hoped that some of that spirit and skill they had observed on the Atlantics' team during its earlier western tour would rub off on their team through the leadership of the old pro. The veteran brought his team home in fourth place, with a record of 39–29. Henry Chadwick, who that year criticized all the teams except Boston's champions, tersely wrote that in St. Louis it "would have been a more successful [season] than one that it was . . . with better management."

When the St. Louis club joined the new National League in 1876, Pearce was retained as shortstop but not as captain. He appeared in only 25 games and batted .206, a far cry from his earlier days.

Still Dickey played on. In 1877 he captained the Rhode Island club of Providence before returning to St. Louis at the end of the season. The rule change that eliminated the "fair foul" that he had used so well did not enhance his average any. Although the local professional club folded at the end of the season, Pearce stayed in St. Louis for three more summers, playing on Sundays for the semi-professional Browns before retiring back to Brooklyn in 1881.

His days as a baseball player, spanning three decades, were finished. Pearce had shaped the shortstop position in his own image. *Spalding's Official Base Ball Guide* for 1878 explained how each position should be played. Its description of a shortstop paid anonymous tribute to Dickey.

> Backing up the other players when the ball is thrown is part of the short-stop's duty which too many neglect. The weak point in the play in this position last year was the failure to run out after short flies. The player who hopes to fill the position well should practice making that class of catches known as "running with the ball," where it appears as if the ball went over the player's shoulder. The short-stop . . . should put his whole mind on getting the ball to the ground "choking it down," as it is called. If he cannot get his hand fairly on it the first time, he will often have time enough to make the play if he can make it bound down in front of him anywhere.

Pearce had done all that for twenty-two years, and this pioneer was the game's best at shortstop.

Back home in Brooklyn, Pearce was not forgotten. The Atlantics, now a minor league club, staged a twenty-fifth anniversary benefit game for him on July 29, 1881, giving Dickey one last chance to play the position he had made famous for the club he had done so much to make even more famous. The proceeds from the game helped Pearce, a married man, to set up a "wine saloon" in Brooklyn named Atlantic Shades.

Still hoping to maintain a place in the game he loved, he also tried umpiring. But this could be a thankless job, even for an old baseball star. In 1885, he was struck by a player who disputed a call. The owners, reluctant to take strong action, accepted the player's apology and thereby excused his actions. One wonders if Pearce remembered his own playing days and his flashing temper, which had gotten him into trouble back in the long-ago 1860s. As late as 1889, Dickey occasionally "was seen on the field in the capacity of umpire."

A combination of Bright's disease and a severe cold, caught during his attendance at the Old Timers' Day at Peddock Island in Boston Harbor, laid Dickey low in September 1908. By then, the sport that he had so nourished had grown to become the national pastime. His role in it had been nearly forgotten, as new players and new stars took the field where he had played so brilliantly decades before. When his cold became pneumonia, the end was near, and he died on September 18 in Onset, Massachusetts.

Nearly a month later, on October 13, the Brooklyn *Eagle* carried an obituary, appropriately in the sports section. It described Pearce as very "active for a man of his years," and one who was very popular with old-time lovers of the game. Pearce, the writer noted, was "undoubtedly the greatest shortstop of his day," and the first man to introduce the bunt hit. Appropriate, too, was the statement on his death certificate, which listed his occupation simply as "Professional Base Ball Player."

REMEMBERED FOR HIS SERIES-ENDING HOMER, DAZZLIN' MAZ SHOULD BE CELEBRATED AS THE GREATEST DEFENSIVE SECOND BASEMAN IN HISTORY— AND AS A CLASSIC BASEBALL CHARACTER

Bill Mazeroski: An Appreciation

JIM KAPLAN

♦ ♦ ♦

In one of baseball's supreme ironies, Bill Mazeroski's greatest moment as a player forever obscured his true greatness as a player.

It wasn't the Shot Heard 'Round the World, but it was equally dramatic and more symbolic than the celebrated Bobby Thomson hit. On October 13, 1960, Mazeroski, the Pittsburgh Pirate second baseman, socked a ninth-inning homer over the brick wall 406 feet from home plate in Forbes Field and beat the Yankees 10–9 in the seventh game of the World Series. Waving his cap in circles, Mazeroski had to fight his way through a crowd to reach home plate. Elsewhere in Pittsburgh, people snake-danced down the streets and stalled trolleys by throwing tons of paper out windows. Worried police closed bridges and tunnels. Swamped hotel managers shut their lobbies. Finally breaking away from the celebration, the quiet hero grabbed his wife and ran off to a Pittsburgh hill to sit still for a few moments and take stock of what had happened.

Plenty had happened. The only homer ever to end a World Series, Mazeroski's blast also concluded one of the wildest seventh games ever (remember the double-play grounder that hit a pebble and clipped Tony Kubek in the throat?). Maz's swing also ended what many consider the

156

best-played era in baseball history. The majors had integrated in 1947 without altering their two-league, 16-team format: hence, the golden era of 1947–60. In 1961 the American League would add two teams, the Nationals would follow in 1962, and baseball would head down the road to dilution, divisional play, the DH, and the domes. Mazeroski's homer would stand symbolically at the peak of baseball history.

But the more he thought about what he'd done, the less delirious Maz became. What a shame, he told friends later, that he'd be remembered for his bat rather than his glove.

That's being modest: It's a shame the greatest defensive second baseman in baseball history should be remembered for a single at bat.

Not that Max couldn't hit. Playing in a low-average era (1956–72), he batted .260 with 2016 hits. A good power hitter for a middle infielder, he had at least 10 homers six times. A great clutch hitter—his homer won the first game of the '60 Series as well as the last—he had 80 or more runs batted in twice. But his superb fielding forever distinguished him from his peers.

The second baseman is the most underrated player on the field. He routinely averages as many chances per game as his more celebrated running mate, the shortstop. Second basemen, moreover, execute baseball's most critical defensive maneuver—the pivot on most double plays.

"I never worried about anything but catching the ball and throwing it to Maz," says Dick Groat, Mazeroski's shortstop in 1956–62. "He'd make the DP after getting a perfect throw or a terrible one.

"He was as good as I've ever seen at turning the double play," says former Cub shortstop Don Kessinger. "They called him No Touch because he threw so quickly he never seemed to touch the ball."

On one memorable occasion the Pirates were a run ahead of the Astros with one out in the ninth and men on first and third. A Houston player hit a high hopper to shortstop Gene Alley, who made the only play possible and threw to Maz for the force. Girding for extra innings, the Pirates leaned back on the bench and conceded a run. Seconds later they realized the game was over: Maz had relayed to first in time for the DP.

"That was one of the best double plays I ever made," says Mazeroski, who retired from coaching in the eighties after helping Julio Cruz become a fine second baseman at Seattle and Tim Wallach a top third baseman at Montreal. "Everyone wound up on the ground. Alley fell down making the throw, I turned it with my feet in the air, and Donn Clendenon hit the ground stretching for the ball at first. I'm lucky I have such a strong arm. I never had to wind up to throw, and that helped me a lot on the double play."

Just another DP turn by Bill Mazeroski

Mazeroski's best friends on the double play were his powerful right wrist and forearm, which enabled him to relay to first with a quick flip. With nimble and strong legs, the 5' 11½", 185-pound Mazeroski could reach the base well ahead of the throw and push off before the runner arrived.

A purist, Maz believed that the most efficient way to make the pivot was to go straight at the runner ("Any other way lengthens your throw"). He hung in so tough that teammates called him Tree Stump. When an opponent crashed into him, they had to bring out a stretcher—for the runner.

"He was the best second baseman I've ever seen," says Red Sox executive Johnny Pesky, a former shortstop who teamed with Hall-of-Fame second baseman Bobby Doerr in Boston and later coached for the Pirates when Maz was playing. "One night he dropped the ball. The next night he took one hundred grounders and never missed one. 'Hit it to Maz,' we used to say. 'Hit it to Maz.'"

In one of his most spectacular fielding plays Maz ran down a grounder past first, fielded it near the right-field line, and made a turnaround, off-balance throw of some 120 feet to nip the Mets' speedy Tommie Agee trying to score from second.

Bill Mazeroski's baseball background is Baseball Classic. His first instructor was his father (isn't it always like that?); the late Lew Mazeroski was himself a prospect on the verge of a tryout with Cleveland when a lump of hardrock coal smashed his foot in a mining accident. Bill reported to his high school team in Tiltonsville, Ohio as a freshman, and his coach, Al Barazio, told him, "I'm going to make a big leaguer out of you." Like many great second basemen, Maz was switched there from shortstop (by Branch Rickey, of course). Maz also supplied the personal touches we associate with old-fashioned ballplayers. Leaving church the day he was married, Mazeroski stuck a chaw of tobacco in his cheek. Maz has hunted and golfed and fished in his time; in fact, he was called Catfish as a kid.

Major leaguers had other names for him. By the time he made his first All-Star team in 1958, the twenty-one year-old Mazeroski was already being called Dazzlin' Maz and The Boy Bandit. When he took infield practice, stars from both leagues stopped to watch him—the fielding equivalent of watching Ted Williams hit.

Baseball people love to listen to him, too. If pressed, Maz can discuss his gloves like a jockey describing his tack: "I used only two or three gloves in my career. I'd break in one in practice and use my main one in games. Some guys have a new one every year; you can't get the feel that way. I also used a small glove. When you reached for a ball, it was there. We were already putting the index finger outside the glove in those days. That creates an air pocket. When the ball hits the glove, it's cushioned."

"Bill Mazeroski's defensive statistics are probably the most impressive of any player at any position," *The Bill James Historical Baseball Abstract* reports. Maz led the league in putouts five times, total chances eight, assists a record nine, range factor ten. He holds major league double-play marks by a second baseman for a season (161), career (1706), and years leading the league (8). His lifetime fielding average of .983 trails only his Pirate successor, Dave Cash (.9836), and a few others among National Leaguers. Cash played most of his career on artificial turf; Maz played most of his on what author and ex-pitcher Jim Brosnan described as the league's worst infield.

In the 1983 *Baseball Research Journal*, Jim McMartin created some all-time defensive listings using such factors as league leadership in putouts, assists and DP's, and the Bill James range factor (putouts and assists divided by games); McMartin's figures established that old number nine was the most efficient middle infielder ever. In *Players' Choice*, second basemen past and present rated him the best glove ever at their position.

There are those who will go further and declare Mazeroski the greatest fielder ever to hang up his spikes. In their highly respected book, *The Hidden Game of Baseball*, John Thorn and Pete Palmer devised a fielding formula for "defensive wins" at every position but pitcher. Maz finished first. (The only active player likely to pass Mazeroski, says Thorn, is St. Louis shortstop Ozzie Smith.)

So why isn't Maz in the Hall? "I don't get carried away about that because I don't know if I belong," he says in his mild way. "I always thought you had to do it all—hit, run, field, throw—to make it."

But isn't it a fact, he was asked, that many players made the Hall on their bats alone? "That's true. Seems it's an offensive place. If I had the records offensively that I do defensively, I'd be in."

The recent enshrinement of Brooks Robinson, Luis Aparicio, and Pee Wee Reese, who were as celebrated for their fielding as their offense, augurs well for the future. "Maybe the tide is starting to turn," Maz says hopefully.

Not fast enough. "It's an absolute disgrace," says Groat, his voice rising to a shout, "that Bill Mazeroski isn't in the Hall of Fame!"

Little-Known Facts

Babe Ruth, in the year he was traded from the Boston Red Sox to the New York Yankees, hit a home run off one of his own pitches. As a result, he won and lost the pennant that year by one game. . . . In 1929, Peoria pitcher Tiger Bright struck out 27 men in a nine-inning game with a yo-yo. . . . George (Rightly) Wilson, pitcher for the really old Orioles, won 86 games in 1886 at the age of eighty-six.

Conrad Horn

EDDIE GAEDEL: "HE ENDED UP WITH THE WRONG CROWD"

The Sad Life of Baseball's Midget

JIM REISLER

♦ ♦ ♦

In an undistinguished grave at St. Mary's Cemetery on the southwest side of Chicago is buried a man immortalized as the answer to one of baseball's better trivia questions.

He lies in one of the older, more crowded parts of the cemetery, made especially pretty in the summer by the trees that shade the graves. In some ways, it is fitting that Eddie Gaedel is there; in section G, grave number X-363B, he may finally have found the peace he never knew when he was alive.

Much is known of the day that Gaedel, 3'7" and sixty-five pounds, stepped up as the St. Louis Browns' first batter in the second game of an August 19, 1951 doubleheader against the Detroit Tigers, walked, and ended his career as quickly as he had started it. But for a game as well-documented as baseball, it is ironic that virtually nothing is known about the man.

The fact is that he died tragically, the victim of a mugging on a south-side Chicago street corner. Fewer than fifty people attended his funeral.

"It was a pretty sad situation all the way through," says Bob Cain, the Detroit pitcher who faced Gaedel. "It's a shame he had to die the way he did but I guess he got in quite a bit of trouble off and on. He ended up with the wrong crowd."

Few baseball people besides then Browns owner Bill Veeck even knew Gaedel. Those who did met him only briefly. Bob Broeg, the longtime St.

Eddie Gaedel sits between Matt Batts (l) and Jim McDonald (r) in the Browns' dugout after drawing a walk

Louis baseball writer who wrote the game story for the next morning's local paper, was one.

After the game, he found the diminutive slugger, dressed in a yellow sports shirt and a tan jacket, sitting on a counter in the Sportsman's Park press box.

"I asked him two or three questions and he gave kind of routine answers," Broeg recalls. "Then I said to him that he's what I wanted always to be, an ex-big leaguer. He suddenly jumped down, thrust out his chest and seemed very proud of himself. Then he shook hands and was gone. I never saw him again."

At first, at least, he made out well, appearing in the following few weeks on television shows, including Ed Sullivan and Bing Crosby. The shows earned him $17,000, "a tremendous amount in those days," according to Bob Fishel, later executive vice president of the American League and then a Browns official.

"Bill Veeck was looking for a midget, not a dwarf or somebody with a large head," Fishel says of Gaedel's agreement to a $100 contract. "We got him from [Cleveland talent coordinator] Marty Caine, a short guy himself. When we saw him, there was no question that Eddie was right. He was actually a very attractive guy."

However, for the few days that he knew Gaedel, also the only man in big league history to wear a fraction as a uniform number (⅛), Fishel admits "I didn't think the world of him." He won't elaborate.

On September 2, 1951—about three weeks after his big league appearance—Gaedel got into trouble on a Cincinnati street corner when he was caught screaming obscenities and then tried to convince a police officer he was a big league ballplayer. He was arrested for disorderly conduct, released on $25 bond, and received a suspended sentence.

According to an interview with his widowed mother, Helen, published in a four-part Louisville *Courier-Journal* series in 1971, Eddie's size had gotten him in trouble for a good part of his life.

Born to a healthy Chicago family that included a 5'6" brother, Robert, and a 5'11" sister, Pearl, Eddie's growth was stunted from the age of three by a thyroid condition. "He was picked on as a kid, [not excluding] small kids too who ganged up on him," Helen was quoted as saying. Nonetheless, Eddie made it through Spaulding High School on Chicago's Southside, and was working as an errand boy at *Drover's Daily Journal,* a defunct Chicago newspaper, when he got to the Browns.

He appeared to have made the most of his size. He worked as the Buster Brown shoe man, appearing at shoe-store openings around the Chicago and St. Louis areas. In the 1950s, he appeared in the Ringling Brothers Circus, and as a promotion man for Mercury Records, but refused to go with the company to California, because, according to his mother, "he was scared to go out."

In April 1961, nearly ten years after appearing for the Browns, Gaedel was briefly back in the news when Veeck, by then the owner of the White Sox, took note of the fans' constant complaints about vendors blocking their views, and hired him and seven other midgets to work as salesmen in the box-seat sections of Comiskey Park for opening day.

But the end was near. By then, Gaedel was suffering from high blood pressure, an enlarged heart, and the effects of frequent falls. On June 18, 1961, he was mugged on a southside Chicago street corner. According to the *Courier-Journal* story, the $11 he had in his wallet was taken from him.

Afterwards, he apparently staggered home and died in his bed of a heart attack. Paramedics were unable to revive him. A coroner's report said that Gaedel also had bruises on his knees and his face.

The article points out that Helen Gaedel, nearly penniless and out of touch with her other children, was devastated. Adding insult to injury, she was swindled out of Eddie's bats and Browns uniform by a man purporting to represent the National Baseball Hall of Fame. The curators at the Hall say their only remnant of Eddie Gaedel's brief big league career is the famous photograph showing him crouching with his tiny bat cocked at homeplate with the catcher, the late Bob Swift, on his knees to receive a pitch.

Gaedel's death attracted little notice beyond the obligatory wire story and a brief mention in Broeg's column the following day. Pitcher Cain was the only baseball representative to attend the funeral.

"I never even met him, but I felt obligated to go," says Cain, who by then was retired from his six-year major league career. "It kind of threw me for a loop that no other baseball people were there."

Only the trivia buffs seem to remember. "Four or five times a year, I'll get a call from somebody wanting to know about him," says Jim Delsing, the Browns' regular right fielder who became an addendum to a trivia question by pinch-running for baseball's only midget.

Delsing says that after he went in to run for Gaedel, "I never met him or never heard from him again, except for what I read in the paper. It was unbelievable what happened to him. And sad, so very sad."

At Bob Cain's home in Cleveland, there is a three-foot vestibule covered with religious artifacts. Occupying a small place in the arrangement is a palm card from the funeral:

"Blessed are they that mourn, for they shall be comforted. May Jesus have mercy on the soul of Edward Gaedel: Departed June 18, 1961."

Hall-of-Fame Managers, Hall-of-Fame Nicknames

JAMES K. SKIPPER JR.

♦ ♦ ♦

Fully fourteen of the sixteen Cooperstown skippers had calling cards. See if you can guess the people from their nicknames:

The Old Roman. When his White Sox won their first pennant in 1901, journalist Hugh Keogh began referring to their owner, who had managed in four leagues, as "The Old Roman." Thomas Shea, author of a 1946 book on baseball nicknames, suggests that the nickname was a composite of his characteristics—breeding, a patrician bearing, shrewdness, and a noble mane of white hair that crowned a classical profile. *(Charles Comiskey)*

The Old Fox. The name was probably given him by an opponent. It derives not from his wiliness as a manager and executive, but from his days as a pitcher, when he was guilty of much chicanery. "For a little fellow he was pretty good," umpire Bill Bryan observed. "He used to stand out there on the rubber and spend minutes knocking the ball against his spikes, pretending there was dirt on them, and meanwhile scuffing the cover of the ball." *(Clark Griffith)*

The Tall Tactician. The 6'1", 170-pound Athletics manager, a master of baseball strategy, was an unforgettable sight for more than half a century—sitting on the bench in suit, tie, and straw hat, and directing his players by waving a score card. *(Connie Mack)*

165

Little Napoleon. The nickname referred to the Giant skipper's height (5'7") and authoritarian and military style of managing. *(John McGraw)*

The "Tall Tactician," Connie Mack

The Mahatma. The Browns and Cardinals manager always thought he had something important to say. He liked to lecture players individually and collectively, using catchy phrases and parables that often were over their heads. As a Dodger executive in the 1940s, he reminded sportswriters of India's orator-turned-statesman, Mahatma Gandhi, and they began to refer to him in print as "The Mahatma." *(Branch Rickey)*

Uncle Robbie. Managing the Dodgers from 1914 to 1931, the portly ex-catcher was a lax disciplinarian. This, combined with a fatherly attitude toward his players, not only won him respect and admiration, but also the nickname "Uncle Robbie." *(Wilbert Robinson)*

Cousin Ed. An ironic nickname for a man who liked to pick fights, "Cousin Ed" derives from "Cousin Egbert," a name given the 1920s-era Yankee general manager by sportswriter W.O. McGeehan. *(Edward Barrow)*

Bucky. The player-manager of Washington's 1924–25 championship teams, he was first called "Bucky" as a kid basketball player. "I had a couple of players on my back in a rough game," he related. "When I shook them off and shot a basket [a friend named Gary Schmeelk] said I bucked like a tough little bronco." *(Stanley Harris)*

The Mighty Mite. The 5'6½" Yankee skipper more than earned the name for controlling such strong-willed players as Babe Ruth, Joe Bush, and Jumpin' Joe Dugan. *(Miller Huggins)*

Marse Joe. Managing the Cubs in the 1920s, he was given the nickname by Chicago sportswriters. "Marse" is a variation of "Massa," a term for "master" once used by slaves. The manager may have first been called "Marse Joe" when he fired Grover Cleveland Alexander for breaking curfew regulations. *(Joe McCarthy)*

Deacon. The only manager to direct three teams (St. Louis, Cincinnati, and Pittsburgh) to pennants, this softspoken man was, in fact, a deacon in the Methodist Church. *(William McKechnie)*

Casey. He was born and raised in Kansas City, Missouri. According to one of several explanations for his nickname, he arrived in minor-league Kankakee in 1910 with "K.C." on his bags and introduced himself by saying "I'm from K.C." *(Charles Stengel)*

Señor. His managerial skills with the Indians (1954) and White Sox (1959) earned him the respectful "Señor," which is Spanish for "Mister." *(Alfonso Lopez)*

Smokey. As a kid on a grade-school baseball team, the legendary Dodger skipper threw a live fastball. The kids said he put plenty of "smoke" on the ball. *(Walter Alston)*

The other Hall-of-Fame managers, nineteenth-century greats George and Harry Wright, had no distinctive nicknames.

Baseball Joe Matson: The Greatest Player Who Never Was

JACK KAVANAGH

◆ ◆ ◆

Let others praise the literary giants who have brought their skills to baseball fiction. Wolfe, Farrell, Malamud, Harris, Coover, Kennedy deserve kudos. But I toss my cap in the air and shout, "huzzah!" for Lester Chadwick, the author who invented the exploits of the Baseball Joe series.

The canon covering Baseball Joe's career is contained in fourteen novels, published by Cupples & Leon, from 1912 to 1928. These differ from other juvenile books about baseball as they trace the personal and professional history of the principal character from his early teens in *Baseball Joe of the Silver Star*, to his ultimate major league achievement in *Baseball Joe, Pitching Wizard*.

Joe Matson is fifteen years old in the first book and thirty-four when the series ends. He moves from town team to prep school and into Yale. Unlike Frank Merriwell, who remained an undergraduate at Old Eli for dozens of dime novels, Joe Matson left after a single season of varsity pitching to enter professional baseball.

A season in the Central League and he is drafted by the St. Louis Cardinals. His potential as a rookie catches the eye of the New York Giants management and a trade is arranged which brings Baseball Joe to the team of his role model, Christy Mathewson.

Chadwick drew extensively on the actual events of baseball to provide Baseball Joe the circumstances of the books. The series runs approximately parallel to a passing scene which saw the transition from the dead ball era to the lively ball and the advent of the home run. In the course of the fourteen novels we find Joe Matson touring the world as a member of the world champion Giants, resisting the temptations of the Federal League, being shamed by the Black Sox, and adapting to the lively ball.

Although the backgrounds and circumstances changed with the times, the plots did not. The books are formula-written with a villain for each, either with a conspiracy to frame Joe for a crime or to kidnap him so he will miss "the big game." Joe never failed to show up for any crucial game, often dragging a covey of villains behind him.

If you are looking for unique plotting, you'll not find it in these books. If complex personalities intrigue you, you'll be disappointed to know Baseball Joe Matson is a one-dimensional demi-god.

However, the Baseball Joe series was only intended to serve boys coming to maturity from 1912 until the eve of World War II. As the books were passed down from older brother to younger, they imparted tidbits of the actual history of the game, playing tips, strategy insights, and an understanding of the framework of organized baseball. These are peripheral values to hero-worshipping young readers. Foremost, Baseball Joe is the best of pitchers, steals bases when he wishes, and develops into a batter with the "hit 'em where they ain't" adroitness of Willie Keeler and the power to drive the ball a tad farther than Babe Ruth.

Joe combines the skills of Cobb, Speaker, Lajoie, and Wagner. About the only thing he didn't do was go behind the plate. The author was probably stumped on how to have Joe pitch to himself.

The Baseball Joe books were among the first juvenile novels I ever read, taking them in random order in the early 1930s. I doubt if all fourteen trickled down from older family members whose hand-me-downs in juvenile literature kept me enthralled during my pre-teen years.

However, I recently borrowed the entire series from a friend who has collected them all. I was able to read my way from the time when young Joe Matson and his family move to Riverside, a town on a river coursing somewhere through New England, until the last book, published sixteen years later. Read in maturity, these books are amusingly arcane. However, they also are tinged with a personal nostalgia for a time which was disappearing as my own adolescence began.

I am sure my own interest in baseball's past was first awakened by these books. Chadwick, a pen name borrowed knowingly from The Father of baseball writers, Henry Chadwick, injects considerable historical information into his stories. For example, while Joe is traveling by train to spring training, he meets an old man who says he played right field for the Cincinnati Red Stockings of 1869. The old-time ballplayer tells Joe about the early years of the game, adding he was in the lineup the day Paul Hines made the first unassisted triple play.

Contemporary historians are quick to deny this and can show box scores to back up their debunking of the accomplishment. However, Lester Chadwick was quoting the beliefs of his time and, as the books are works of fiction, the Hines unassisted triple play makes a better story.

Throughout the novels, Joe Matson experiences events which served to teach the juvenile reader the realities of life in professional baseball. Joe resents the fact that his contract can be sold without his consent, but accepts this as necessary "for the good of the game."

Joe can always see the other fellow's viewpoint, but stands with the establishment whenever a crisis occurs. A boy reading the books for excitement, for accounts of games played, for the suspense as Joe escapes one dastardly plot after another, unconsciously absorbs a great deal of baseball background.

Chadwick blended fact and fiction. He barely hid the actual identity of real-life players: Hornsby was Mormsby; Ruth was Roth ("look out for his beanball") as a pitcher and Kid Rose, later, as a slugger. Joe's idol and mentor on the Giants was Hughson, famous for his fadeaway. McRae is the bellicose Giants manager.

Baseball Joe Matson began playing in New England, as a boy, on a town team, after his family had moved to Riverside. The Matson family consisted of the father, an inventor and early-century wimp. He is constantly being swindled by evil partners whose ill intent is always apparent to his son. Mother Matson, who hopes young Joe will enter the ministry, flutters from crisis to crisis, and presumably found Joe, and his sister, Clara, a year younger, under a leaf in the cabbage patch.

The family is 110 percent four square in every virtue, but Joe is the first to recognize he has been living in the twentieth century for a decade. Even so, Joe's boyhood transportation is by bike, with an oil lamp on the handlebars, or by hiring a livery rig from the town stable to chase fleeing villains.

Joe's athletic skills are utilized from time to time by the author to resolve a crisis. Joe enables a man to escape a burning building by hurling up a ball of yarn and attaching a stout rope to it so the man can slide down to safety.

In another situation, Joe first meets Mabel Varley, the romance of his life, when she caroms past him, helpless in a carriage lurching behind a runaway horse. Joe stops the animal in its tracks by throwing a stone and hitting the horse in the head, knocking it unconscious.

This first meeting with Mabel begins a succession of appearances in subsequent books which even the most juvenile of readers realized must lead Baseball Joe to the altar. Actually, Joe's courtship of Mabel extends from *Baseball Joe in the Central League,* through four intervening books, until Joe and Mabel finally tie the knot in *Baseball Joe, Home Run King.*

There was a break in the series after 1918, due, most likely, to the First World War and the scarcity of paper for juvenile books. Although the books parallel the real events in baseball, the author seems to have overlooked World War I. Unlike Matty, the obvious counterpart for the fictionalized Matson, Baseball Joe not only doesn't go to war, he is oblivious of it.

It is quite likely that the Edward Stratemeyer "fiction mill" changed horses behind the pseudonym, Lester Chadwick, at this point. To give this project a literary mystique it doesn't deserve—after all, we're not going to divide into camps over authorship (no Baconians need apply)—it can be observed that the books from 1912 to 1918 contain vastly more baseball historical references. Also, the dialogue is characteristically dotted with what I will suggest is "the Stratemeyer stammer."

This is a dialogue device, in which the personal pronoun is repeated, to connote stress and determination: "I—I'd rather fight than give in."

But more significant in the books from 1922 on is that Joe's upward mobility, having been attained on the Giants, no longer serves as the book's achievement pinnacle. Where Joe had been able to end each book looking forward to a coming season played at a higher level—sandlot, to prep, to college, to minors, to majors, to the Giants—once with New York, each successive season had to top the last. This was to lead to problems for the author, whoever wielded the pen behind the pen name.

Eventually, Baseball Joe had done it all. He rarely won a crucial game without pitching a no-hitter. When a base hit would do, he customarily belted the ball out of sight. He had been carried off the field in triumph by his teammates so often they were becoming stoop-shouldered by the task. Whether it was ordained that *Baseball Joe, Pitching Wizard* was to be Joe Matson's swan song, instead of another of a continuing series of extraordinary accomplishments, is left to conjecture by those familiar with the publishing world. I think it was.

There had been a lapse of three years since Baseball Joe had left his readers agape in wonderment. In 1925's *Baseball Joe, Champion of the League,* the Giants win more games than any team ever had. Joe, of course, pitches the final victory and, for a variation on the theme of personal contribution, doesn't hit a home run. Instead, he scores from first base on a single.

This caps a season in which Joe Matson leads the league in niceness, decency, and celibacy; and, incidentally, batting average, home runs, stolen bases, and, when pitching, strikeouts and earned run average. It didn't seem possible for Joe to exceed the excess of success in the future.

Sensibly, the author behind the series—let's credit Edward Stratemeyer with blocking out these books, if not providing the final manuscript—tried to phase Joe out. Missing from the list of Baseball Joe books in the Grobani bibliography is the 1926 *Baseball Joe, Club Owner.*

Joe leaves the major leagues with a sore arm, the consequence of evil doings by the villains in the prior volume. This plot seems to be an effort to close the circle of novels at twelve. When the publisher agreed to permit Joe to leave the big leagues, there was a tacit awareness this would deprive the books of the most attractive elements for juvenile readers. We—for I was among them—wanted Joe to conquer more baseball worlds, not settle down in a front-office job in a minor league city.

Joe is back in his boyhood hometown, Riverside, now strangely relocated in the Midwest. It might be that a new hand has taken up the pen behind the pseudonym and didn't remember Riverside was in New England, or the marketing people at Cupples & Leon may have thought it better for circulation to locate in mid-America.

Joe buys the franchise and finds three of his old Silver Star teammates still in the lineup. He encounters a new set of blackguards and reveals himself as a closet bigot. At one point he explains, about Moe Russnak, the book's bad guy, "He's a Jew that lives in Pentolia [rival city]. Not that I have anything against him because of his race. Our shortstop, Levy, is a Jew and he's as fine a fellow as there is on the team."

Having delivered himself of the classic brotherhood bromide, but not introduced Levy to his sister, Clara, who will wed Joe's best friend, another WASP, Joe manages the team, in a nonplaying role, to the pennant. He then gives the franchise to his dependent father, whose patents have been stolen again and again during the series, and his brother-in-law, Mabel's brother, Reggie Varley. The series might have ended at that point, but someone decided, in 1928, to bring Joe back to the major leagues, his arm restored. One can sense Lester Chadwick chafing at having to find more worlds—and World Series—for his protagonist to conquer. Possibly it crossed the author's mind to have Baseball Joe tumble off Coogan's Bluff, locked in combat with the book's villain, as Conan Doyle, bored by the exploits of Sherlock Holmes, had sent him over Reichenbach Falls in the clutches of Professor Moriarty.

In the end, Chadwick used a more appropriate means and more diabolical. He gave the plot a final twist by writing *finis* to a series with a climax that could never be exceeded in a subsequent book.

Joe had purged baseball of two teammates who had accepted bribes from gamblers. Despite having to replace them with two untested rookies, the Giants win yet another pennant and provide Joe with an obligatory encore in the subsequent World Series. Baseball Joe's readers know their hero will win; we read only to learn how he will do it this time.

Joe is concerned about the two rookies who have replaced the crooked veterans. He worries how they will stand up to the pressure of championship games and fears they will embarrass themselves by making crucial errors on balls hit to them. Joe has the solution. He avoids the risk of shaky-handed fielders by not allowing the ball to be batted to them. His solution? *He methodically strikes out all 27 batters as they come to the plate.*

If there's to be a plaque honoring Baseball Joe Matson erected in the Baseball Hall of Fiction Fame, let it be noted that Joseph Matson, born in 1894, died of over-achievement in 1928. The series ended at that point. The books remained in circulation for a decade or more longer and still appear in secondhand bookstores. They are fun to read, loaded with historic detail, and, if they were part of your own boyhood, leave you awash in nostalgia.

George McBride: "I Took Honus Wagner's Job"

LAWRENCE S. RITTER

♦ ♦ ♦

The way I started in the American League? See, that was kind of peculiar—couldn't happen that way today. I was raised in Milwaukee but in 1901 I went out to South Dakota to play some ball. Our season closed out there a little early, so I came back home. A fellow named Wid Conroy had been playing shortstop for the Milwaukee club in the American League, but he sprained his ankle a day or two before I got home. Well, when the newspaper people found out that I was back from South Dakota, they called up and said bring your glove and shoes and your underwear to the ballpark . . . might be a chance for you to play today!

Well, I went out there and sat in the bleachers right behind first base and Hughie Duffy, the manager, he called me in and said, you're going to play today . . . shortstop. Well, I guess the rules were different in those days, cause I wasn't on the roster, and I didn't even have a contract. I was a third baseman, but they played me that day at shortstop. Then, of course, I signed up and played a game or two more till the end of the season.

In 1951, we had a fiftieth anniversary party for the American League, over in Boston. All the charter members of the American League got an invitation. Twenty-nine players came to the affair. Now, I guess all but ten of them are dead. Connie Mack, Cy Young, Hughie Duffy, fellows like that, all gone. The Milwaukee club was transferred to St. Louis for 1902 and the next move of a big league club was when the Braves came in '53! 'Course the old Milwaukee club wasn't the Braves, but the Brewers.

After 1901 I went back to the minors for a few years. Made the rounds a little bit: Milwaukee in the American Association, Kansas City, St. Joe, and then in 1905 the Pirates bought me. I'd shifted to shortstop by then.

Took Honus Wagner's job . . . at least that's why I went up. But they played me as a utility man till they traded me to St. Louis—the Nationals— and then I went back down to Kansas City.

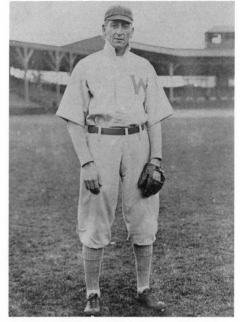

George McBride in 1909

Now, there's a funny parallel between me and Joe Cronin. I was with Pittsburgh and went to Kansas City. About twenty years later, Joe was with Pittsburgh and went to Kansas City. I went from Kansas City to Washington and he went from Kansas City to Washington. That's where the parallel ends. He was supposed to be a bad fielding shortstop, but he looked like a promising hitter. A scout had been looking at Cronin for Clark Griffith and finally got to talking to Joe and signed him up. Well, he telephones Griff and tells him he signed Cronin. "What?" he says. "That sieve? That fellow can't field. He isn't even hitting too well." But Joe went back up there, married Griff's daughter, hit real well, and Griff sold him to Tom Yawkey for, supposed to be, $250,000!

Now, I never improved my hitting too much. But I could field all right, I guess. I played the players differently according to the pitch and the speed. I could play way back at short, you know. Always had a good arm.

Walter Johnson came to the Senators in the fall of '07 and I came in the fall of '08. They were rough on some rookies, but I never had any trouble. But, see, I'd come up and been down and got my bumps and been around, so sure wasn't cocky-like. Cobb had a lot of trouble. He fought them back, though. If you come up cocky-like, why they'd get on you all right. But I know that when I come up to that Washington club, I was well-received and for the twelve or fourteen years Walter and I were there, why we'd always receive the rookies and try to help them out.

Yep, during Walter Johnson's greatest years I played shortstop behind him. I think he was the greatest pitcher I ever saw. And he was just as nice a man as he was a pitcher. Never heard him swear. When he got mad, maybe he'd say, "Gracious sakes alive!" That was when he was really high and really cussing! But it's true that he didn't like to hit anybody. He didn't like them to hang over the bag like Cobb did and Frank Robinson does. Saw him pitch those four games in three days, over at the old Highlanders, in 1908. Pitched three shutouts in three playing days. 'Course there was a Sunday in between, but still, that's something. Twelve hits in the three games. Just a kid, too.

His curveball was never too much, you know. There was a period of about two years where Gabby Street wouldn't ever call for that curve. He learned to throw a changeup, but he threw almost all fastballs. Amazing, too, for such a young fellow to come right to the big leagues with the control that he had. Had it from the beginning. I managed him one year, you know. He was a great big boy. If they were all like Walter Johnson, a manager wouldn't have any trouble at all.

In 1912, Jake Stahl was manager of the Red Sox, and Griff was our manager at Washington. Well, they tried to create a little excitement. Smokey Joe Wood was going for his sixteenth in a row and Johnson had already gotten sixteen in a row and his streak was ended. Stahl and Griff fixed it so they would pitch against each other up in Boston. Wood beat Johnson one to nothing. Very highly publicized. Crowd was right up to the baselines. Had mounted police to come in and keep them back as far as they could. Hits were few. I remember because I got a two-base hit which was considered something. Yep. They beat Johnson one to nothing. In those days, you know, to fill up a park like that was something. Yes, very highly publicized.

Eddie Ainsmith and Gabby Street and John Henry, who was a graduate of Amherst, were the catchers on that team when I came up. Germany Schaefer and Nick Altrock were there. Nick was still pitching. I played with him in the Association in 1902, that was when he was just starting. Went up to the Red Sox and then to the White Sox. A character. He was a great fielding pitcher.

Clyde Milan was on the team too. He and Cobb were great friends. Both come from the South. Milan had a nickname: Zeb. Cobb'd say, Zeb I'm going to beat that record [the single-year stolen base record of 88, which Milan had set in 1912]. And he did, too: he got 96 in 1915. Milan was a great player, one of the best center fielders I ever saw. I remember once we played an exhibition game. The outfield was Cobb, Speaker, and Milan, three center fielders.

Joe Judge came up later and was a very underrated ballplayer. He was a little man. Always hit .300, and he was fast, a good fielder.

We had Chick Gandil for several years. Tough. But I always found him a pretty good sort of chap. See, Felsch and Jackson were . . . were victims of circumstance. But Gandil . . . 'Course it broke Cicotte's heart. Very sad happening.

Yep, I played during the years when Cobb was in his prime, and I was a shortstop. But I never had any trouble with Cobb and those spikes of his. Got it in the glove and threw it down to the base. That's all. Went over to Detroit with him as a coach for a few years after I got through playing with Washington. Some say as he was a dirty ballplayer, but I say he was a good hard ballplayer. There are some players who didn't like him, but you know he was a ballplayer's ballplayer. He hustled out there. I think he was as fast as anybody, from home to home. I mean, all the way around. Good strong arm. Baserunner . . . oh, boy. He'd steal on those pitchers.

'Course I played with Honus Wagner, too. He was a great ballplayer. Awkward, but he had everything. Good legs, big hands. Cobb was a different type. Cobb was a harder ballplayer than Wagner. I think Cobb was the best I ever saw, really. 'Course Ruth was another type. He was a great pitcher. I hit against him, and he was a great pitcher. Great *ballplayer.* When he first come up, he was just a great big boy. They soon saw that if they could put him in there every day he'd be a wonder.

Hal Chase was one of the few first basemen that played the deep first base. He would play away and still be able to get back to the base. He'd catch that ball on the run and, oh, you saw a lot of one-hand playing. 'Course now, that's all they do, that one-handing. But Chase played first base with a little tiny glove. Bigger than what we wore, but tiny. Sisler was another great first baseman. Saw him play third base one day. Last day of the season, last two innings, he went over and played third base. Left-handed!

Joe Cantillon was my first manager. He was a real character. Was an umpire, you know. Managers left you alone much more than they do now. Now it's 2–0 and 3–1 and you're told what to do with the bat! Those days, they didn't do that at all. Sometimes now it's 3–1 and I see them busting away with a man in scoring position! 'Course in those days, you played for one or two runs more than you do now. We had the spitball and the emery ball. Stole more bases in those days. Relied on stolen bases. And we weren't told when to steal—had to make our own strategy, so to speak. 'Course there's things they do now that we couldn't do. I can't really say that we thought more or that we were better. I think you have more good ballplayers now. Got more ballplayers altogether.

Cobb, when he was a manager, he had a theory of his own for everything. Knew as much baseball as anyone, but it's an exception when a great ballplayer makes a great manager too. I didn't like managing too much. I sort of eased into it. See, I was captain of that team down there in Washington for twelve years! In 1920, I was Griff's coach and utility man. Played eight or ten games. Griff went scouting, you know, and I managed the team the last month or two in '20. Had to go in there and play a few times, too. [The next year, Griffith stepped aside and McBride managed the Senators to a fourth-place finish.]

In those days baseball wasn't considered as respectable as it is now, but it was the aim of all the youngsters to go to the big league. 'Course, salary didn't mean a thing. I got $150 a month as a rookie, not bad money for those days. Oh, you got the same money you'd get today, all right, just not as much of it! You know, even if you were a rough or tough character in those days, to play in the big leagues was an education for you. You'd meet nice people, travel all over. Always did stay at the best hotels and travel in the best way, too. It was an education.

I was pretty fortunate. My investments in the stock market have taken care of me pretty well. Never did any more baseball after 1929. I'll be eighty-one in November [1964].

I have no regrets in baseball. The fall of the year came, and you were glad to get home, but when spring rolled around, why you were glad to get out and start all over again.

When Immortals Returned to the Minors

LAWRENCE S. KATZ

♦ ♦ ♦

When the skills of stars like George Brett, Don Mattingly, and Wade Boggs have diminished, they will undoubtedly be eyeing positions in private industry, broadcasting, management, and even ownership. They would no more return to the minor leagues than to the womb.

There are several reasons. First, big leaguers of this stature are well aware of the marketability of their identities and skills, and the lucrative pastures that lie beyond in business and industry. Secondly, the minor leagues of today exist almost exclusively as training grounds for future major league prospects.

At one time, however, the minor league system comprised a world unto itself. Long before urbanization, expansion, and the electronic media focused mass attention on the big leagues, the minors formed the core of baseball activity in cities and towns throughout the nation.

As *Minor League Baseball Stars* (Volume l), pointed out:

[T]he major leagues have hardly been representative of America over most of the last century. Big league clubs were concentrated primarily in the Northeast and Middle West. . . . Major expansion to [the west and south] did not come until l957 in California and in l962 in Texas.

The Bill James Historical Baseball Abstract has noted:

While the major leagues were, as a whole, the best baseball going, there was not, as there is today, a one-to-one relationship between a ballplayer's abilities and major league status. A conservative assessment is that some of the players who made their living in the minor leagues were just as good as some of those who played for years in the majors.

In an earlier era it was without shame that so many greats of the game closed out their careers by taking that bumpy road down to the minors. Those familiar only with major league record books might be surprised at the list of Hall of Famers who closed out their careers this way.

Some made the trip back down for just one last "cup of coffee," despite its sometimes bitter taste. Each time this happened, fans in some of the country's remotest regions were treated to the sights of stars they had only read about.

Some were making fleeting final encores. Others were building second careers as minor league stars long after their niches in baseball history were secured.

The reasons for their return were varied. Undoubtedly, some played to earn a shot back to the bigs. Some became playing managers. Others simply returned to their home towns and continued playing the game they loved.

In any event, none of the Hall of Famers listed here ever played in the majors again.

Hall-of-Fame regulars who went down for a short bow include Earl Averill, Home Run Baker, Dave Bancroft, Jim Bottomley, Roger Bresnahan, Jimmy Collins, Kiki Cuyler, Bill Dickey, Hugh Duffy, Elmer Flick, Jimmie Foxx, Goose Goslin, Gabby Hartnett, Billy Herman, Harry Hooper, Rogers Hornsby, Willie Keeler, Joe Kelley, George Kelly, King Kelly, Ernie Lombardi, Al Lopez, Heinie Manush, Rabbit Maranville, Joe Medwick, Orator Jim O'Rourke, Ray Schalk, George Sisler, Enos Slaughter, Tris Speaker, Joe Tinker, Arky Vaughan, Paul Waner, Zack Wheat, and Hack Wilson. Pitchers include Grover Cleveland Alexander, Chief Bender, Pud Galvin, Lefty Gomez, Burleigh Grimes, Walter Johnson, Rube Marquard, Robin Roberts, Warren Spahn, Ed Walsh, and Mickey Welch.

A surprising number of players, with their bronze plaques in escrow, hit that dusty trail in a big way.

Slugging first baseman **Jake Beckley,** forty years old and 70 hits short of 3000, left the St. Louis Cardinals in the middle of the 1907 season, never to return. Beckley went on to establish a more-than-respectable career as a player-manager before retiring at the age of forty-four:

Year	Club	League	Pos	G	AB	R	H	2B	3B	HR	SB	BA
1907	Kansas City	A.A.	1B	100	378	65	138	10	4	1	12	.365
1908	Kansas City	A.A.	1B	136	496	66	134	19	5	1	13	.270
1909	Kansas City	A.A.	1B	113	428	41	120	16	3	1	12	.280
1910	Bartlesville	W.A.	1B	70	249	21	64	15	0	0	13	.257
1910	Topeka	West.	1B	63	233	19	60	11	0	1	1	.258
1911	Hannibal	C.A.	1B	98	355	50	100	7	4	0	22	.282

In 1906, **Jesse Burkett,** a .342 lifetime hitter with three seasons over .400 and 2872 major league hits, returned to Worcester, Massachusetts, where he had played in 1889. He promptly won the batting title and led the team to four consecutive New England pennants.

Year	Club	League	Pos	G	AB	R	H	2B	3B	HR	SB	BA
1906	Worcester	N. Eng.	OF	98	363	59	125	21	7	1	—	.344
1907	Worcester	N. Eng.	OF	52	195	23	66	8	1	1	9	.338
1908	Worcester	N. Eng.	OF	97	375	49	110	11	5	1	8	.293
1909	Worcester	N. Eng.	OF	75	218	30	71	10	1	1	6	.326
1910	Worcester	N. Eng.	OF	38	72	3	24	3	0	0	1	.333
1911	Worcester	N. Eng.	OF	76	243	42	83	8	1	1	1	.342
1912	Worcester	N. Eng.	OF	28	60	6	21	4	0	0	0	.350
1913	Worcester	N. Eng.	OF	19	42	4	10	3	0	0	0	.238
1916	Low.Law. Hart.	East.	OF	24	38	5	8	—	—	—	—	.211

Big **Dan Brouthers,** hitting .330 with Philadelphia in 1896, left in mid-season to join Springfield of the Eastern League at age thirty-eight and hit an even .400. The next year, he won the Eastern League batting championship.

Year	Club	League	Pos	G	AB	R	H	2B	3B	HR	SB	BA
1896	Springfield	East.	1B	51	205	42	82	—	—	—	9	.400
1897	Springfield	East.	1B	126	501	112	208	44	13	14	21	.415
1898	Spring. Toro.	East.	1B	50	189	42	63	10	2	4	2	.333
1899	Spring. Roch.	East.	1B	45	170	27	40	5	4	3	2	.235

Following a four-year retirement, Brouthers returned to the majors in 1904 at the behest of his friend, John McGraw. After going 0-for-5 with the New York Giants in 1904, he returned to the minors and closed out his career at the age of forty-seven:

Year	Club	League	Pos	G	AB	R	H	2B	3B	HR	SB	BA
1904	Pough-keepsie	Hud. R.	1B	—	424	—	158	—	—	—	—	.373
1905	Pough-keepsie	Hud. R.	1B	—	308	—	91	—	—	—	—	.295

Twenty-two games into the 1897 season, slugging first baseman **Roger Connor** left the St. Louis Browns and began a seven-year descent into the minors. Purchased by Waterbury of the Connecticut League the following year, he served as the club's manager-first baseman while his wife worked in the box office and his adopted daughter sold tickets. The next year, he led the league at the age of forty-two with a .392 average:

Year	Club	League	Pos	G	AB	R	H	2B	3B	HR	SB	BA
1897	Fall River	N. Eng.	1B	47	171	32	49	—	—	—	9	.287
1898	Waterbury	Conn.	1B	95	—	—	—	—	—	—	—	.319
1899	Waterbury	Conn.	1B	92	347	79	136	28	2	5	18	.392
1900	Waterbury	Conn.	1B	83	286	54	82	9	3	2	20	.287
1901	Water. N.Hav.	Conn.	1B	107	411	58	123	—	—	—	—	.299
1902	Springfield	Conn.	1B	62	224	25	58	7	1	1	15	.259
1903	Springfield	Conn.	1B	75	279	28	76	12	3	0	12	.272

Thirty-six hits short of 3000, **Sam Crawford** departed the major leagues in 1917 for his adopted state of California. At thirty-eight, he joined the Pacific Coast League Los Angeles Angels and played four seasons, including 535 games in his last three years:

Year	Club	League	Pos	G	AB	R	H	2B	3B	HR	SB	BA
1918	L.A.	P.C.	1B/OF	96	356	38	104	14	7	1	8	.292
1919	L.A.	P.C.	OF	173	664	103	239	41	18	14	14	.360
1920	L.A.	P.C.	OF	187	719	99	239	46	21	12	3	.332
1921	L.A.	P.C.	OF	175	626	92	199	40	10	9	10	.318

Batting star and base-stealer extraordinaire **Billy Hamilton** left the majors in 1902 at age thirty-five with a .344 lifetime mark and 937 steals. Among the three minor league batting titles won by this player-manager during the next decade was a .412 mark in 1904, leading all of organized baseball:

Year	Club	League	Pos	G	AB	R	H	2B	3B	HR	SB	BA
1902	Haver-hill	N. Eng.	OF	66	243	67	82	23	2	2	26	.337
1903	Haver-hill	N. Eng.	OF	37	132	37	60	15	2	4	27	.446
1904	Haver-hill	N. Eng.	OF	113	408	113	168	32	8	0	74	.412
1905	Harris-burg	Tri.St.	OF				(No record available)					
1906	Haver-hill	N. Eng.	OF	14	51	1	10	1	0	0	—	.196
1906	Harris-burg	Tri. St.	OF	43	155	33	43	5	1	0	16	.278
1907	Haver-hill	N. Eng.	OF	91	324	50	108	16	4	0	29	.333
1908	Haver-hill	N. Eng.	OF	85	300	63	87	19	0	1	39	.290
1909	Lynn	N. Eng.	OF	109	376	61	125	17	2	0	23	.332
1910	Lynn	N. Eng.	OF	41	112	14	28	1	2	0	5	.250

The first of **Nap Lajoie's** two post-major-league seasons opened with a glorious tour around the eight-city International League circuit in which the Toronto player-manager was showered with gifts and ovations. The season closed with a batting title and a pennant.

Year	Club	League	Pos	G	AB	R	H	2B	3B	HR	SB	BA
1917	Toronto	Int.	1B	151	581	83	221	39	4	5	4	.380
1918	Indianapolis	A.A.	1B	78	291	39	82	12	2	2	10	.352

Several Hall-of-Fame pitchers made the transition and became productive minor leaguers.

At the age of forty, **Mordecai (Three Finger) Brown** returned to the minors for four years. After the first two, Brown returned to the Terre Haute club he broke in with eighteen years earlier. He spent the rest of his playing career as a pitcher-manager:

Year	Club	League	G	IP	W	L	Pct	H	SO	BB	ERA
1917	Columbus	A.A.	30	185	10	12	.455	167	61	51	2.77
1918	Columbus	A.A.	12	50	3	2	.600	49	13	9	2.70
1919	Terre Haute	I.I.I.	33	175	16	6	.727	161	72	20	2.88
1919	Indianapolis	A.A.	6	34	0	3	.000	39	9	11	—
1920	Terre Haute	I.I.I.	13	80	4	6	.400	74	42	13	2.59

Billy Hamilton's counterpart on the mound was undoubtedly **Joe (Iron Man) McGinnity,** who "retired" at the age of thirty-seven to a minor league career as a player-manager that lasted until he was fifty-four:

Iron Joe McGinnity

Year	Club	League	G	IP	W	L	Pct	H	SO	BB	ERA
1909	Newark	East.	55	422	29	16	.644	297	195	78	—
1910	Newark	East.	61	408	30	19	.612	325	132	71	—
1911	Newark	East.	43	278	12	19	.387	269	77	53	—
1912	Newark	Inter.	37	261	16	10	.615	293	62	43	—
1913	Tacoma	N.W.	68	436	22	19	.537	418	154	66	—
1914	Tacoma	N.W.	49	326	20	21	.488	295	105	73	—
1914	Venice	P.C.	8	37	1	4	.200	42	7	5	—
1915	Tacoma	N.W.	45	355	21	15	.583	291	58	39	—
1916	Butte	N.W.	43	291	20	13	.606	340	95	63	—
1917	Butte-Gr.Fls.	N.W.	16	119	7	6	.538	119	28	25	—
1918	Vancouver	P.C.-I.	9	—	2	6	.250	47	31	14	—
1922	Danville	I.I.I.	16	79	1	6	.143	117	12	12	—
1922	Dubuque	Miss. V.	19	91	5	8	.385	94	19	19	—
1923	Dubuque	Miss. V.	42	206	15	12	.556	268	41	44	—
1925	Dubuque	Miss. V.	15	85	6	6	.500	119	22	18	—

Rube Waddell's great career ended with a four-year stint in the minors:

Year	Club	League	G	IP	W	L	Pct	H	SO	BB	ERA
1910	Newark	East.	15	97	5	3	.625	73	53	41	—
1911	Minneapolis	A.A.	54	300	20	17	.541	262	185	96	—
1912	Minneapolis	A.A.	33	151	12	6	.667	138	113	59	—
1913	Virginia	North.	15	84	3	9	.250	86	82	20	—

Waddell only lived another year, dying of tuberculosis in 1914 at the age of thirty-seven.

The minor leagues have been an integral part of organized baseball since 1877, when, one year after the formation of the National League, the International Association was established. Seven years later, the oldest minor league still in existence, the International League, was created. It was then known as the Eastern League.

The minors experienced their most dramatic growth in the first half of the twentieth century. From 1903 to 1913, the number of minor league clubs grew from 13 to 40. Three decades later, there were over 50 minor leagues in existence.

But social forces were already at work by this time, and the scope and stature of minor league baseball began a steady decline. By 1947, a "bonus baby" named Joe Tepsic quit baseball altogether rather than report to the farm club after spending all of one year with the Brooklyn Dodgers!

Stealing First and Fielding with Your Head

PETE WILLIAMS

♦ ♦ ♦

Classic psychologists like Jung and Ranke, as well as more recent social scientists like Joseph Campbell, have emphasized the importance of archetypes in human culture and in the human mind. If humans think in terms of archetypes, as these and other thinkers contend, we are likely to demand, era by era, individual manifestations of universal types. To borrow terms from sociology, the archetypes are general "slots" into which we feel a continuing need to place individual "fillers." We "fill" archetypal "slots" with real individuals, whether or not the process is completely fair to the individual—was Gerald Ford really an inept klutz? was Helen of Troy really much more than a chubby little Greek girl?—and we do it in sport as surely as in any other area of public life.

There is no orthodox number of categories, or archetypal "slots," in sport, but the three most usually discussed are hero, villain, and fool, to which might be added trickster. Thus, baseball's wily managers (Stengel, Weaver, Martin, Herzog) are tricksters; Yogi Berra, though the judgment is very unfair, is a fool; Ruth is a hero, some of his unsavory behavior unreported in the press, and Joe Jackson, who led all batters and made no errors in the 1919 World Series, is a villain, no matter what Gropman or Kinsella try to do about it.

There are secondary categories, too: Heroes can be Apollonian (noble souls, like Walter Johnson), Dionysian (revelers of large appetite, like Ruth) or Adonic (martyrs, like Lou Gehrig). Fools can be either jesters or dolts, the distinction here being one of intent (the term "fool" itself can denote either stupidity or the wisdom of the Fool in *Lear*). It's probably best to use a separate term for the fool who knows what he's up to and to call him a clown. Germany Schaefer's image is that of a clown, while we look at Babe Herman as a fool, despite the fact that both players deserve to be taken a good deal more seriously.

Take Herman. Do you know that until he got sidetracked by baseball, he was set on going to college, and that his choice was Berkeley? That he was, like his neighbor and friend Casey Stengel, a very good business-man? That one of his sons ran a large opera company, and that Herman himself was an accomplished botanist who developed new varieties of or-chids? In fact, Herman's intelligence was recognized, if not emphasized, throughout his career. A biographical sketch dated March 9, 1933, con-cludes with this:

Handles money carefully and he is shrewd salesman of own talents. In this depression year, he will be one high-salaried player who will draw higher wage than ever before. And yet there are fellows around who call him dumb.

Much later, in a column called "So Babe Herman's Smart," Harry Rob-ert says Herman "must have been the greatest genius at camouflaging in-tellect who ever lived." The problem with Robert's witticism, of course, is that he's got it backwards. It was the writers who camouflaged Herman's intellect. There was an opening for an archetypal fool, a slot to be filled, and Babe Herman, once he was given that position, was never allowed to quit it.

Why was he chosen in the first place? Probably for three reasons: He was certainly guilty of being absent-minded, and his mental lapses were not infrequent; he was, when he was starting out, a lousy fielder, al-though he improved quickly (and he was always a fine runner), and he had a gift for making dumb remarks.

Of the remarks Herman made, some are undoubtedly apocryphal, in-ventions of the writers embellishing the legendary figure they'd created; others are probably genuine. In this, we can't fail to see the resemblance between Herman and that contemporary "fool," Yogi Berra. Here, for ex-ample, is a Hermanism which was probably devised by some writer des-perate for good copy:

A Herman yarn that gained wide circulation involved Babe bragging to his teammates about the "smartness" of his five-year-old son Bobby. To prove his point to the fellows on the bench, Babe subjected Bobby to a quiz program.

"How much is six times two?" asked Babe.

"Ten," answered Bobby.

"See that," exclaimed Babe triumphantly, "He only missed it by one."

Some others, however, sound as though they could be genuine:

The fey quality of the Babe's utterances contributed not a little to his "image." There was the scorching day he stepped out of the elevator in a St. Louis hotel clad in a crisp ice cream suit.

"My, but you look cool, Mr. Herman," the young lady at the cigar counter observed admiringly.

Herman tried a bit of gallant repartee.

"You," he replied with a courtly nod, "don't look so hot yourself."

There are so many Babe Herman stories. Like the time a book salesman tried to sell him an encyclopedia. "It will help your children get to college," pleaded the salesman. Said Babe: "Nothing doing. They can walk to school."

A few days before the season ended, a reporter asked Herman what he was going to do in the off-season. "A rich friend of mine invited me to go on a trip around the world with him, but I told him I'd rather go somewhere else," replied Herman.

Herman was a bad fielder early in his career, but always denied ever being hit on the head by a fly ball, although the writers never let that accusation drop. Maury Allen's obit gives Herman's side:

His image was fixed on a sunny afternoon in Brooklyn when a fly ball struck him and cost the Dodgers a game.

"The ball actually hit me in the shoulder," he said, "but the writer reported it hit me in the head. It made a better story, so I let it go."

In that obit, by the way, Allen adds that "despite his image, Herman was a bright and articulate man.

Herman's fielding improved rapidly, however, and by 1930 he was better than average. "Lank" Leonard wrote a column with the heading, "'Babe' Herman Rapidly Rounding Out Into Dependable Outfielder," in which he said this:

Last year [1929] he made more errors than any other outfielder in the National League. The year before he made more than any outfielder in either major league. That gives you an idea of how much he has improved. . . . They once called him "Boob" Herman, but not today.

In 1931, writing in *Baseball Magazine*, F.C. Lane said that "Herman's antics in the outfield were once the butt of ridicule. They are so no longer"—and Herman himself was fond of pointing out that his lifetime fielding average was ten points higher than Cobb's. John Drebinger even went so far as to say that Herman made one of the three greatest catches he ever saw. But the archetype always takes precedence in these things; the image always supersedes the man, as it does in this interview with Jim Murray in 1973:

> "Now, the fielding was another thing they got all mixed up. Here I was playing first base all those years and, one day, Bizzy Bissonette gets sick and can't play right field. So l say, 'Hell, I'll play it.' You see, it was this awful sun field out there, the toughest sun field in the league, and, the sunset, which came through the opening of the roof there, made it worse. So, we didn't have flip glasses in those days and, when it got dark enough, the sky was murder, and when the ball was hit up, there was this black spot you had to pick out of the sun. What? Oh, the black spot was the ball and you can see sometimes how you could camp under the wrong spot."
>
> Like, the Babe sometimes found himself waiting for a mosquito to come down and while waiting he would feel this Thunk! on the back of his head.

Herman was, however, frequently guilty of mental mistakes. He was prone to bouts of absent-mindedness or daydreaming. Dazzy Vance was referring to this when he cracked that Herman was "a great hitter because he never thinks up there, and how can a pitcher outsmart a guy who doesn't think?"

Once, at the Polo Grounds, the Dodgers were leading the Giants by a run in the bottom of the ninth with two on and one out. Hank Leiber hit a long fly to Herman. Herman caught it, but he thought there were two out, so he turned immediately, stuffed the ball in his hip pocket and started trotting to the clubhouse in center field. Meanwhile two runs scored and the Giants, not the Dodgers, won the game.

And then there was the first game of the doubleheader on August 15, 1926, a day that will live in Kings County infamy. The newspaper account is straightforward:

While both exhibitions were listless at first the 15,000 fans got a kick out of a boob play pulled by the Robins in the seventh inning of the opening encounter. With three on base, Babe Herman delivered a double that scored but one run and eventually developed into a double play, the like of which has seldom if ever been seen in the major leagues.

Butler opened with a single to left and scored on DeBerry's double to the left field corner of the park. Vance beat out a bunt, putting his battery mate on third and "Chick" Fewster was struck by a pitched ball, filling the bases.

Johnny Wertz was yanked and George Mogridge, veteran portsider, relieved him. After Jacobson sent up a puny fly to Mogridge, Herman lashed his double against the right field wall scoring DeBerry. Vance, who was on second, thought that Jimmy Welsh was going to catch the ball and tarried close to the bag before he started to run.

He attempted to score, and seeing the throw to the plate had him trapped started back for third. Fewster and Herman kept tearing around the bases before they realized what had happened and Chick and Babe both pulled in to third as Vance managed to get back safely in the run down. The ball was put on both Fewster and Herman, thereby completing an exceedingly unusual twin killing.

Please note that the chief culprit is Vance. In fact, if you accept Herman's own version from *The Glory of Their Times,* Herman made the right decision when he lit out for third:

Everybody blames me for three men winding up on third base, but it wasn't my fault. Actually, it was Dazzy Vance who caused the whole mess. . . . I hit a line drive to right field and slid safely into second with a double. But while I'm on the ground I looked up and saw a run-down between third and home. Naturally, I figure Chick Fewster is caught in a run-down, so I get up and sprint for third, like I'm supposed to. That way we'll have a man on third even if Chick is tagged out.

But when I got to third, Fewster was already there, which surprised me. And then here comes Vance into third from the other side. That really surprised me.

Anyway, there we were all on third at one and the same time. Vance was declared safe and Fewster and I were both out. If there was any justice, Vance would have been the one declared out because he's the one caused the traffic jam in the first place. But down through history, for some reason, it's all been blamed on me.

Poor Herman. The "strange reason" was that he, not Vance, was the archetypal fool. He drove in the winning run on that play, just as he drove in the winning runs in the first game he played when he came back to the Dodgers in 1945 at age forty-two. Then he tripped on first and fell down, and the headlines, ignoring the fact that he'd won the game for the Dodgers, said, "SAME OLD HERMAN, TRIPS OVER FIRST BASE."

Herman Schaefer's stunts were all intentional. Herman was a man of many nicknames, starting out his career as "Middles," and then "Noodles," before being given the one that stuck, "Germany"—although, after the start of World War I, he dropped "Germany," first for "Prince" (possibly because he was, along with his cohort Nick Altrock, one of the first players to be called a "clown prince"), then for "Liberty." Like Herman, he is remembered chiefly as an eccentric, not as a quality player, and like Herman, he was a lot smarter than people thought.

Some of Schaefer's jokes were just that, the pranks of a compulsive laugh-seeker, like the time he caught an ump asleep at a table in the back room of a Chicago bar. The Detroit writer Malcolm W. Bingay was Schaefer's main chronicler, and he tells the story in the voice of his Lardneresque character, Iffy, the Dopester. The back room in question, a summer kitchen, had been added to the building, and a drainpipe that used to be outside remained on what now was an interior wall:

> Now into the place one night came old Jack Sheridan, famed in song and story as an umpire. In the winter months when the season was over, Jack worked in Chicago as an under-taker. He called 'em in the summer and he buried 'em in the winter. And he did something else. As soon as the baseball schedule had run its course, Jack would settle right down to catch up on his fall drinking.
>
> Well, this night Schaef found Jack back in that summer kitchen sound asleep, sitting on a hard-bottomed kitchen chair. His ear was nestled against the rough and rusty edge of the old drainpipe, just as comfy as though it were a silken cushion. That was enough for Schaef. He climbed up through the hole in the ceiling to the old roof and found the other end of the drainpipe.
>
> Pouring into his ear Jack heard a terrible voice. "Jack Sheridan," it roared, "your time has came!"
>
> Jack Sheridan got right up out of that chair and made the distance to the bar in nothing flat. He downed a couple and stood there waiting to determine, in his own mind, whether it was just something he had et.
>
> After a while he went back to the summer-kitchen seat—and fell

sound asleep once more, with his ear again resting on the drainpipe. For the second time Schaefer climbed the ladder and for the second time there came into Jack's ear the voice from the tomb: "Jack Sheridan, your time has came!"

Jack went right out onto Clark Street in such a hurry he went through Joe Cantillon's Japanese screen, which Joe prized very much as a work of art.

Ruth may never have done it, but Germany Schaefer called his shot at least once, and maybe twice. The less reliable of the two stories involves the tight 1907 pennant race in which Schaefer's Tigers finally finished first, but only 1½ games ahead of the A's. In a key game, Rube Waddell twice struck out Schaefer, who was never much of a hitter. The next time Schaefer came up, Rube got two quick strikes on him. Ossee Schreckengost was catching, and he started needling Schaefer:

"What's the matter, Herman? Didn't you see the last one go by?" asked Schreck.

"Well, have him pitch another like it and I'll ride it right out of the park," said Schaefer.

"I think we can oblige," said Schreck. Calling to Rube, he said, "Another one just like the last one, Rube."

Waddell r'ared back and let go one of his fastest pitches. . . . Schaefer, who occasionally connected for the long ball, swung with might and main. He met the ball perfectly and drove it over the left field fence for one of the longest homers ever seen at Philadelphia's Columbia Park. Herman carried his bat with him as he ambled around the bases. About every five paces he stopped and lifted the bat to his right shoulder as though it were a gun and "shot" the discomfited Rube.

On an earlier occasion, in 1906, Schaefer faced White of the White Sox, and this "shot" is pretty well documented, since everybody in the park heard Schaefer bellow his "call." Schaefer was out of the lineup because, according to Bingay, he "had a sore thumb from using it to take off the cap of a bottle of beer," but he could still pinch hit. Davy Jones tells the story in *The Glory of Their Times:*

Well, Schaefer walked out there and just as he was about to step into the batter's box he stopped, took off his cap, and faced the grandstand.

"Ladies and gentlemen," he announced, "you are now looking at Herman Schaefer, better known as Herman the Great, acknowledged by one and all to be the greatest pinch hitter in the world. I am now going to hit the ball into the left field bleachers. Thank you."

It goes without saying that Schaefer, swinging on White's second pitch, did exactly that. Jones goes on:

Boy oh boy, you should have seen him. He stood at that plate until the ball cleared the fence, and then he jumped straight up in the air, tore down to first base as fast as his legs would carry him, and proceeded to slide headfirst into the bag. After that he jumped up, yelled "Schaefer leads at the quarter!" and started for second. He slid into second—yelled "Schaefer leads at the half!" and continued the same way into third and then home. After he slid into home he stood up and announced: "Schaefer wins by a nose." Then he brushed himself off, took off his cap, and walked over to the grandstand again.
"Ladies and gentlemen," he said, "I thank you for your kind attention."
Back on the bench everybody was laughing so hard they were falling all over themselves.

McGraw, who was of substantial help to Schaefer when Germany was stricken with TB, was very fond of the prince, and when he took the Giants on a world barnstorming tour in 1913 he arranged to put Schaefer on the opposing White Sox squad (Germany played in an infield that included Buck Weaver and Hal Chase). Before they sailed for Japan in November, their train went from Ohio to California, stopping along the way in small towns where, according to McGraw's syndicated (and obviously ghosted) column, the local kids all clamored for a glimpse of Matty. Matty, a shy man, refused to come out, so a stand-in was found:

"Germany" Schaefer . . . was little Johnny-right-out-on-the platform, and, of course, the crowd, not knowing Matty, except from his pictures, thinking Schaefer was Big Six, would set up a howl.
"Oh, you, Matty! Yea, Matty! How are you, Big Six?"
Then the inimitable Schaefer would spread his hands for silence.
"Ladies and gentlemen," he would begin, "I see here before me the flower of the society in this town, and I don't see how such grand specimens could be raised in this cold climate except in a conservatory. (Cheers.) I want to compliment you on your wonderful health and beauty giving climate, on your pretty girls, your beautiful

women and your well-paved streets."

As a rule, the streets would be ankle-deep in mud. But "Germany" always got the big hand and left a trail of oratory clear across the continent to Matty's credit. I'll bet William

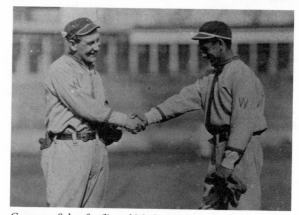

Germany Schaefer (l) and Merio Acosta

J. Bryan has nothing on Big Six's reputation as a speaker in the towns both Mr. Bryan and Schaefer have played.

On the trip back from Japan, the athletes were getting rusty, so Schaefer and some others devised some shipboard exercise:

> Several of the players Thorpe, Magee, Slight, Weaver, Lobert . . . Schaefer . . .—have invented some new indoor training stunts. . . . Perhaps the most novel of the strange stunts, certainly the most amusing, is the "horse" racing in the dining salon. The game is played with any number of "horses" and riders. The favorite "horses" are Thorpe [and] Schaefer. . . . The "horses" have to go on their hands and knees and the riders are not allowed to touch their feet on the floor. The races take place along the various aisles in the dining salon, which are about sixty feet in length. . . . Jim Thorpe has won a good share of the contests because of his great strength and his ability to excel in all athletic exercises.

And there was the time Schaefer unsuccessfully tried to get Billy Evans to call a game the Tigers were losing:

> With Detroit playing the Indians, Schaefer tried to induce the ump to call the game on account of rain. It was the first half of the fifth. At the time, Cleveland was winning 5–1. If the game were called before 4½ innings had been played, the game would have been declared no contest. But the umpires insisted that the game go on. When Detroit took the field in the fifth, Schaefer with great dignity strode to his

place at second base wearing a long raincoat. He played through the inning dressed just like that. At the end of the fifth inning, the game was officially washed out with the Indians in the lead 6–1.

I wonder if Stengel was thinking of Schaefer when he came out of the dugout carrying a flashlight in an effort to get a game called on account of darkness some years later. At any rate, Schaefer's humor here certainly served a legitimate strategic purpose, as it did when he committed his most renowned stunt, stealing second, then first, then second again. Davy Jones was watching this remarkable performance from third. Here's how he tells it.

> It was during those years . . . that I saw Germany Schaefer steal first base. Yes, first base . . . I saw him do it. . . .
> We were playing Cleveland and the score was tied in a late inning. I was on third base, Schaefer on first, and Crawford was at bat. Before the pitcher wound up, Schaefer flashed me the sign for the double steal. . . . Well, the pitcher wound up and pitched, and sure enough Schaefer stole second. But I had to stay right where I was, on third, because . . . the Cleveland catcher . . . refused to throw to second, knowing I'd probably make it home if he did.
> So now we had men on second and third. Well, on the next pitch Schaefer yelled, "Let's try it again!" And with a bloodcurdling shout he took off like a wild Indian back to first base, and dove in headfirst in a cloud of dust. He figured the catcher might throw to first since he evidently wouldn't throw to second and then I could come home same as before.
> But nothing happened. Nothing at all. . . . Everybody just stood there and watched Schaefer, with their mouths open, not knowing what the devil was going on. Me, too. Even if the catcher had thrown to first, I was too stunned to move, I'll tell you that. . . .
> So there we were, back where we started, with Schaefer on first and me on third. And on the next pitch darned if he didn't let out another war whoop and take off again for second base. By this time the Cleveland catcher evidently had enough, because he finally threw to second to get Schaefer, and when he did I took off for home and both of us were safe.

It's obvious that when he stole first Schaefer was after runs, not laughs, and it's also obvious that his strategy worked. It should be added that the umpires checked the rule book before allowing the play to stand, and that nothing was found forbidding running the bases backwards.

Schaefer undoubtedly knew this. The rules were changed shortly afterward, as a direct result of this play.

Schaefer was an aggressive ballplayer (he and Cal Griffith were once suspended for protesting a bad call) who knew the game. He was a good coach who once even wrote an article on coaching. Had he not died young, this player/coach who had John McGraw's respect might well have ended up managing a major league club. Still, his obit in *The New York Times* on May 17, 1919, has this sub-head: "Baseball Comedian Passes Away." Once you've been assigned an archetypal "slot," it's very difficult to get the public to view you in any other way.

Babe Herman knew this, and he knew where the blame should be placed. The writers are fans like any others, and they need to view players as archetypes, too; the writers also need good copy, which gives them an additional motive to exaggerate the characteristics of individual players. One of the Herman obits points out that the Tales of Herman "were embellished and embroidered by imaginative New York newspapermen until the boundary between fact and fiction became fuzzy," and Arthur Daley himself admitted that Herman "has been victimized by some base canards." When asked why the Dodgers were called "daffy" if they were really less loony than, say, Frisch's Cardinals, Herman said, succinctly, "Well, mostly it was the writers. They gave us the image." When Herman talked to the writer who'd written that the fly ball had bounced off his head when the writer knew it had only hit him on the shoulder, Herman asked him why he'd written that. The writer was succinct, too. "It made a better story," he said.

Herman recognized that his image would probably keep him out of the Hall, even though contemporary writers have often supported his candidacy, making statements like, "he was a lot more ballplayer than clown," and "evidence doesn't support the myth that he was a dumb baseball player." A couple of years before he died, Herman gave an interview that concluded with these comments. They illustrate how neither Babe Herman nor Germany Schaefer, world without end, can ever be taken seriously:

"In 1944 I was talking to Casey [Stengel]," recalls Herman, "and he told me that some writers were going to put me into the Hall the next year. . . . [But] all the people who had truly seen me and knew the legends were just legends, were gone-dead or retired. . . . There were a bunch of guys who had never seen me at my peak. So all they can go on is records, which don't tell I never got hit on the head with a fly ball, and the legends are stronger than the records."

"FORCED TO DRINK WHISKY
AT THE POINT OF A GUN"

The Kidnapping of Flint Rhem

J O H N   T H O M

♦ ♦ ♦

Through the years, pennant races have provided baseball with many exciting games, memorable performances, and unexpected goats and heroes.

Close races have given the game some of its oddest moments as well. For one, there is the tale of the old-time pitcher who was kidnapped on the eve of a crucial series in order to give the home team an advantage against the visitors. It is a story that has survived for sixty years and it deserves an encore here.

Unfortunately, the only admitted witness to the episode was the pitcher himself, so, like his team's manager, we will have to accept his account of the crime at face value. We can, however, draw our own conclusions.

First, to appreciate the story fully, let's look at the important events surrounding his team. That team was the 1930 St. Louis Cardinals, a good club which played inconsistent ball during the early months of the pennant race. The Cards, the defending champion Chicago Cubs, John McGraw's New York Giants, and the upstart Brooklyn Robins, nee Dodgers, had taken turns leading the National League into the unusually hot days of this particular summer.

Then the Cards seemed to draw energy from the hot weather and in August started to play at a sizzling winning pace that put them into contention early in September. Under the guidance of rookie manager Charles "Gabby" Street, a top-to-bottom lineup of .300 hitters, and a gritty pitching staff that included hard-throwing Wild Bill Hallahan, the stormy Burleigh Grimes, veteran Jesse "Pop" Haines, and former 20-game-winner Flint Rhem, the team could hardly lose.

On September 12, after taking three games out of four from the Giants at the Polo Grounds, St. Louis pulled to within a half game of first place. The following day the Cards beat the Boston Braves, 8–2, behind Pop Haines and moved into first, tied with Brooklyn. The Cubs were a half game back. St Louis had reeled off 33 victories in its last 43 games, a winning percentage of .767. On Sunday the 14th, the Cards split a doubleheader in Boston and slipped to a half game behind the Robins, who were also hot, winners of 10 straight games.

After the twin bill, the Cardinals boarded a train for New York to play a three-game series with the Robins, a surprise contender in the pennant race. Like the Cardinals, no one had given Brooklyn much hope for the flag this year, but a heavy-hitting attack led by Babe Herman and the gutsy pitching of veterans Dazzy Vance and Dolf Luque put Brooklyn in the thick of the race.

There were just two weeks left on the schedule in September 1930 as the Cards headed for Brooklyn and the much-heralded series. The two teams were at a crossroads. The pennant might be decided during the mid-week series if one team or the other could win all three games. It was the talk of the town. But it was not the only topic of conversation.

In September 1930 the country was both celebrating ten years of prohibition and debating—very heatedly—whether the "Noble Experiment" had overstayed its welcome. On the street, in the home, in the pulpit, in the halls of Congress, in newspapers and magazines, even, yes, in thousands of speakeasies, it was "wets" vs. "drys." Stated simply, all alcoholic beverages were illegal under the force of the Eighteenth Amendment and many people in the country were arguing for repeal.

Even some ballplayers could be counted as "wets." One of those was twenty-nine-year-old Charles Flint Rhem, tall right-hander of St. Louis who had just defeated the Giants in the recent series finale. Rhem had been known to seek the comfort of prohibition gin . . . and rum . . . and whisky . . . and, well, you get the idea. But he also exhibited a high sense of duty as it related to the national experiment of a drink-free society and its effect on his colleagues. Once, when he was teamed with another well-known "wet," the famous Grover Cleveland Alexander, Rhem was stopped one night returning late to his hotel by his coach, the same Gabby Street, now managing the Cards. who inquired into his apparently drunken condition.

"Sarge," he countered, "you can't blame me this time. I was with Alexander and I was only trying to drink his share to keep him sober." That was pure Flint Rhem. And now the legend was about to turn another page.

The St. Louis-Brooklyn series was set to begin Tuesday, September 16, at Ebbets Field, giving the Cards an off-day on Monday, their first on this four-city eastern swing. The Robins worked on Monday, walloping the Cincinnati Reds, 15–5, for their 11th victory in a row. The win gave Brooklyn a full game lead on St. Louis.

Monday also brought potential disaster for Bill Hallahan. The powerful left-hander had a taxi door close on his hand—his right hand—blistering his fingers. For a time, it looked as though he might have to miss his turn against the Robins.

The Borough of Brooklyn, the whole city of New York, the entire baseball world was poised to watch the unfolding panorama of this series, easily the most important of the year. There were also, according to the police report filed on behalf of the central character of this story, two other very interested individuals watching the comings and goings of the players, one player in particular.

The Tuesday afternoon game approached amid extraordinary excitement and partisanship by Robins fans. Ebbets Field's capacity of 25,500 was taxed to its limits, and an unruly crowd outside made conditions unsafe. The more disreputable patrons inside resorted to a fusillade of verbal abuse and bottle-throwing against the Cardinals.

Someone, however, was missing. Cardinal pitcher Flint Rhem, who was penciled in as the starter because of Hallahan's hand injury, did not appear for game one of the series. His absence, of course, was not without precedent. Called the Baron Munchausen of the Barleycorn League by one observer of the day, Rhem had taken other unscheduled days off in years past. Nevertheless, Rhem's disappearance on the eve of such a crucial set of games raised an alarm in the Cardinals' camp. The police were notified and a search began. In the meantime, the Cards defeated the Robins, 1–0, in ten innings.

Good ol' Flint missed one of the greatest games in pennant-race history. A patched-up Hallahan retired the first twenty Robins he faced, then lost his perfect game when he fumbled a tapper back to the mound by Babe Herman. The Robins made their first hit in the eighth inning when Johnny Frederick singled. But he was out at second on a throw from catcher Gus Mancuso when Mickey Finn missed a hit-and-run sign. Finn followed with a single but was out trying to stretch it into a double, colliding hard with Card shortstop Charley Gelbert.

Brooklyn got two more hits in the ninth and again failed to score. Al Lopez singled to open the inning and was safe at second when Card third baseman Sparky Adams tried to force him on Vance's sacrifice. Eddie Moore also bunted but his attempt popped easily to Mancuso. Lopez lost attention momentarily and wandered too far away from second, giving Mancuso just enough time to throw quickly and double him off. Wally Gilbert singled, but the rally ended when Herman flied to left.

Hallahan was pitching out of trouble, and Gabby Street was patiently waiting for his Cards to break through against Dazzy Vance. St. Louis had two good scoring opportunities cut short. In the fourth, with two on and two out, Taylor Douthit drove the ball up the alley in right center, but Herman, not noted for his fielding, raced over from right field and made a spectacular catch on the dead run.

Two innings later the Cards came within a few inches of taking the lead. Adams was on third base with two outs in the sixth. With two strikes on Chick Hafey, Adams broke for home. Vance, seeing Adams coming down the line, threw at the surprised Hafey, who did not move far enough away and was hit by the pitch before Adams could cross the plate. Adams had to return to third base on the dead ball and was stranded there when George Watkins fouled out.

The Cardinals struck quickly in the top of the tenth inning. Andy High, who was delivering key hits for St. Louis down the stretch, doubled for Gelbert, who was sidelined with a black eye following his collision with Mickey Finn. High moved to third on a sacrifice by Hallahan and scored on a single by Douthit.

Brooklyn nearly pulled the game out in the bottom of the tenth. Hallahan went to the mound to face Glenn Wright, who opened with a screaming double to the center-field bleacher fence. The crowd was roaring. Hallahan walked Del Bissonette, then Frederick advanced the runners to second and third on a sacrifice.

Reserve Jake Flowers, batting for Finn, was walked to load the bases, bringing up Lopez with only one out. Lopez hit a hard smash to Adams, who had moved over to short from third base when Gelbert had to leave the game. Handcuffed by the hard-hit ball, Adams knocked it down with his bare hand, recovered quickly, and threw the ball to Frankie Frisch at second, who made a perfect pivot and got the ball to Bottomley at first just before Lopez planted his foot on the bag. A game-ending double play. The crowd was stunned.

Brooklyn was beaten. Two more close losses for the Robins on Wednesday and Thursday dashed their hopes for the flag. Ultimately, their losing streak reached seven games and dropped them to fourth place.

But what about Flint Rhem? Where was he? He was scheduled to pitch the Wednesday game, wasn't he? The Cards were back in their hotel in New York after their exciting victory on Tuesday when Flint finally showed up looking somewhat the worse for wear.

Flint Rhem's well-earned reputation always preceded him, and Gabby Street could have anticipated just about any explanation. What he heard from poor Flint, however, strained even Gabby's credulity. There are several versions extant of the conversation between Street and Rhem and all of them are colorful. One goes something like the following.

"I was standing outside the hotel yesterday, Skip, waiting on a taxi-cab," Rhem began in his quaintest South Carolina drawl, "when this car came by and two fellas called to me. I went over there and before I knew it they pulled guns on me and pushed me into their car. They drove me to a house over in New Jersey and held guns on me and forced me to drink whisky all day. They must not have wanted me to pitch against the Robins."

Ring Lardner wrote that Rhem kept saying over and over to Street, "It was terrible, Sarge, it was just awful."

Another report of the return of the prodigal had it that Rhem told Street, "But that wasn't the worst of it. They forced me to drink glass after glass of liquor—rye, or maybe Scotch, I wouldn't know. It might have been gin."

Dan Daniel in the New York *Telegram* quoted our ill-starred hero as confessing that, "I am ashamed to say that I got drunk. Imagine me getting drunk!" Street was beside himself. Rhem went on, Daniel wrote, saying, "I pleaded with the bandits not to make me drink hard liquor, which you know I abhor, but they would not listen to me. I was in their power. I drank and drank—always at the point of a gun, always threatened. It was horrible."

The story got around that gambling interests spirited Rhem away in order to give Brooklyn an edge in the games against St. Louis. If that were the plot, they should have kidnapped Hallahan or High.

The league was poised to open an investigation into Rhem's charges of kidnapping owing to the close pennant race and the appearance of unsavory conduct. But Branch Rickey, business manager of the Cardinals, went to National League President John Heydler to tell him the Rhem story was bunk. Heydler wisely decided not to proceed with an inquiry.

The undaunted Rhem could not help police locate the house in Jersey, but the ploy did not aid the cause of the Robins. Though Rhem did not pitch in any of the games, the Cardinals swept the series and sent Brooklyn reeling.

The irrepressible Nick Altrock, former pitcher and famous baseball comic, later said that he rushed into the streets of New York hoping to be mistaken for the Cardinal pitcher by gunmen or anyone else who could provide the necessary whisky. He reported that he had no luck along these lines.

Years later, Rhem reminisced about the old days and thought it would be a good idea to "set the record straight" about the famous incident in his past. He said he roomed with Bill Hallahan and that the two "were a lot alike. We liked to roam about at the amusement parks, take roller coaster rides and take a drink or two and live a little bit."

Flint said he knew he was scheduled to pitch one of the games in the important series. "Oh," he said, "it [the pennant race] was closer than planks in a floor that year." Indeed, four teams still had a good chance at the flag.

"The night before the series," Rhem continued, "we went out. Now, it wasn't a big party or anything like that. Just something to eat and maybe, I don't remember exactly, a couple of drinks. Well, the next morning when I woke up, I was sicker than I have ever been in my life. It was horrible. It must have been some bad piece of meat I'd eaten the night before."

Isn't it always the food? Ill, Rhem stayed in his hotel all day. "The next day," he said, "Mr. Rickey came by our hotel room and knocked on the door. I was still sicker than a mule. Mr. Rickey came in the room and sort of left the door cracked a little bit, about two feet. Outside in the hall I could see some sportswriters standing around trying to listen.

"'Shad,' Mr. Rickey asks me, 'what's the matter with you? I guess somebody kidnapped you.' I was still pretty green around the gills when I looked up at him. 'You can call it what you like,' I said. 'All I know is I'm sicker than can be.' Now that's all I said, so help me.

"Well, those writers outside the door took that little conversation and built up this story, I don't know if Mr. Rickey helped them or not, that I had been kidnapped and taken to New Jersey where the kidnappers fed me whisky to get me so drunk I couldn't pitch in the Brooklyn series. All the while I was supposed to be sick. I was in my own hotel room. So help me, that's what happened."

By Saturday the 20th, Rhem was back in the good graces of his teammates and pitched a complete-game victory over the Philadelphia Phillies, 9–3, holding the hit-happy Phils to just seven hits. His last appearance in the regular season was three days later when he started against the same Phillies. Though he was credited with a victory again, it was not so pretty. He went four-plus innings in a 19–16 win, a game more typical of the awesome hitting and run-scoring of 1930. The Cards made twenty-six hits in the game, two by Rhem. Interested onlookers included the American League champion Philadelphia A's, getting a look at their World Series opponents.

The kidnapping (or whatever it was that happened to Flint Rhem in New York) was behind him at season's end, and forgotten by Street as well. Gabby even handed Flint the ball in the second game of the World Series against the A's. Down one game to none, Rhem was asked to get the Cards even. He couldn't. Overmatched by the powerful and pitching-laden A's, he and the Cards fell, 6–1.

The A's went on to win the series in six games. Rhem went on to pitch in the majors until 1936. He was never kidnapped again.

Flint Rhem was a 20-game winner in 1926, won more than 100 games in his big-league career, and appeared in four World Series. But he probably found more to celebrate on December 5, 1933, than anything he ever did in his baseball career. For it was on this day that Prohibition vanished from the land.

Little-Known Facts

One-Finger Murphy, St. Louis catcher and pitcher during baseball's Blue Period, was fined for spitting more times than any other major league ballplayer; on three separate occasions he was arrested and held without bail. . . . A right-handed batter usually hits better against a left-handed pitcher than a left-handed batter. . . .

Conrad Horn

RICKEY PLANNED TO SIGN SEVERAL
BLACKS AT ONCE

Jackie Robinson's Signing: The Untold Story

JOHN THORN AND JULES TYGIEL

♦ ♦ ♦

It was the first week of October, 1945. In the Midwest the Detroit Tigers and Chicago Cubs faced off in the final World Series of the World War II era. Two thousand miles away photographer Maurice Terrell arrived at an almost deserted Lane Field, the home of the minor league San Diego Padres. Terrell's assignment was as secretive as some wartime operations: to surreptitiously photograph three black baseball players wearing the uniforms of the Kansas City Royals, a Negro League all-star team. Within three weeks one of these players would rank among the most celebrated and intriguing figures in the nation. But in early October 1945, as he worked out with his teammates in the empty stadium, Jackie Robinson represented the best-kept secret in sports history.

Terrell shot hundreds of motion-picture frames of Robinson and his cohorts. A few appeared in print but the existence of the additional images remained unknown for four decades, until unearthed in 1987 at the Baseball Hall of Fame by John Thorn. This discovery triggered an investigation which has led to startling revelations regarding Brooklyn Dodger President Branch Rickey's original plan to shatter baseball's longstanding color line; the relationship between these two historic figures; and the still controversial issue of black managers in baseball.

The popularly held "frontier" image of Jackie Robinson as a lone gunman facing down a hostile mob has always dominated the integration saga. But new information related to the Terrell photos reveals that while Robinson was the linchpin to Branch Rickey's strategy, *in October 1945*

204

Rickey intended to announce the signing of not just Jackie Robinson, but several stars from the Negro Leagues at once. Political pressures, however, forced Rickey's hand, thrusting Robinson alone into a spotlight which he never relinquished.

The path to these revelations began with Thorn's discovery of the Terrell photographs in a collection donated to the Hall of Fame by *Look* magazine in 1954. The images depict a youthful, muscular Robinson in a battered hat and baggy uniform fielding from his position at shortstop, batting with a black catcher crouched behind him, trapping a third black player in a rundown between third and home, and sprinting along the basepaths more like a former track star than a baseball player. A woman with her back to the action is the only figure visible in the vacant stands. The contact sheets bore the imprinted date October 7, 1945.

The images perplexed Thorn. He knew that the momentous announcement of Jackie Robinson's signing with the Montreal Royals had not occurred until October 23, 1945. Before that date his recruitment by Brooklyn Dodger President Branch Rickey had been a tightly guarded secret. Why, then, had a *Look* photographer taken such an interest in Robinson two weeks earlier? Where had the pictures been taken? And why was Robinson already wearing a Royals uniform?

Thorn called Jules Tygiel, the author of *Baseball's Great Experiment: Jackie Robinson and His Legacy,* to see if he could shed some light on the photos. Tygiel had no knowledge of them, but he did have in his files a 1945 manuscript by newsman Arthur Mann, who frequently wrote for *Look.* The article, drafted with Rickey's cooperation, had been intended to announce the Robinson signing but had never been published. The pictures, they concluded, had doubtless been shot to accompany Mann's article, and they decided to find out the story behind the photo session. Tygiel set out to trace Robinson's activities in early October 1945. Thorn headed for the Library of Congress to examine the Branch Rickey papers, which had been unavailable at the time Tygiel wrote his book.

The clandestine nature of the photo session did not surprise the researchers. From the moment he had arrived in Brooklyn in 1942, determined to end baseball's Jim Crow traditions, Rickey had feared that premature disclosure of his intentions might doom his bold design. Since the 1890s, baseball executives, led by Commissioner Kenesaw Mountain Landis, had strictly policed the color line, barring blacks from both major and minor leagues. In 1943, when young Bill Veeck attempted to buy the Philadelphia Phillies and stock the team with Negro League stars, Landis had quietly but decisively blocked the move. Rickey therefore moved slowly and deliberately during his first three years in Brooklyn. He informed the Dodger owners of his plans but took few others into his confidence. He began to explore the issue and devised elaborate strategies to cover up his attempts to scout black players.

In the spring of 1945, as Rickey prepared to accelerate his scouting efforts, integration advocates, emboldened by the impending end of World War II and the recent death of Commissioner Landis, escalated their campaign to desegregate baseball. On April 6, 1945, black sportswriter Joe Bostic appeared at the Dodgers' Bear Mountain training camp with Negro League stars Terris McDuffie and Dave "Showboat" Thomas and forced Rickey to hold tryouts for the two players. Ten days later black journalist Wendell Smith, white sportswriter Dave Egan, and Boston city councilman Isadore Muchnick engineered an unsuccessful audition with the Red Sox for Robinson and two other black athletes. In response to these events the major leagues announced the formation of a Committee on Baseball Integration. (Reflecting Organized Baseball's true intentions on the matter, the group never met.)

Amidst this heated atmosphere Rickey created an elaborate smokescreen to obscure his scouting of black players. In May 1945 he announced the formation of a new franchise, the Brooklyn Brown Dodgers, and a new Negro League, the United States League. Rickey then dispatched his best talent hunters to observe black ballplayers, ostensibly for the Brown Dodgers, but in reality for the Brooklyn National League club.

A handwritten memorandum in the Rickey Papers offers a rare glimpse at Rickey's emphasis on secrecy in his instructions to Dodger scouts. The document, signed by Charles D. Clark and accompanied by a Negro National League schedule for April–May 1945, is headlined "Job Analysis," and defines the following "Duties: under supervision of management of club:

1. To establish contact (silent) with all clubs (local or general).
2. To gain knowledge and abilities of all players.
3. To report all possible material (players).
4. Prepare weekly reports of activities.
5. Keep composite report of outstanding players. . . . To travel and cover player whenever management so desire."

Clark's "Approch" [sic] was to "Visit game and loose [sic] self in stands; Keep statistical report (speed, power, agility, ability, fielding, batting, etc.) by score card"; and "Leave immediately after game."

Curiously, Clark listed his first "Objective" as being "to cover Negro teams for possible major league talent." Yet according to his later accounts, Rickey had told most Dodger scouts that they were evaluating talent for a new "Brown Dodger" franchise. Had Rickey confided in Clark, a figure so obscure as to escape prior mention in the voluminous Robinson literature? Dodger superscout and Rickey confidante Clyde Sukeforth has no recollection of Clark, raising the possibility that Clark was not part of the Dodger family, but perhaps someone connected with black baseball. Had Clark himself interpreted his instructions in this manner?

Whatever the answer, Rickey successfully diverted attention from his true motives. Nonetheless, mounting interest in the integration issue threatened Rickey's careful planning. In the summer of 1945 Rickey constructed yet another facade. The Dodger President took Dan Dodson, a New York University sociologist who chaired Mayor Fiorello LaGuardia's Committee on Unity, into his confidence and requested that Dodson form a Committee on Baseball ostensibly to study the possibility of integration. In reality, the committee would provide the illusion of action while Rickey quietly completed his own preparations to sign several black players at once. "This was one of the toughest decisions I ever had to make while in office," Dodson later confessed. "The major purpose I could see for the committee was that it was a stall for time. . . . Yet had Mr. Rickey not delivered . . . I would have been totally discredited."

Thus by late August, even as Rickey's extensive scouting reports had led him to focus in on Jackie Robinson as his standard bearer, few people in or out of the Dodger organization suspected that a breakthrough was imminent. On August 28 Rickey and Robinson held their historic meeting at the Dodgers' Montague Street offices in downtown Brooklyn. Robinson signed an agreement to accept a contract with the Montreal Royals, the top Dodger affiliate, by November 1. Rickey, still concerned with secrecy, impressed upon Robinson the need to maintain silence until further preparations had been made. Robinson could tell the momentous news to his family and fianceé, but no one else.

For the conspiratorial Rickey, further subterfuge was necessary to keep the news sheltered while continuing the arrangements. Rumors about Robinson's visit had already spread through the world of black baseball. To stifle speculation Rickey "leaked" an adulterated version of the incident to black sportswriter Wendell Smith. Smith, who had recommended Robinson to Rickey and advised Rickey on the integration project, doubtless knew the true story behind the meeting. On September 8, however, he reported in the Pittsburgh *Courier* that the "sensational shortstop" and "colorful major league dynamo" had met behind "closed doors."

"The nature of the conferences has not been revealed," wrote Smith. "It seems to be shrouded in mystery and Robinson has not made a statement since he left Brooklyn." Rickey claimed that he and Robinson had assessed "the organization of Negro baseball," but did not discuss "the possibility of Robinson becoming a member of the Brooklyn Dodgers organization."

Smith hinted broadly of future developments, noting that "It does not seem logical [Rickey] should call in a rookie player to discuss the future organization of Negro baseball." He closed with the tantalizing thought that "it appears that the Brooklyn boss has a plan on his mind that extends further than just the future of Negro baseball as an organization." But the subterfuge succeeded. Neither black nor white reporters pursued the issue further.

Rickey, always sensitive to criticism by New York sports reporters and understanding the historic significance of his actions, wanted to be sure that his version of the integration breakthrough and his role in it be accurately portrayed. To guarantee this he expanded his circle of conspirators to include freelance writer Arthur Mann. In the weeks following the Robinson meeting, Mann, Rickey's close friend and later a Dodger employee, authored at the Mahatma's behest a 3000-word manuscript to be published simultaneously with the announcement of the signing.

Although it is impossible to confirm this, it seems highly likely that Maurice Terrell's photos, commissioned by *Look*, were destined to accompany Mann's article. Clearer prints of the negatives revealed to Thorn and Tygiel that Terrell had taken the pictures in San Diego's Lane Stadium. This fits in with Robinson's fall itinerary. In the aftermath of his meeting with Rickey, Robinson had returned briefly to the Kansas City Monarchs. With the Dodger offer securing his future and the relentless bus trips of the Negro League schedule wearing him down, he had left the Monarchs before season's end and returned home to Pasadena, California. In late September he hooked up with Chet Brewer's Kansas City Royals, a postseason barnstorming team which toured the Pacific Coast, competing against other Negro League teams and major and minor league all-star squads. Thus the word "Royals" on Robinson's uniform, which had so piqued the interest of Thorn and Tygiel, ironically turned out not to relate to Robinson's future team in Montreal, but rather to his interim employment in California.

For further information Tygiel contacted Chet Brewer, who at age eighty still lived in Los Angeles. Brewer, one of the great pitchers of the Jim Crow era, had known Robinson well. He had followed Robinson's spectacular athletic career at UCLA and in 1945 they became teammates on the Monarchs. "Jackie was major league all the way," recalls Brewer. "He had the fastest reflexes I ever saw in a player." With Brewer's Royals, Robinson was always the first in the clubhouse and the first one on the field. "Satchel Paige was just the opposite," laughs Brewer. "He would get there just as the game was about to start and come running on the field still tying his shoe."

Robinson particularly relished facing major league all-star squads. Against Bob Feller, Robinson slashed two doubles. "Jack was running crazy on the bases," a Royal teammate remembers. In one game he upended shortstop Gerry Priddy of the Washington Senators. Priddy angrily complained about the hard slide in an exhibition game. "Any time I put on a uniform," retorted Robinson, "I play to win." The fire in his playing notwithstanding, Robinson maintained his pledge to Rickey.

Jackie Robinson in his secret major league try-out

Neither Brewer nor any of his teammates suspected the secret that Robinson faithfully kept inside him.

Brewer recalls that Robinson and two other Royals journeyed from Los Angeles to San Diego on a day when the team was not scheduled to play. He identified the catcher in the photos as Buster Haywood and the other player as Royals third baseman Herb Souell. Souell is no longer living, but Haywood, who, like Brewer resides in Los Angeles, has vague recollections of the event, which he incorrectly remembers as occurring in Pasadena. Robinson had befriended Haywood the preceding year while coaching basketball in Texas. He recruited the catcher and Souell, his former Monarch teammate, to "work out" with him. All three wore their Royal uniforms. Haywood found neither Robinson's request nor the circumstances unusual. Although he was unaware that they were being photographed, Haywood still can describe the session accurately. "We didn't know what was going on," he states. "We'd hit and throw and run from third base to home plate."

The San Diego pictures provide a rare glimpse of the pre-Montreal Robinson. The article which they were to accompany and related correspondence in the Library of Congress offers even rarer insights into

Rickey's thinking. The unpublished Mann manuscript was entitled "The Negro and Baseball: The National Game Faces A Racial Challenge Long Ignored." As Mann doubtless based his account on conversations with Rickey and since Rickey's handwritten comments appear in the margin, it stands as the earliest "official" account of the Rickey-Robinson story and reveals many of the concerns confronting Rickey in September 1945.

One of the most striking features of the article is the language used to refer to Robinson. Mann, reflecting the blind racism typical of postwar America, insensitively portrays Robinson as the "first Negro chattel in the so-called National pastime." At another point he writes, "Rickey felt the boy's sincerity," appropriate language perhaps for an eighteen-year-old prospect, but not for a twenty-six-year-old former army officer.

"The Negro and Baseball" consists largely of the now familiar Rickey-Robinson story. Mann re-created Rickey's haunting 1904 experience as collegiate coach of black baseball player Charlie Thomas, who, when denied access to a hotel, cried and rubbed his hands, chanting, "Black skin! Black skin! If I could only make 'em white." Mann described the search for the "right" man, the formation of the United States League as a cover for scouting operations, the reasons for selecting Robinson, and the fateful drama of the initial Rickey-Robinson confrontation.

Other sections, however, graphically illustrate which issues Rickey deemed significant. Mann repeatedly cites the financial costs incurred by the Dodgers: $5,000 to scout Cuba, $6,000 to scout Mexico, $5,000 to establish the "Brooklyn Brown Dodgers." The final total reaches $25,000, a modest sum considering the ultimate returns, but one which Rickey felt would counter his skinflint image.

Rickey's desire to dispel the notion that political pressures had motivated his actions also emerges clearly. Mann had suggested that upon arriving in Brooklyn in 1942, Rickey "was besieged by telephone calls, telegrams, and letters of petition in behalf of black ball players," and that this "staggering pile of missives were so inspired to convince him that he and the Dodgers had been selected as a kind of guinea pig." In his marginal comments, Rickey vehemently objected to this notion. "No!" he wrote in a strong dark script, "I began all this as soon as I went to Brooklyn." Explaining why he had never attacked the subject during his two decades as general manager of the St. Louis Cardinals, Rickey referred to the segregated conditions in that city. "St. Louis never permitted Negro patrons in the grandstand," he wrote, describing a policy he had apparently felt powerless to change.

Mann also devoted two of his twelve pages to a spirited attack on the Negro Leagues. He repeated Rickey's charges that "They are the poorest excuse for the word league" and documented the prevalence of barn-storming, the uneven scheduling, absence of contracts, and dominance of booking agents. Mann revealingly traces Rickey's distaste for the Negro Leagues to the "outrageous" guarantees demanded by New York booking agent William Leuschner to place black teams in Ebbets Field while the Dodgers were on the road.

Rickey's misplaced obsession with the internal disorganization of the Negro Leagues had substantial factual basis. But in transforming the black circuits into major villains of Jim Crow baseball, Rickey had an ulterior motive. In his September 8 article, Wendell Smith addressed the issue of "player tampering," asking "Would [Rickey] not first approach the owner of these Negro teams who have these stars under contract?" Rickey, argued Smith in what might have been an unsuccessful preemptive strike, "is obligated to do so and his record as a businessman indicated that he would." As Smith may have known, Rickey maintained that Negro League players did not sign valid contracts and became free agents at the end of each season. The Mahatma thus had no intention of compensating Negro League teams for the players he signed. His repeated attacks on black baseball, including the Mann article, served to justify this questionable practice.

The one respect in which "The Negro and Baseball" departs radically from common perceptions of the Robinson legend is in its depiction of Robinson as one of a group of blacks about to be signed by the Dodgers. Mann's manuscript reveals that Rickey did not intend for Robinson, usually viewed as a solitary standard bearer, to withstand the pressures alone. "Determined not to be charged with merely nibbling at the problem," wrote Mann, "Rickey went all out and brought in two more Negro players," and "consigned them, with Robinson, to the Dodgers' top farm club, the Montreal Royals." Mann named pitcher Don Newcombe and, surprisingly, outfielder Sam Jethroe as Robinson's future teammates.

As Mann's report indicates, and subsequent correspondence from Rickey confirms, *Rickey did not plan to announce the signing of just one black player.* Whether the recruitment of additional blacks had always been his intention or whether he had reached his decision after meeting with Robinson in August is unclear. But by late September, when he provided information to Mann for his article, Rickey had clearly decided to bring in other Negro League stars.

During the first weekend in October Dodger Coach Chuck Dressen fielded a major league all-star team in a series of exhibition games against Negro League standouts at Ebbets Field. Rickey took the opportunity to interview at least three black pitching prospects, Newcombe, Roy

Partlow, and John Wright. The following week he met with catcher Roy Campanella. Campanella and Newcombe, at least, believed they had been approached to play for the "Brown Dodgers."

At the same time Rickey decided to postpone publication of Mann's manuscript. In a remarkable letter sent from the World Series in Chicago on October 7, Rickey informed Mann:

> We just can't go now with the article. The thing isn't dead,—not at all. It is more alive than ever and that is the reason we can't go with any publicity at this time. There is more involved in the situation than I had contemplated. Other players are in it and it may be that I can't clear these players until after the December meetings, possibly not until after the first of the year. You must simply sit in the boat. . . . There is a November 1 deadline on Robinson,—you know that. I am undertaking to extend that date until January 1st so as to give me time to sign plenty of players and make one break on the complete story. Also, quite obviously it might not be good to sign Robinson with other and possibly better players unsigned.

The revelations and tone of this letter surprise Robinson's widow, Rachel, forty years after the event. Rickey "was such a deliberate man," she recalls, "and this letter is so urgent. He must have been very nervous as he neared his goal. Maybe he was nervous that the owners would turn him down and having five people at the door instead of just one would have been more powerful."

Events in the weeks after October 7 justified Rickey's nervousness and forced him to deviate from the course stated in the Mann letter. Candidates in New York City's upcoming November elections, most notably black Communist City Councilman Ben Davis, made baseball integration a major plank in the campaign.

Mayor LaGuardia's liberal supporters also sought to exploit the issue. Professor Dodson's Committee on Baseball had prepared a report outlining a modest, long-range strategy for bringing blacks into the game and describing the New York teams, because of the favorable political and racial climate in the city, as in a "choice position to undertake this pattern of integration." LaGuardia wanted Rickey's permission to make a pre-election announcement that "baseball would shortly begin signing Negro players," as a result of the committee's work.

Rickey, a committee member, had long ago subverted the panel to his own purposes. By mid-October, however, the committee had become "an election football." Again unwilling to risk the appearance of succumbing to political pressure and thereby surrendering what he viewed as his rightful role in history, Rickey asked LaGuardia to delay his comments. Rickey hurriedly contacted Robinson, who had joined a barnstorming team in New York en route to play winter ball in Venezuela, and dispatched him to Montreal. On October 23, 1945, with Rickey's carefully laid plans scuttled, the Montreal Royals announced the signing of Robinson, and Robinson alone.

The premature revelation of Rickey's racial breakthrough had important ramifications for the progress of baseball's "great experiment." Mann's article never appeared. *Look,* having lost its exclusive, published two strips of the Terrell pictures in its November 27, 1945 issue accompanying a brief summary of the Robinson story. The unprocessed film negatives and contact sheets were loaded into a box and nine years later shipped to the National Baseball Hall of Fame, where they remained, along with a picture of Jethroe, unpacked until April 1987.

Newcombe, Campanella, Wright, and Partlow all joined the Dodger organization the following spring. Jethroe became a victim of the "deliberate speed" of baseball integration. Rickey did not interview Jethroe in 1945. Since few teams followed the Dodger lead, the fleet, powerful outfielder remained in the Negro Leagues until 1948, when Rickey finally bought his contract from the Cleveland Buckeyes for $5,000. Jethroe had two spectacular seasons at Montreal before Rickey, fearing a "surfeit of colored boys on the Brooklyn club," profitably sold him to the Boston Braves for $100,000. Jethroe won the Rookie of the Year Award in 1950, but his delayed entry into Organized Baseball foreshortened what should have been a stellar career. To this day, Jethroe remains unaware of how close he came to joining Robinson, Newcombe, and Campanella in the pantheon of integration pioneers.

Beyond these revelations about the Robinson signing, the Library of Congress documents add surprisingly little to the familiar contours of the integration saga. There is one letter of interest from Rickey to Robinson, dated December 31, 1950, in which the old man offers some encouragement to Jackie's budding managerial ambitions. But by the time he retired in 1956, Robinson's personal ambition to manage had faded, though he never flagged in his determination to see a black manager in the majors. The Rickey Papers copiously detail his post-Dodger career as general manager of the Pittsburgh Pirates, but are strangely silent about the critical 1944–48 period. Records for these years probably remained with the Dodger organization, which claims to have no knowledge of their whereabouts. National League documents for these years remain closed to the public.

In any case, Robinson's greatest pioneering work came as a player. Though Rickey apparently intended that Jackie be just one of a number of black players signed at one time, the scuttling of those plans laid the success or failure of the assault on Jim Crow disproportionately on the capable shoulders of Jackie Robinson, who had always occupied center stage in Rickey's thinking. While this greatly intensified the pressures on the man, it also enhanced his legend immensely. Firmly fixed in the public mind as the sole pathfinder, rather than group leader, he became the lightning rod for supporter and opponent alike, attracting the responsibility, the opprobrium, and ultimately the acclaim for his historic achievement.

THE CUBS WON 23 MORE GAMES
THAN THE WHITE SOX IN 1906

The Greatest Series Upse of All Time

PETER M. GORDON

♦ ♦ ♦

Although the last decade has produced a number of surprises
World Series and some commentators labeled the Dodgers' 1988
over the Athletics the greatest upset in World Series history, the t
that actually deserves that title occurred more than four score ye
the victory of the White Sox over the Cubs in 1906.

In that bygone era between the Spanish-American War and
War I, major league baseball teams played in wooden parks for t
part, and overflow crowds stood behind ropes on the outfield gr
peace between the American and National Leagues, like the airpl;
only three years old. And independent professional and amateur
proliferated throughout the country. These leagues were so n
that the popular *Spalding* and *Reach Base Ball Guides* covered
ploits as well as those of the majors. Henry Chadwick, writin
Spalding Guide in 1906, even felt compelled to defend the "mer
ganized base ball" in order to justify the greater space devoted
league coverage.

Despite the official peace between the leagues, in Chicago tl
between the National's Cubs and the junior circuit's White
more intense each year. The Cubs, as the National League hei
Anson's White Stockings, claimed the loyalty of many traditic
The White Sox, owned by former star player Charles Comiskey,
many Cub adherents with their success in the young America

While the Cubs languished in the second division, the Sox won the AL's first two pennants in 1900 and 1901, always remained in contention, and missed by just two games the opportunity to play the Giants when the World Series resumed in 1905.

Not having won a pennant themselves since 1886, the Cubs hired Frank Selee, who had won five flags with Boston in the 1890s, to manage the team in 1902. Also arriving that year were rookie infielders Joe Tinker and Johnny Evers and center fielder Jimmy Slagle. All three were excellent fielders, and the development of young Johnny Kling into an outstanding defensive catcher gave the Cubs the best up-the-middle defense in baseball. Selee also shifted former catcher Frank Chance to first base, where he blossomed into a team leader and all-around star. The acquisition of hard-hitting Frank Schulte in late 1904 boosted the offense.

To build his pitching staff, Selee brought two college stars with little or no professional experience to the Cubs, Carl Lundgren (University of Illinois) and Ed Reulbach (Notre Dame). But his boldest move was trading his 1903 ace Jack Taylor to the Cardinals for a raw rookie named Mordecai "Three Finger" Brown.

The Cubs rose to second place in 1904, but ill health forced Selee to resign in mid-season in 1905. Frank Chance took over as manager and over the winter traded his best veteran pitcher, Jake Weimer, for third baseman Harry Steinfeldt. Feeling that he needed one more key piece to complete his lineup, Chance then convinced new owner Charles Murphy to trade four players to Brooklyn for left fielder Jimmy Sheckard. Sheckard filled the number-two slot in the batting order to perfection, setting the National League record for sacrifices in a season in 1906 and giving the Cubs the best lineup in the league.

Further strengthening his pitching with mid-season trades for Orval Overall and Jack Taylor, Chance's team rode roughshod over the rest of the league. They took over first place for good on May 28 and edged the second-place Pirates twice by 1–0 scores on the Fourth of July to boost their lead to 4½ games. Exactly one month later they still led by 4½ but then launched the hottest sustained streak in history, winning 37 of their next 39 to end the race.

Winning by a final margin of 20 games, the Cubs dominated the league statistically, leading in runs scored, fewest runs allowed, batting average, and fielding average, all by wide margins. They set new records for fewest errors made (194), runs allowed (2.5 per game), and shutouts (31). Steinfeldt led the league in hits, Chance in runs and stolen bases, and Shulte in triples. And in the single most important indicator of a team's superiority—games won—the 1906 Cubs rank as the greatest of all time with 116 victories.

Across town, meanwhile, the White Sox were not even in the American League pennant race for much of the summer. They trailed by 9 games on July 28 while the Philadelphia Athletics, New York Highlanders, and Cleveland Naps battled for the league lead. But starting on August 2, the White Sox ran off a 19-game winning streak that catapulted them into first place by 5½ games. The Highlanders won 15 in a row and passed the Sox in early September, but Chicago won 14 out of 21 on a long homestand in the final month and clinched the pennant with four games left to play.

Mordecai "Three Finger" Brown

Managed by their fiery center fielder, Fielder Jones, they were a group of tough, veteran ballplayers (average age: thirty) who knew how to win. Shortstop and cleanup hitter George Davis was in his seventeenth year in the majors and was the team's best clutch hitter. Third-place hitter Frank Isbell's .279 average was the team's best, although his defense at second base was not outstanding. Lee Tannehill at third base and Jiggs Donohue at first gave the Sox outstanding defense at the corners, although Tannehill hit only .183 for the season. Billy Sullivan was the leader during the games and considered the best defensive catcher in the league. Bill O'Neill led the outfielders with a .248 average but lost his job in left when the Sox acquired veteran Patsy Dougherty from New York. Center fielder Jones and right fielder Eddie Hahn could not top the .230 mark, but both were outstanding baserunners, and Jones was a superior flyhawk.

What was particularly amazing about their pennant was the fact that the White Sox finished last in the league in batting with a .230 average, which earned them their famous nickname, "The Hitless Wonders." But they had the best pitching and defense in the league, going the Cubs one better by posting 32 shutouts for a mark that still stands today. Their pitchers, righties Frank Owen and Ed Walsh and southpaws Nick Altrock and Doc White, were all capable of brilliant performances. And manager Jones squeezed every last drop of ability out of his players. It seemed to contemporary observers like Henry Chadwick that the team "won on generalship alone."

Everyone expected the immensely powerful Cubs to demolish their crosstown rivals in the World Series. Indeed, the disparity between the two teams, on paper, was the greatest in World Series history. The Cubs won twenty-three more games than the White Sox. By instructive contrast, in 1988 the A's had won just ten more games than the Dodgers, the Orioles in 1969 had only won eight more games than the Mets, and in 1914 the Athletics had won just five more games than the "Miracle Braves." While the Sox pitching and defense were impressive, most observers believed that the Cubs' were even better. And of course the Cubs could hit. The Cubs scored 135 more runs than the Sox, allowed 79 fewer, and out-hit them by 32 points. The Cubs dominated the Sox in every offensive and defensive category except walks allowed. As if the mismatch between the two teams wasn't enough to favor the Cubs, the White Sox received word on the eve of the Series that George Davis, their best (indeed, some would say only) hitter, would be out indefinitely with a bad cold. Although the Cubs would also be missing leadoff man Jimmy Slagle, oddsmakers still favored them as much as 3 to 1.

To no one's surprise, Manager Chance confidently predicted victory. "Every man [on the team] is fit to play the game of his life. I believe we will win." However, Fielder Jones also anticipated a win, saying "I expect the Cubs to meet their Waterloo." Chance probably dismissed Jones' prediction as posturing, but Fielder Jones had seen his team beat the odds all year. He also expected that because the Cub batters weren't used to seeing left-handers and spitballers in the National League, Altrock, Walsh, and White could nullify the Cubs' hitting advantage. The Chicago *Daily News* felt this was a strong enough possibility to spend an entire article refuting it.

The likelihood of a Cub sweep could not diminish the "Base Ball Fever" that gripped Chicago in anticipation of the day of the first game on October 9. Employers complained that no one would work or buy; employees and patrons only wanted to discuss the game. The morning dawned clear but bitterly cold. Despite the below-freezing temperature, fans began to arrive at the West Side Grounds, the Cubs' home park at the corner of Lincoln and Polk, by 12:45 P.M. for the 3:00 P.M. game. The West Side Grounds had a wooden grandstand and pavilion behind the plate and was encircled by a wooden fence. Those lucky enough to get a seat paid the impressive sum of $1.50 for the grandstand, $1.00 for the pavilion, or 50 cents for the bleachers. One could also pay 50 cents for the privilege of standing behind ropes along the foul lines. As game time approached many stores stopped doing business altogether, and the entire town went "Base Ball mad."

For the first game the Cubs replaced Slagle with utilityman Solly Hofman, and the Sox moved the slick-fielding Tannehill to shortstop, placing George Rohe at third. Otherwise, the teams played their regular lineups throughout the series. Manager Chance warmed up both Brown and Lundgren, but no one was surprised when he started Brown, his ace all year. Fielder Jones never had any doubts who his first starter would be: left-hander Nick Altrock. Remembered today (if at all) as a famous baseball clown with the Senators in the '20s and '30s, his 20 wins in 1906 marked the third straight season the dark, thin, gutsy southpaw had won 19 games or more. Monte Cross had intimated to Fielder Jones earlier in the season that, while the Sox staff was strong, it lacked a pitcher "steady enough to do justice to himself and his team" in an important game. Jones replied that in any clutch situation "I would send Nick Altrock to the slab, and show me any pitcher in the league who is better acquainted for just such an emergency."

By 3:00 P.M. the temperature had dropped below freezing, and snow flurries began to fall. While the cold may have led the less hardy to forsake the ballpark for the comfort of McVicker's Theatre or the First Regimental Armory downtown, where the Chicago Tribune arranged play-by-play boards, the West Side Grounds still filled with 12,693 fans. The enthusiastic crowd appeared equally divided between Cub and White Sox fans, as they screamed and waved multicolored pennants on almost every pitch.

Altrock justified Jones' faith by matching Brown out for out at the start of the game. The cold appeared to bother batters from both teams, as the hurlers threw no-hit ball for the first three innings. "Wildfire" Schulte broke up the dual no-hitter with two out in the bottom of the fourth by beating out a Baltimore chop to Isbell at second. Although Schulte was safe stealing second when Isbell dropped Sullivan's throw, Altrock got Chance to tap back to the mound to end the inning.

In the top of the fifth, replacement George Rohe became the hero of the game by pulling a Brown fastball down the left-field line and into the bottom of the bleachers for a triple. With Rohe on third, Brown bore down and struck out Jiggs Donohue, and got Patsy Dougherty to tap an easy roller back to the mound. However, in his anxiety to get Rohe at the plate, Brown threw wide to Kling, thus letting Rohe score the first run of the game. The Sox added an insurance run the next inning, when Altrock walked and moved to second on a sacrifice by Hahn. Nick was out at the plate trying to score on Jones' single, but Jones took second, moved to third on a passed ball, and came in on Isbell's single.

Altrock tried to finesse the Cubs in the sixth, and began by walking Kling. Three Finger Brown helped himself by bouncing a single up the middle. Following the accepted baseball practice of the time, Hofman sacrificed Kling and Brown up a base. Altrock, a bit nervous, threw a fastball over Sullivan's head back to the screen behind home plate, scoring Kling, but then the Sox defense saved the game. Jimmy Sheckard hit what appeared to be a game-tying Texas leaguer over short, but Tannehill, despite playing in on the grass, went back and caught the ball over his head in short left. Rohe almost went from the hero to the goat on the next play, when he threw Schulte's grounder wide of first, but Donahue stretched his full six feet, one inch and barely caught the ball for the third out. Given a reprieve, Nick steadied and disposed of the Cub machine handily over the last three innings. After Steinfeldt flied to Jones in center for the last out, the deliriously happy Sox fans rushed onto the field and carried off their heroes on their shoulders.

The teams moved to the White Sox home, South Side Park, for Game Two the next day. (Because both teams were from Chicago, there were no days off for travel.) The Sox kept the grass high and the ground soft in their infield to slow the ball down and make it easier to field. Many sportswriters felt that the South Side Park helped the Sox win the pennant by greatly reducing the hitting ability of visiting teams. Indeed, the Sox had a .701 winning percentage at home, compared to .527 on the road. The Cubs topped both marks with a good .727 percentage at the West Side grounds, and an amazing .800 on the road.

The mercury dropped even farther before Game Two, and the cold wind blowing off Lake Michigan led the Chicago *Daily News* to recommend that fans wear fur coats. The game figured to be another pitching duel, matching Ed Reulbach, who led the NL in winning percentage, against southpaw Doc White, who led the AL in ERA. Doc White (who actually had a dental degree) held the record for most consecutive shutouts until Don Drysdale broke it in 1968. The 12,500 fans that turned out despite the freezing weather saw a pitcher's duel—for the first inning. The cold made it difficult for White to grip the ball, although it did not seem to bother Reulbach very much. After retiring the side in order in the first, White struck out Chance to start the second, but gave up a hard single to left by Steinfeldt. As expected, Tinker bunted for a sacrifice down the third-base line, but unexpectedly beat out Rohe's throw. The field did slow down Evers' grounder to Isbell, but the second baseman's hurried throw to force Steinfeldt at third went wide of the bag and Steinfeldt scored. White walked Kling to load the bases and pitch to Reulbach. Reulbach laid down a perfect suicide squeeze to score Tinker, and then Hoffman drove in the third run by beating out an infield hit.

White, unstrung, allowed another run in the third and was replaced by Frank Owen in the fourth. Reulbach, on the other hand, pitched a one-hitter, winning easily, 7–1.

The weather warmed up on October 11 as the teams returned to the West Side Grounds. After their easy victory the day before the Cubs confidently expected to roll over the Sox. But they hadn't counted on twenty-four-year-old spitballer (and future Hall of Famer) Ed Walsh pitching one of the greatest games in World Series history. Both Walsh and the Cubs' Jack Pfiester baffled opposing batters early on, striking out at least one hitter each inning.

The pitchers strung goose eggs until the seventh, when Tannehill got his first hit of the series, a single just past Steinfeldt at third. Pfiester pitched around Walsh to keep him from sacrificing and ended up walking him. Disconcerted by his failure, Pfiester hit Hahn with the next pitch to load the bases. Pfiester took a deep breath and went back to his best pitch, the curve ball. He got manager Jones to swing at a sweeping curve and foul out to Kling for the first out. He then threw three straight curves past Isbell, who flung his bat down in frustration. With bases loaded with two down, the Sox had to rely on Game One hero George Rohe. The White Sox fans in the crowd began to despair; it was too much to expect the utilityman to save the day again. However, Rohe had watched Pfiester throw four straight curve balls, and guessed correctly that he would start him off with a fastball. Rohe pulled that pitch down the left-field line and into the temporary bleachers for a bases-clearing triple. That was all the scoring as Walsh fanned twelve to win 3–0 and give the White Sox a 2-games-to-1 lead in the series.

The Sox received a big lift for Game Four when they learned that George Davis could play; Davis took over his customary place at short and cleanup, with new hero Rohe staying at third. Altrock and Brown locked horns again at South Side Park in a replay of their pitcher's duel in Game One. However, this time Brown got the better of it. Altrock's stuff was not quite as overpowering as in the first game, but he compensated with a canny pitch selection that kept the Cubs off balance. Meanwhile, Brown overwhelmed the Sox, pitching a no-hitter through 5⅔ innings. The hurlers matched each other out for out until right fielder Hahn lost Frank Chance's fly ball in the sun in the top of the seventh, allowing it to drop for a single. Steinfeldt and Tinker sacrificed Chance to third, and he scored on the only hard blow of the game, Evers' crisp single to left. That ended the scoring; the 1–0 victory tied the Series again.

The young, cocky Cubs had expected the Series to be over after four games, so suddenly Game Five became the most crucial game. The day dawned bright and warm, perfect for baseball. By noon the streets leading to the West Side Park were clogged with fans waiting to get inside, and over 23,000 fans pushed their way into the park before they had to lock the gates at 1:40. Eager fanatics outside offered the fabulous sum of $20 for a seat. Spectators climbed telephone poles and packed the roofs of the houses surrounding the park. Despite the locked gates, Cub and Sox supporters kept pressing forward and their weight collapsed the left-field bleacher fence. Fans spilled onto the field, and it took a squad of police with clubs 20 minutes to restore order. Finally, with the overflow crowd standing behind ropes in the outfield as well as along the sidelines, the game began.

In an effort to benefit from his team's success in road games, Chance dressed the Cubs in their traveling gray uniforms, despite their being the home team. To further fire up the Cub hitters, a live bear cub was paraded in front of the team bench before the game. At first all of the mumbo jumbo appeared to have worked, as the Cubs took advantage of "rank" fielding (errors by Isbell and Walsh) to score three runs off Walsh in the bottom of the first. With Ed Reulbach on the mound set to repeat his Game Two mastery of the Sox, it looked like the Series might, indeed, be over.

But the Sox, who had beaten the odds all year, were not ready to die. Isbell led off the third with his second double, and then George Davis made his presence felt by doubling into the crowd in right, driving in Isbell. Manager Chance, perhaps overreacting, replaced Reulbach with Pfiester, who started well by striking out Rohe, but then hit Donahue with a pitch. Dougherty then grounded slowly to Tinker, who had to settle for erasing Donahue at second, while Davis took third. On Pfiester's second pitch to Sullivan, Davis and Dougherty pulled off a perfect delayed double steal to tie the score.

In the top of the fourth, the Sox teed off on Pfiester and his replacement Overall, scoring four runs on doubles by Isbell, Davis, and Dougherty. After the first inning, Walsh held the Cubs off through six, but gave way to Doc White, who redeemed his Game Two performance by shutting out the Cubs the rest of the way. Their 8–6 victory in what many observers call "the greatest game of all time" put the Sox ahead in the series three games to two.

Chicago shut down for the sixth game. No one could believe the Cubs were on the brink of elimination, least of all the Cubs themselves. The day was again perfect for baseball, and while the crowd jostling for space in South Side Park was more orderly than the day before, the stadium was still absolutely jam-packed, as 20,000 fans kept up a constant din of horns, bells, and hollers. Their efforts were aided by the thousands of fans who stood in the streets surrounding the park, listening avidly.

The Cubs appeared jittery during infield practice; even Evers looked flat. The Sox, on the other hand, went through a spirited practice to the delight of their fans. Manager Chance, his back to the wall, sent Three Finger Brown to the mound. Although Brown had had only one day of rest after a complete game, such a pitching choice was not unknown back then, when pitchers did not have to throw hard for an entire game. Fielder Jones started Doc White, even though he had hurled three innings in relief the previous day.

Because he had worked the day before, White didn't have his good fastball and relied upon his curve and change. The Cubs reached him for a run in the first, but White steadied and disposed of Chance and Schulte to keep the deficit from growing.

The Sox came out swinging in the bottom of the first, determined to eliminate their "hitless" reputation. Hahn beat out a smash to second, but Jones forced him for the first out. Isbell singled hard to right, sending Jones to second. Davis, batting cleanup, hit a high fly to deep right. It looked as if Schulte would catch it, but at the last second it bounced into the crowd surrounding the outfield for a double. The game was held up while Schulte hotly contended that a policeman holding back the crowd interfered with his attempt to catch the ball. No policeman could be found at that point in the crowd. Neither umpire saw any interference, nor would any of the fans back Schulte's claims. The double stood, leaving runners on second and third with one out.

Chance brought the infield in, and Rohe grounded to Tinker, who cut off Isbell at the plate. However, after Rohe stole second without a throw from Kling, who did not want to chance a repeat of the previous day's double steal, Jiggs Donahue put the Sox ahead with a double into the crowd in left. Brown managed to end the scoring there, but after he got the first two Sox batters out in the bottom of the second the game completely unraveled for the Cubs.

First Ed Hahn lined a single to left. Brown got two quick strikes on Fielder Jones, but then lost his control and walked him. He managed to induce Isbell to hit an easy roller to second. However, in his eagerness to field the ball, Tinker cut in front of Evers, missed the ball, and also managed to obscure Evers' view so that by the time Johnny made the play Isbell was on first, loading the bases for George Davis. Davis swung at the first offering and hit a hard, high liner to short. Tinker leaped and just tipped the ball with his glove, deflecting its flight enough that Sheckard couldn't reach it until Hahn and Jones had scored, Isbell stopping at second. The noise from the crowd drowned out the brass band playing in the box seats as Rohe hit a grounder to short and beat Tinker's throw to load the bases again. Brown, despairing and completely unstrung, was replaced by Overall.

The umpires threw in a fresh ball for the new pitcher, and Donahue promptly hit it over second for a single and the third run. Overall walked Dougherty to force in the fourth run before he steadied and struck out Sullivan to end the inning. White started the second leading by six runs, and although he gave up a run in the fifth, the lead was never in any danger. The Sox kept adding to the score for a final tally of 8–3. As soon as the game ended, the White Sox fans swarmed onto the field just as they did after Game One, and again hoisted their heroes on their shoulders. After parading around the field, the crowd congregated in front of the Cubs' owner's box until Mr. Murphy made a charming concession speech, admitting that the best team won.

From the North to the South Sides Chicago was one big party that night. A crowd of 2,000 fans made the rounds of all of the White Sox' houses to cheer the ballplayers again. Even Frank Chance admitted that the Sox had "fairly won," although he still said he had the better team. Chance was right, which just made the Sox' upset victory even greater.

Fielder Jones correctly anticipated that his pitchers could nullify the Cubs' hitting. The White Sox hurlers held the mighty Cub attack to a minuscule .196 average, enabling them to win despite their own low team average of .198. By the time the Cub batters began to adjust to the Sox staff's unorthodox deliveries, the Series was over. None of the famous Cub stars hit well at all, sub Solly Hofman leading the club with a .304 average.

Without the Cubs' offensive advantage, the teams were nearly equal, and the teamwork and experience of the White Sox enabled them to get the edge over their powerful crosstown rivals. The Sox hit poorly as a team, but got the clutch hits when it counted from Rohe (.333), and veterans Davis (.308), Isbell (.308, four doubles), and Donahue (.333). The Cubs kept taking themselves out of rallies by getting caught stealing, while the Sox, in contrast, tied the crucial fifth game with a perfect double steal. In the crucible of the fifth and sixth games the Cub fielding fell apart, while the Sox fielding remained steady. Although the White Sox victory surprised every contemporary observer, with the possible exception of the team itself, in retrospect perhaps no team in a World Series should be favored by odds as outlandish as 3 to 1. After all, in professional baseball it's not uncommon for last-place teams to take 4 out of 6 from first-place teams. The Sox, after all, had won the pennant against very tough competition. The Cubs' great successes blinded the sportswriters and commentators of the time as to how good the Sox really were.

The Cub juggernaut was just getting rolling, however. The team won three of the next four pennants, and finished second in 1909 despite winning 104 games. Tinker, Evers, Chance, and Brown would go on to the Hall of Fame, and the team's double plays would be immortalized by Franklin P. Adams in baseball's second-most-famous poem. However, despite their achievements you rarely see the team ranked among the greatest of all time, nor do you read much about their surprising loss to the White Sox in 1906.

Their great upset victory was the pinnacle of the White Sox early years. Although the team would win over 90 games in 1907 and 1908, they would finish behind the pennant-winning Tigers. Most of the team would be out of baseball—retired or released—within a couple of years. Altrock's arm went bad in 1907, and he was never again the same hurler who matched outs with Three Finger Brown. Walsh, of course, would go on to a Hall of Fame career, and White would have his record, but most of the Hitless Wonders would fade into obscurity. Still, no one could take away the fact that in 1906 they staged the biggest World Series upset of all time.

THINK UMPIRES TAKE TOO MUCH ABUSE FROM PLAYERS? LATE LAST CENTURY, THEY OFTEN HAD TO FIGHT THEIR WAY OFF THE FIELD

Umpiring in the 1890s

RICH ELDRED

◆ ◆ ◆

Umpiring in the late nineteenth century was often perilous. Virulent and at times violent abuse from players, fans, owners, and reporters was common. Although baseball fans were disgusted by the constant turmoil, the magnates did nothing.

"The pay is good and you can't beat the hours," umpire Tim Hurst said, but in fact few men long endured working a game alone. Half a season, a year, were routine tenures. Most umpires were hired sight unseen by National League president Nick Young, and many were ex-ballplayers with no experience. Young's failure to rotate umpires—one man commonly worked an entire homestand or more—allowed minor tiffs to escalate into running feuds.

In one stretch of 1897, Tom Lynch handled 63 games involving Boston. On Labor Day, manager Frank Selee wrote Young asking for somebody else.

"I can only give decisions as I see them," Lynch told Tim Murnane of the Boston *Globe*. Dropping by the Boston *Herald* office before leaving town, he thanked baseball writer Jake Morse. "If all papers were as fair as the Herald, it would not be such bad work umpiring," Lynch told the *Herald*. Lynch's work was a "treat," Morse wrote on September 8, but he added his opinion that the league should use two umpires.

In times of inertia it takes a crisis to stir some action. One crisis occurred in August 1897 and the league's response had far-reaching implications.

On August 8 the Baltimore Orioles were in Boston. Naturally, Lynch was the umpire. In the eighth inning he kicked Joe Kelley and Arlie Pond off the Orioles' bench. "You're a big stiff," yelled Jack Doyle, Baltimore's first baseman. Lynch looked away. Passing by after the inning, Doyle suggested Lynch would get "trimmed" in Baltimore. Lynch thumbed him.

"Doyle followed Lynch up, thrice applying to him an epithet so vile and offensive as not to excuse but to demand physical retaliation," Bert Smalley wrote in the Boston *Record,* adding, "The epithet Doyle then used was too much to be endured, even by an umpire." When Doyle repeated it the second time, Lynch whirled around. "What's that you say?" As Smalley described it, "A third time the foul-mouthed player flung the insult in Lynch's teeth and Lynch struck him fairly between the eyes. The fierce minute's work that followed before the police and the players could pry the men apart had best be forgotten."

Observed Murnane: "The time will soon come when no person above the rank of garrotter can be secured to umpire a game."

"I for one admire Lynch's pluck and sand," Smalley declared. "Players of Doyle's stripe are fast making the game one that only a prize fighter or a thug has any business in."

The plucky Lynch, unable to open his left eye because of Doyle's head butt, went home to New Britain, Connecticut. He told Murnane that except in Boston, the team owners failed to back the umpires. New York owner Andrew Freedman, who complained that the umpires were incompetent and dishonest, was the worst crank, Lynch said.

Baltimore's owner/manager, Ned Hanlon, illustrated Tom's point. "Is it any wonder after the deal that Lynch gave the Baltimores on Friday that some of the players would have resented it?" he said. "It has been a general roast and this man Lynch is at heart a Boston man and I know it," he told the *Globe.*

Doyle defended his attack on Lynch. "I want to tell you one thing, that all with Irish blood in their veins will never stand being openly assaulted without retaliating," he told the Boston *Post.* "That is the first time in my life I ever raised my hand on the ballfield at any umpire."

Ashamed of the incident, Lynch sent Young his resignation. Nick refused it; he couldn't spare Lynch because umpire Tim Hurst was in jail. (More on this later.)

To fill in for Lynch while he was away, Young hired Bill Carpenter, a twenty-three-year-old umpire in the Maine State League. When Doyle batted, the crowd hissed. "Doyle has a crust like an alligator. . . . He simply faced the pavilion and clapped his hands," Murnane observed. One fan hollered, "Dirty ball, dirty ball." Baltimore catcher Bill Clarke told

Carpenter, "Don't judge us by the action of one man." He's right, Murnane said. "Ed Hanlon must blush at the language used by his men." Carpenter twice called for policemen when he ordered Baltimore players off the field. When Boston's Hugh Duffy ran in from left to argue, the Oriole bench "to a man commenced to cry, 'Police! Police!'"

And why was Tim Hurst in jail? It was because of something that happened in Cincinnati.

You could buy a mug of beer at the park in Cincinnati. Occasionally, unhappy fans gave the umpire a "crystal shower."

Later, explaining what had happened that fateful day, Hurst said, "I am sorry . . . but it is done and cannot be helped now. . . . The crowd kept jeering me but I paid no attention until a heavy beer mug struck me on the foot. I turned in time to see another coming. I picked up the first one and threw it underhanded into the crowd. I did not throw it at any particular person. . . . I lost my temper and this is the result." The "result" was that a fan was hospitalized with severe head injuries.

Hurst was arrested and charged with assault to kill. He put up a $300 bond and left town, but the man's condition slipped and, at the request of the Cincinnati police chief, Hurst was picked up during the Pittsburgh-St. Louis game. After spending the night on a bed in the jury room, he was released on $500 bond.

Reappointment is out of the question, Murnane thought. "Hurst is a most companionable fellow, the wittiest of entertainers and a good friend. He never drinks or uses tobacco." But "public sentiment will condemn him."

Despite his occasional problems Hurst had long success, and it wasn't owing to gentle diplomacy. One time, Bert Smalley wrote in the Boston *Record* on July 28, 1897, Tim "put his mouth close to the player's ear and said coolly, 'Now you're getting a bit chesty, I see you've made a couple of good stops, knocked out a couple of hits and you think you're solid with the crowd. Well, I'll just tell you something. I'll give you the key to my room at the hotel, where everything is nice and quiet, and when we get in there alone I'll break that jaw of yours so you can't kick for the rest off the season. I'll see that you get out quietly so you can explain your injury by saying you fell down somewhere.'" The kicker didn't take the key.

Joe Kelley told Hurst, "If I was Hanlon you'd never umpire another game in Baltimore."

"What? Not be allowed to umpire in this city for a lot of swell gentlemen like your crowd? Now, Kel, don't say that, old boy, for you know all the umpires are stuck on you people."

Hurst called a Brooklyn player out at home. The player retorted, "You're a nice duck, ain't you. Why, he didn't come within a yard of me. Say, Tim, I know your girl in Philadelphia." Hurst whipped out his notebook and pencil. "When any of my friends so forgets themselves as to speak to such a yellow ballplayer as you, I scratch them," he said as he erased the name.

As Hurst explained to Tim Murnane, "You see, I don't let these people bother me in the least. . . . If a man takes these ballplayers seriously it is only a matter of a very short time until they drive him to drink or to a madhouse."

But unfortunately for league president Young, the players were winning. Jack Sheridan quit and Bob Emslie was hurt. Four of Young's seven-man staff were in trouble.

"Altogether I am very badly off for umpires and don't know where to look for recruits," Young said. "I sincerely hope there may be extenuating circumstances in Hurst's case."

Young, sitting in his Washington office (besides serving as league president he worked as a clerk for the Treasury Department), reflected on "the toughest week for umpires in all my experience," which dated from 1871. Heaving a sigh and looking forlorn, he remarked, "I don't know where to get acceptable men to umpire if this thing continues. . . . Here is Connolly of the New England League, said to be one of the best men in the business, [he] positively declines to accept an appointment." (Connolly had refused in '96 also.) "And Dan Campbell begged off until umpiring was semi-respectable. . . . John Sheridan sat in a chair right at my desk and vowed he could not stand the personal abuse heaped on him by certain players, managers and newspapers. He vowed to me that he had not taken a drink of liquor since the season began, notwithstanding the charge made against him by Ned Hanlon."

Young noted that he'd be in a "pretty fix" if not for Bob Emslie and Lynch. "Lynch is a sick man and he needs a few weeks' rest. He intended to go to the seashore to build up his constitution," but could not be spared. "Bob Emslie received a sharp blow over his left lung and coughed up a large clot of blood," but was still calling them. Al Reach recommended John Kelly of the Pennsylvania Interstate League, and Nick signed him pronto.

Eventually, Young felt himself compelled to resign from his federal sinecure to give full attention to the umpire problem.

The *Globe*'s Tim Murnane went to New Britain, Connecticut, to talk with Tom Lynch. (Lynch, who worked at the Opera House during the winter and was "considered a man of executive ability," was himself the National League president years later.) Murnane and Lynch discussed

Jack Sheridan. "The players simply broke poor Jack's heart," Lynch said. "I saw him at the Ashland House yesterday and he told me the players abused him until he could stand it no longer. While he was in Pittsburgh I sent him a telegram telling him to stick it out. . . . He told me that the message cheered him up for several days. . . . The poor fellow cried like a child as he went over his troubles for Sheridan and was the soul of honor," Lynch said. Murnane concurred: Sheridan was "always impartial and fearless until slimy-tongued players abused him and he lost heart for the position."

On August 9, Murnane reviewed the season up to then, and one wonders why only Sheridan quit.

Early on, Cleveland's Jesse Burkett, "well educated by [manager Patsy] Tebeau," threatened to "whip" Michael McDermont after a game. A Louisville crowd mobbed Sheridan and when he called Lajoie out for deliberately getting hit by a pitch, several Philadelphia players tried to slug him.

In Pittsburgh, a mob "grossly insulted" Tim Hurst. Tim knocked down one fan, precipitating a general row, and fifteen police escorted him out. "A block away a man hit Hurst in the back of the head and the umpire promptly sent his assailant to the grass too. The mob was closing in now and Hurst, breaking through, jumped on a trolley car and took the first train out of town."

When McDermont forfeited a game to New York and fined Pittsburgh's Dick Padden, Frank Killian, and Pat Donovan $25 each, the Pirates kicked out the dressing-room windows. Later, McDermont fired a punch at Jim Rogers of Louisville.

In Chicago, Lynch called a Colt safe at home. Boston catcher Fred Lake protested and Cap Anson got into it. Lake tried to bop Cap. "Lynch, in trying to separate the belligerents, handled the 'old man' [Anson] a bit roughly, whereupon Anse squared off at him. Lynch then grabbed the broom with which he swept the plate and made a swipe at the Chicago captain, who ducked. Then Lynch put Anson out of the game." The police dragged Monte Cross off the field and fined him $25.

On July 10, Sheridan was pelted with rotten eggs. On the same day, in Louisville, Lynch tossed Clarke and Davis out of the first game of a doubleheader, then, after a "wild row," refused to umpire the second game. Jim Wolf filled in. New York, Louisville's opponent, was ahead 7–2 in the ninth when Mike Sullivan and then Amos Rusie lost the plate. When Tom McCreary walked, forcing in the tying run, and the Giants surrounded Wolf, the crowd charged the field. "Joyce tried to punch Wolf and Parke Wilson struck Hach of Louisville in the face. In the midst of the row, when a policeman was hauling Wilson off the field, Pickering of Louisville scored the tying run."

On July 22, Pink Hawley of Cincinnati decked Sheridan with a shot to the jaw. Jack ejected him. In the second game, the crowd brought bags of rotten eggs and bombarded Sheridan again. In another game, Heine Peitz, the Reds' catcher, charged Hurst. Tim jolted him in the tummy with his mask and Peitz smashed Hurst in the mouth, drawing blood.

Murnane concluded: "There are more games lost by woodenheaded players failing to exercise their alleged 'thinkers'. . . than by erroneous decisions of the umpires." About the latter, Murnane said, Hurst, Lynch, and Emslie were the best men. Sheridan was before he went backsliding. "O'Day is honest but loses his head too easily," McDonald is good if he's left alone, and McDermont is "just fair."

But not all men were as nifty with their fists as Mr. Hurst, and the $1,500 salary wasn't attracting anyone. Cincinnati pitcher Frank Dwyer donned the mask for a day. The Reds were down 3–2 in the ninth with two out and the bases loaded. Dwyer called Bid McPhee out on strikes. "The air became blue," Murnane wrote. "Dwyer's associates were hot enough to mob him. Few players would have acted as honestly as Dwyer." (Dwyer and Bill Carpenter later became full-time umpires.)

With all this happening, the time was never better for strong, united action by the magnates. Typically, they did nothing.

Lynch returned to his post. Hurst, found guilty of attempted murder in Cincinnati (the victim recovered), was fined $100 plus court costs. Jack Sheridan was gone for good.

In September, Andrew Freedman docked in New York City, fully rejuvenated from his annual European vacation, and immediately blasted his favorite targets.

The Giants would be second except for rotten umpires in Cincinnati, he told Murnane. "The players there are a lot of loafers and the umpires we had to submit to were thoroughly incompetent." Who was to blame? "Nick Young. He is dominated by a bad influence [John T. Brush]. When we were in the west we were furnished with the worst and now that we have returned home we have two umpires and always the best the league affords. I have no complaint to make to this, because we play only clean ball." Sure you do, but what about the Reds? "They are a lot of loafers and will not receive any courtesies from me. They have won game after game by unfair means and their tactics are sanctified by the Cincinnati management. . . . As long as that team is in the hands that it is, it will not succeed."

The other owners were not pleased with Freedman's comments. "Mr. Freedman has made some serious charges in his recent interviews," said Brooklyn owner Charles Byrne. "He has charged umpires with being drunk," and picking on New York. ". . . He is reckless and doesn't care what he says."

In case he hadn't assured his termination, Tim Hurst chattered away with Murnane: "What do you think of that stiff Freedman? Here he goes and abuses Mr. Young as if he were a pickpocket. . . . Why that man works 20 out of every 24 hours of his life for the National League. . . . Making such cracks about Nick Young is enough to give a decent man the pip. The league ought to get after this Bowery boy and throw him into a tank."

The *Herald*'s Jake Morse concurred: "The league could not replace Mr. Young."

But of course they could replace Mr. Hurst.

The American League, just over the horizon in the late 1890s, succeeded where others failed, for many reasons. By 1900 people were sick of lawless National League ball. Ban Johnson's reputation was that he brooked no challenge to the umpire's authority, and the press expended barrels of ink extolling him in 1901, when Ban faced similar troubles. While Johnson's disciplinary actions were tempered by box-office considerations, he won nearly unanimous approval in print, even from National League partisans. And across the tracks, Andy Freedman banned umpire Billy Nash from the New York grounds and openly mocked and threatened Nick Young. The contrast wasn't lost on the fans.

Maybe the American League would have made it even if the National League had run a tighter ship, but no other rival had.

One of Johnson's original umpires was Tommy Connolly, who had twice turned Young down. He lasted until 1931 and was elected to the Hall of Fame in 1953.

"I am glad to have the opportunity to be with Johnson," Connolly told *Sporting Life.* "I'll get a chance to get backed up. In my last venture in the National League, I fined eleven men in two weeks and not a fine went. All the rules in the world will not help the game if the umpires are not supported."

Johnson also hired Jack Sheridan. On the way to his first assignment, Jack got off the train in Missouri and began directing an imaginary game in the middle of Main Street. He was hospitalized for "mental derangement." Drink was responsible, Johnson lamented. Fortunately, Sheridan recovered rapidly and went on to umpire fourteen years in the American League.

After being fired by Nick Young, Hurst signed on as manager of St. Louis for 1898. His team had a dismal (39–111) record. Amazingly, Hurst was rehired by Young.

He didn't last long. This time, Murnane wrote, Hurst "has himself to blame for his luck, for besides poor umping, he has added a foul mouth to his work."

There's no backing, Tim told his pal Jake Morse. "I got tired of it. What's the use? There was only one way—grin and bear it."

Even on the fringes of baseball, Hurst was beloved by the scribes and remained one of sport's most quoted men. Annually, Morse and others wondered why Ban Johnson didn't grab such a fine ump. In 1905 Ban broke down and signed him up.

But Tim's pugnacious, both-guns-blazing approach was not what Johnson wanted. When Tim spat in Eddie Collins' face, "because I don't like college men," Ban let him go.

In a way it was the end of an era. There have been incidents since then, but never again would an umpire have to brawl his way to the top or face the relentless barrage of scorn that defined umpiring in the 1890s.

Did the Babe Call His Shot? (Part I)

PETE WILLIAMS

◆ ◆ ◆

When I think back over the great deeds of sport that I have witnessed and think particularly of the ones that have warmed my heart and made it glow beyond all cynicism, I remember with most pleasure the last World Series in which Ruth played, back in 1932, and which involved the New York Yankees and the Chicago Cubs. The game took place in Chicago, and Root was pitching for the Western team. The Cubs were giving Ruth an unmerciful riding down on the field, and the sallies were deliberately vicious and foul, having chiefly to do with his origin, upon which, as I have indicated, there may be considerable speculation. He had already hit one home run, and when he came to bat in the latter part of the game, the entire Cub bench came out to the edge of the dugout and began to shout filth and abuse at him.

Root put over the first pitch and Ruth swung at it and missed. There was a great roar of delight from the partisan crowd, which hated everything that came from New York, and the players redoubled their insults. Ruth held up one finger so that everyone could see it. He was indicating that that was just one strike. The crowd hooted him. Root pitched again and Ruth missed for the second time, and the park rocked with laughter. The Cub players grew louder and more raucous. The Babe held up two fingers. The crowd razzed him, and there was nothing good-natured about it, because his magnificent effrontery was goading them badly.

Two balls, wide pitches, intervened. And at this point, Ruth made the most marvelous and impudent gesture I have ever seen. With his forefinger extended *he pointed to the flagpole in center field, the farthest point removed from the plate. There was no mistaking his meaning. He was advising crowd, pitcher, and jeering Cubs that that was the exact spot where Root's next pitch would leave the park.*

The incensed crowd gave forth a long drawn-out and lusty "Booooooo!" Ruth made them choke on it by slugging the ball out of the premises at exactly that point, the center-field flagpole, for his second home run of the day and probably the only home run in the entire history of baseball that was ever called in advance, as to both time and place.

—Paul Gallico, 1938

Gallico was writing six years after the event, in his book *A Farewell to Sport*. The sportswriter is the ultimate fan, and Gallico can serve as a convenient and typical example. The sportswriter can willingly suspend disbelief. He can make his villains more loathsome and his heroes more divine. And sometimes he can go further than the simple distortion of reality to create a new reality—a falsehood that becomes popularly accepted truth and genuine myth. This is precisely what happened when my father, the late Joe Williams, reported on Babe Ruth's fifth-inning home run at Wrigley Field in the 1932 World Series. Whatever happened on the field that day was transformed by Williams and writers who followed his lead into a Bunyanesque tall tale so powerful that reasonable men like Gallico, even when they were shown it was false, refused to, or could not, abandon belief.

When the Yanks arrived in Chicago after sweeping the first two games of this unforgettable fall classic, the fans were in a mood to install a new god. Indeed, they already had their candidate picked out. John Drebinger reported in *The New York Times* on the throng that greeted their train at the La Salle Street station: "At once a great roar went up for Babe Ruth, who was almost swallowed up by the crowd the moment he alighted from his car." And these were Cub fans. The public mood was such that a miracle, while presumably not specifically expected, would certainly be received without cold and rigorous scrutiny.

The inning-by-inning account in *The New York Times* said that Ruth "hit a tremendous drive . . . for his second homer of the game." But there were hints that some writers had seen something more. Robert Creamer, the author of the critically acclaimed biography *Babe*, quotes the account in the *San Francisco Examiner* as saying Ruth "called his shot." *The Times*'s Drebinger wrote, "Ruth came up in the fifth and in no mistaken motions the Babe notified the crowd that the nature of his retaliation would be a wallop right out [of] the confines of the park." But the New York *World-Telegram's* Williams was the only writer who said this:

> The Bambino hit two homers during the day, each of them a record breaker, and on the occasion of his second round-tripper even went so far as to call his shot. . . . In the fifth, with the Cubs riding him unmercifully from the bench, Ruth pointed to center field and punched a screaming liner to a spot where no ball ever had been hit before.

Nobody else has said Ruth had pointed to center. In fact, the headline over Williams's column said, with little ambiguity: "RUTH CALLS SHOT AS HE PUTS HOMER NO. 2 IN SIDE POCKET." Creamer notes this column and goes on to say, "Williams was a positive, opinionated observer and a vigorous journalist. . . . I believe that Williams' strong personality and the wide circulation given his original story in Scripps-Howard newspapers got the legend started and kept it going."

Now the other writers jumped on the bandwagon. Two days after the game was reported in the press, Tom Meany of the *World-Telegram* wrote the Babe had "pointed out the spot in which he intended hitting his homer." Gallico wrote "He pointed like a duelist to the spot where he expected to send his rapier home." One day later, another New York writer, Bill Corum, said Ruth "pointed out where he was going to hit the next one, and hit it there," although, as Creamer points out, Corum said no such thing when he wrote the game up on October 2. That these first few days established the myth firmly is reflected in the fact that both the *Reach* and the *Spalding Guides* for 1933 assume that Ruth called his shot.

The mythmaking was not quite over. Some three weeks later the one called shot became two. Again Williams was the reporter, although the source of the larger fiction seems to have been either Ruth or a nameless scriptwriter. The occasion was a radio show on which Ruth appeared, and which had been arranged by Williams's close friend, the flamboyant press agent Steve Hannagan. Were these Hannagan's words, spoken by the Babe?

> Mr. Ruth was asked if he really believed he was going to hit those home runs when he came to the plate.
>
> "I knew I wanted to hit them, but of course I wasn't sure. That's what gave me such a big kick—hitting 'em after saying I was going to. I've hit more than 650 home runs, but those two I hit off Charlie Root will always stand out above them all."
>
> As an afterthought Mr. Ruth roared into the mike:—
>
> "Can you imagine what a mug I would have been if I had missed them? Say, those people in Chicago would be laughing at me yet—and I wouldn't blame them, either."

This amplified version of the legend lasts, at least in Williams's columns and mind, for nearly three years. The last mention of *two* called shots occurs in May 1935, in a piece Williams devotes to athletes who "had the stuff to back up" their boasts:

> There was Ruth that time he called his shots against the Cubs in the 1932 World Series, twice driving home runs to the exact spot he designated, this being probably the most spectacular demonstration of self-belief in the history of baseball.

No serious revision of the legend begins until 1937, nearly five years after the event. There are primarily three versions of what Ruth actually did. One, he gestured toward the Cub dugout, threatening to slice a pitch in the direction of his hecklers; two, he was simply raising his finger to indicate he had one strike left; three, the gesture (and maybe it was also a raised middle finger) was meant for Root.

The first of these gains considerable legitimacy in that it is the version adopted in 1937 by Ruth himself, and offered to reporters while he was playing golf. According to Williams:

> In the course of the round, somebody brought up the inevitable question—his greatest thrill. He wasn't sure. The day he fanned Cobb, Crawford and Veach on nine pitched balls with the bases full would always linger in his memory. So would that home run he hit against the Chicago Cubs in the 1932 World Series. This was when he pointed to the center field flag pole, announced to one and all the next pitch would go exactly there for four bases—and it did.
>
> To many people this was the most dramatic moment in the history of modern baseball. To the Babe, it develops, it was a fluke. He wasn't trying to hit a home run at all. He was trying to hook a ball into the dugout of the Cubs, who had been riding him for an hour or more.
>
> "That Grimm and those other guys were giving me hell, so I thought I would foul off a couple into the dugout just to have some fun. The first two pitches were outside—at least I thought they were—but the umpire called them strikes. The next one was in the same spot. I said to myself, 'He may call this one a strike, too, so I'll cut it into the dugout.'
>
> I swung too true. The ball went over the fence. True enough, I had pointed there, but what I wanted to do was ram the ball down Grimm's throat."

The obvious inconsistency here is that Ruth said he did point to the fence, but doesn't explain why. Still, he plainly says he was trying to slice one into the Cubs' dugout. This version is possibly supported by two columns written the day after the game, both quoted by Creamer. Philadelphia writer Jimmy Isaminger said the homer was preceded by "a satiric gesture to the Cub bench," and Westbrook Pegler said Ruth made "a warning gesture of his hand to [Guy] Bush" just before hitting it. After the fans had begun tossing lemons on the field in the second inning, Ruth had *successfully* fouled a ball into the stands. Wrote Williams:

> Sewell got a base on balls. . . . This brought up Ruth and a grandstand fan let go a lemon at him. Ruth retaliated with a three-cushion shot of a curve ball, which went into the stands and caused no inconsiderable amount of ducking and scurrying.

This is the version accepted by both Gehrig and Ruth's buddy, boxer Mickey Walker, as reported by Williams:

> The most fascinating stories, unhappily, are not always true. Biographers assure us George Washington felled no cherry tree, the she wolf did not wet nurse Romulus and Will Tell wasted no arrows shooting apples off junior's noggin. And now comes reliable testimony that Babe Ruth didn't call that celebrated home run.
> It comes, singularly, from a prize fighter, yet not so singularly when it is pointed out that Mickey Walker and the Babe were the best of pals.
> There came a night when the Babe and Walker and a kindred soul, Jack Schaefer, a hotel man and ardent sports follower, were sitting around nibbling on nutritious, body-building scotch, and the fighter put the question flatly to the old King of Swat, then retired: Did he or did he not call the home run he hit off Charley Root in the 1932 World Series? He didn't.
> "I had two strikes on me and the pitcher was levelling with speed curves," the fighter quotes Ruth. "We were kiddin' one another and I swept my arm, motioning to the outfield, trying to rib him into a fast ball. I was waiting for the pitch and when it came I belted the ball over the center-field fence."
> The ball went into the center-field bleachers, not out of the park. . . . There *was* an immense amount of "kiddin'" (except it was razzing) and the ringleader was Guy Bush, another Cub pitcher, who, propped against a dugout, was directing a flow of invective at Ruth through cupped hands. And Ruth did make the gesture: in fact, he made several gestures, some even before the second strike.

It was just as easy to believe Ruth had actually called the shot as not and it made a wonderful story, so the press box went along with it. First intimation I got that not everybody in baseball concurred was at a dinner in Newark one night. I happened to be seated between Lou Gehrig and Joe McCarthy. I disremember how the subject came up, but Gehrig laughed: "The gestures were meant for Bush. Ruth was going to foul one into the dugout, but when the pitch came up, big and fat, he belted it." McCarthy only smiled quizzically.

The second revision of the legend, that Ruth was indicating he had two strikes on him and therefore one chance left, was Gabby Hartnett's. The Cub catcher's book was reviewed by Williams in 1950:

> From now on it's going to take some mighty powerful persuasion to convince Virginia there's a Santa Claus. Particularly after what Gabby Hartnett's done to the most fantastic of all the Babe Ruth legends—you know, the one about him calling his shot in the '32 World Series.
>
> It came in the fifth-inning. . . . All the while Ruth was at bat the Cubs, led by Guy Bush, a pitcher, had been trying to heckle the big fellow. Ruth was more amused than annoyed. From time to time he'd look toward the enemy dugout back of third, jabber something and laugh like crazy. He made several gestures. I have a distinct memory that once he pointed the bat at Bush who stood on the top step in the dugout. And just before he hit the home run from which Hartnett would now divest of the grand, matchless theater which has been associated with it for so many years, he did motion in the general direction of the stands in right center. I can still see him doing it. . . .
>
> But Hartnett says, no, that's not the way it was. Ruth waved his hand across the plate toward the Cub bench. At the same time he said—and I think only the umpire and myself heard him—'it only takes one to hit it.'

The third possibility, that Ruth was gesturing at Root, is mentioned in Tom Meany's 1947 biography of Ruth.

We do know this: One, Root was a Cub. Two, Root was standing directly between Ruth and center field. And wouldn't this explain the apparent contradiction in Ruth's own account? If Ruth was threatening only the Cub bench, he would be gesturing only in that direction; couldn't he have been threatening Root, too?

I have a recent letter from Ruth's teammate, outfielder Ben Chapman. Chapman's version, which sounds remarkably like Ruth's, suggests just such an interpretation. "Root knocked Babe down and Babe pointed at center field," says Chapman, "but he was telling Root what he thought— he really let him have [it], *but* he did not call his shot."

Was the myth suffering because of these new revelations? Not on your life. While the writers were viewing the events of October 1, 1932 in a more coldly factual light, the hero they had created was keeping the fiction alive. In his autobiography Ruth embellished further. Not only had he called the homer, Ruth wrote, but he'd planned it the night before the game. The writer-fans who had forced the story on the Babe no longer believed it, but the Babe, ironically, had by now become a man of the faith.

Did Ruth call his shot? It's yesterday's news that he probably did not. My father, forgetting his seminal column, later maintained he did not. Did Ruth think he had called it? My father told me Ruth had gradually come to think he did. So their roles over the years had become reversed. Does it make any difference? Maybe Ruth was right in adhering to the story as a higher truth: a romantic vision. As late as 1965 Gallico reaffirmed his orthodoxy by remembering in *The Golden People* "that fantastic day in Chicago, when Root of the Cubs had two strikes on him and the Babe called his shot by pointing to the flagpole in center field and then hit the next pitch to the very same spot for a home run. Not only the World Series crowd and those of us in the press box, but practically every home in America thrilled as though the feat had been accomplished by our own son.

And even long after he came to see there was no truth to one of baseball's most celebrated legends, a legend whose seeds he had inadvertently sown, my father had this to say:

This much I do know. Even if Ruth didn't mean it, the thunderous drama still lives in my memory. And no amount of testimony to the contrary is ever going to change it in the slightest. I always was a pushover for wonderful fairy tales, anyway.

NOT ONCE, NOT TWICE, BUT . . . .

Did the Babe Call His Shot? (Part II)

DON BELL

♦ ♦ ♦

Forty years after Babe Ruth's death, a unique home movie of his famous 1932 called-shot home run surfaced in Louisville, Kentucky. The film was shot by a Chicago printer, Matt Kandle, who was sitting behind home plate at Wrigley Field with a 16-mm Kodak box camera during the third Yanks vs. Cubs World Series match when Ruth apparently signalled his intention, then hit the ball out of the park. Now in the possession of his great grandson, Kirk Kandle, an advertising copywriter with the Louisville Courier-Journal, *the film, which had been stored over the years in the family film archives and more or less forgotten, has been seen by only a handful of people.*

Don Bell, a Canadian writer and baseball buff who heard about the film, flew to Kentucky to look at the rare footage, the only visual record known to exist of Ruth hitting his controversial homer. This is an excerpt, with a few added details, from his story which appeared in the New York Village Voice.

I must confess, my first viewing of the film on the WAVE-TV control-room monitor was a disappointment, and for a brief panicky moment I thought that the trip to Louisville would end up as a strikeout. Fanned with the bases loaded. Great expectations—then *whiff!* Mired in some drought-stricken wasteland, miles from home plate. Kentucky is for horses and asses, not baseball smurfs.

Yes, Ruth is seen pointing in the batter's box, a wonderful, sweeping theatrical gesture, once simultaneously as Cubs catcher Gabby Harnett scoops up a low outside pitch, and again as Hartnett fires the ball back to Charlie Root. Bat in his left hand, resting on his right shoulder, and his right hand extended, very distinctly, pointing, not once but *twice.*

Problem is, this is followed by another pitch, a called strike, and it's only on the third of the three pitches we see in the sequence that Ruth homers. If this is the case, then it would, technically, destroy the legend that Ruth pointed just before his swing. Back to the boondocks, kiddo, no story.

"Uh . . . Kirk . . . I. . . ."

"Didn't you see it?"

"What?"

"He pointed just before he creamed the ball. But it happened so fast."

We asked technician Steve Prince if he could put the film through again.

"There. You see."

"He did something . . . but it's so quick. It's too bad we can't watch it in slow motion."

"That would be interesting," Kirk said. Up to now, nobody had ever seen the film in slow motion. On his home videocassette, he could stop the film completely, but it produced a fuzzy, streaky image, hard to evaluate. Steve said that if we dubbed the old print onto videotape and watched it on the station's Tektronix color monitor, we'd be able to slow it down, watch it at our own pace, frame by frame if so desired.

So Kirk, setting the condition that the videotape be erased immediately after the screening, told Steve to go ahead, and in a few minutes we're watching it on the color monitor, and, by God, it's like connecting for a game-winning homer on a tricky curve ball that seemed just out of reach.

What the film shows (It runs two minutes and 25 seconds) is this—let's take it from the top:

It opens with scenes of a band marching on the field. There are atmosphere shots of players, fans, and the temporary outfield bleachers, which validates this as a World Series. Bunting hangs all around the grandstand decks. Then there's a burst of patriotism as players troop across the infield holding the edges of an enormous, undulating Stars and Stripes.

Eventually, we see Ruth, the game's third hitter, standing at the plate; the film doesn't record it but it is known that every time Ruth came to bat, he was met with hoots, catcalls, and lemons that were thrown on the field. We see him reacting by clouting his first homer, a three-run shot deep into the right-center-field bleachers.

Next comes a bit where Matt, always the funster, ran footage of a player circling the bases backwards: home plate, third, second, first, batter's box. It may be Gehrig, who also hit two homers in the game.

The next thing on the film is the called-shot sequence. Now let's watch very carefully what happens:

First, we see the outside pitch, most likely a ball, which Harnett drops. This is the sequence we already mentioned. Ruth points twice, defiantly, like an animal; you can almost feel his growling, though there's a bit of horseplay in the gesture as well. More than anything, he looks like a wrestler expressing exaggerated theatrical savagery. It's hard to believe he's only calling the count, which has often been suggested: he's pointing with his right hand, but in the language of baseball, a left hand or no hand at all signifies a ball, the right hand a strike. Yet there doesn't seem to be any concrete meaning to the gesture. Maybe he's just brusquely replying to the Cubs bench jockeys and the fans who are berating him.

The next pitch is a called strike. Then there seems to be an in-camera edit. Of course. Matt's style wouldn't be to run the film continuously. According to the literature of the called shot, Ruth stepped out of the box before the crucial pitch; most likely he did step out and Matt, intent only on capturing Ruth's at bat and not wanting to waste any film, stopped the camera. He also changed the angle just slightly, resuming his shooting over the left shoulder of the fan seated in front of him rather than the right. But everything else is in place: Ruth, the catcher, and the umpire are exactly where we left them.

Now watch closely. The film is slowed down. Slow, slow. . . . Charlie Root is starting his wind-up.

And then Ruth points!

Very quickly—his right hand off the bat for just an instant. But he *points!*

And then he points *again,* just before Root pitches, but not as he pointed after the first pitch, not an extended, arm-sweeping motion.

Rather, he points like he's cocking a gun, like he means it, a killer gesture; his arm levered, then a staccato wrist movement, like a marksman aiming a pistol, or a duelist! The arm up in the air, then down. Then pumped up and down once more, blindingly fast, the instant before Root releases the ball. *Bang, bang,* bye-bye. . . .

A split second later—this is all part of the majestic arithmetic of the movement—the pitch is made and the Babe lifts up his leg and pounds the pitch with every drop of juice he has, twisting around after he connects. Oh, what a sublime, consummate swing! He just remains there for an instant in baseball heaven, corkscrewed up and frozen, and Charlie

Root too is still, paralyzed, shoulders slumped (yup, he should have brushed him back). And then the Bambino is off and running toward first base. Halfway, we lose him for a second—the spectator in front of Matt has stood up—and then we catch him again as he rounds first. But now everyone is standing and all Matt can catch on his little camera are backs, plenty of backs. End of movie.

What can we conclude? My feeling after watching the film some twenty times at various speeds and stopping it at will is that Ruth, in fact, called his shot *four* times. Twice in the first sequence, which was more a flamboyant, general statement of intent than anything telepathic. But more definitely, more precisely, in the two cocking-the-gun-and-shooting gestures just before Root hurled the ball.

There is an interesting irony in the fact that baseball's most celebrated home run should be termed the called "shot." The word *shot*. The Yankees' Murderers' Row. *Bang*. Okay, fellas, this is Babe offering you his Saturday Night Special and you'll never forget it.

Babe was pure beast, "the most uninhibited human being I have ever known," as *The New York Times*'s John Drebinger described him. His home run was nonverbal, a no-mind *action*. A supernal celebration, an electrifying, pure event. A summation of everything the Slambambino stood for.

The only other at bat that rivals Ruth's for sheer drama and mythmaking is Casey's. But the fictional slugger of Mudville let everyone down in the crunch by biting the dust—he didn't live up to expectations. Ruth did. Forty-one years after his death, fifty-seven years after his homer, we still remember him as arch-hero, not loser. The world is full of Caseys, but there was only one Ruth.

As the Babe himself often replied when asked what he would have done if he'd whiffed on the pitch, "I'd surely have looked like an awful ass, wouldn't I?"

MAJOR LEAGUE BASEBALL'S ONLY FATAL INJURY

The Ray Chapman Beaning

R I C H A R D   D E R B Y

♦ ♦ ♦

Ray Chapman, the only player killed in a major league game, was one of the most popular performers ever to wear a Cleveland uniform. From the time he joined the Indians late in the 1912 season at age twenty-one until his death, he was the club's regular shortstop. He broke in by hitting .312 in 31 games in 1912 and during the eight seasons that followed he hit .300 or better three more times. In 1917 Ray batted .302, stole 52 bases, and scored 98 runs. Two seasons later he hit an even .300, and he was a few points over that level at the time of the 1920 tragedy.

Although he was only twenty-nine, Chapman was thinking of quitting the game after the 1920 season in favor of a business career. He had earlier married Kathleen Daly, the daughter of the president of the East Ohio Gas Company. "I'll play next year [1920] because I want to help give Tris [manager Tris Speaker], Mr. Dunn [owner James Dunn], and Cleveland the first pennant the city has ever had," he was quoted as saying. "Then I will talk about quitting, but I want to help bring that championship here first."

On Monday, August 16, 1920 the Indians were engaged in a game against the Yankees on a gloomy, rainy day in the Polo Grounds. Carl Mays was pitching for New York. Mays was not a popular player with either his opponents or his teammates and had a reputation as a headhunter.

Chapman led off the fifth inning. He had a habit of crowding the plate, and Mays may have decided to pitch inside to avoid Ray's drag-bunt specialty. As the first pitch was delivered Chapman stood motion-

Carl Mays   *Ray Chapman*

less with his head nearly over the plate. The pitch struck him on the head. He made no attempt to back away from the pitch and presumably was fooled by the delivery.

There is considerable confusion as to what happened next. Roger Peckinpaugh, who was playing shortstop for the Yankees, claimed the ball was fielded by third baseman Aaron Ward. Other versions have Muddy Ruel, New York's catcher, fielding the ball. Still others, including Jack Graney, Chappie's roommate who was watching from the Cleveland bench, claim the ball was fielded by Mays. This latter version is supported by accounts in the Cleveland *Plain Dealer.*

A few moments after being struck, Chapman regained consciousness and was helped to his feet. He tried to walk but could not and slumped to the ground in deep unconsciousness, bleeding from both ears. A doctor hurried from the grandstand and gave first aid. Chapman was carried to the clubhouse and then taken to St. Lawrence Hospital.

Cleveland held a 3–0 lead at the time and, with Stan Coveleski owning a four-hit shutout going into the ninth inning, eventually won, 4–3. Ironically, the run set up by the mishap turned out to be the decisive margin. Harry Lunte went in to run for Chapman and was forced at second base by Speaker. Larry Gardner singled Speaker to third, and Steve

O'Neill then knocked in what proved to be the winning run. Mays continued to pitch for New York until being lifted for a pinch-hitter in the eighth inning.

Later that evening, some eight hours after the accident, New York surgeons operated on Chapman. His skull was crushed in on one side and X-rays showed a fracture on the opposite side. By five o'clock the following morning Ray was dead.

His body was returned from New York on a train and removed at the East 105th Street station. Accompanying the body back to Cleveland were Mrs. Chapman, Speaker, and Joe Wood. Mrs. Chapman had been summoned to New York but had not arrived until a few hours after Ray's death. To lessen her grief, friends convinced her not to view the remains until returning to Cleveland.

Ray was buried on August 20. Many baseball notables attended the funeral, which was held at St. John's Cathedral. Thirty-four priests participated in the service. On Chapman's grave was placed a blanket made of more than 20,000 blossoms purchased by his fans at a dime apiece. Speaker and Graney were so overcome by grief that they could not attend the funeral.

The tributes to Chapman were many. "I can't say the things Ray Chapman deserves," declared his closest friend, Speaker. "He was an inspiration to the whole team both with his playing and his personality. . . . I would not mind losing the pennant if it meant Ray was coming back next year."

"There wasn't a better man anywhere," commented Nap Lajoie, the retired former Cleveland star. "He loved the game and even now hadn't reached his best. He was the kind who was continually improving and learning."

Yankee manager Miller Huggins offered this tribute: "The game has lost one of the finest men who ever wore a uniform. He was a credit to baseball as a man and as a player. Second only to Speaker himself, Ray Chapman was the man we had to fear at bat and in the field. He was one of the fastest in the game and off the field one of the best. Baseball has lost a man it will be hard to replace."

The death of Chapman completely demoralized the club for a spell. At the time the Indians were engaged in a tight three-team race. The victory on the day of the tragedy left them in first place with a 71–40 record, followed by the White Sox at 72–42 and the Yankees at 72–44. Because of Ray's death, the August 17 game was called off. The Indians then lost to the Yankees the following day, 4–3, when Wally Pipp tagged Jim Bagby for a two-run homer in the ninth inning. According to Chapman's roommate Graney, "We feel as if we did not care if we ever played baseball again. . . . We cannot imagine ourselves playing with Chapman dead. We did not sleep last night and we cannot eat today." The Indians' staunchest supporters gave them up as pennant contenders.

But the club struggled on. Speaker finally returned to action on August 22 although he was almost too weak to swing the bat. With the addition a short time later of pitcher Duster Mails and Joe Sewell, who took over Chapman's shortstop spot, the Indians gained a new lease on life and fought their way to the first pennant in Cleveland's history.

Did Mays intend to hit Chapman? Speaker said the Cleveland players did not feel that Mays was to blame. According to Graney, "While we feel it was solely an accident that took Chappie from us, we are unanimous in not wanting ever to bat against Carl Mays again. We don't think Mays tried to dust Chappie off. Neither did he try to dust any of the other boys off yesterday, but we think he has in the past. A batter has a chance to dodge the fastball thrown by an ordinary pitcher, but Mays has a freak delivery and his fastball has a sudden dip to it that never gives a batter a chance to dodge."

Ty Cobb, although not present, expressed much the same opinion. "I will say that Carl Mays and I never got along," the Detroit star said. "I dodged a lot of them from him, which gave me dark suspicions. Yet keep in mind that he was a submariner with a delivery that started around his knees, resulting in curious breaks of the ball and a tendency for it to sail toward a batter's skull. I believe it is for no one to say that there was purposeful intent behind that pitch."

Perhaps the most eloquent of all were the words attributed to Mays himself as quoted in the November 1920 issue of *Baseball Magazine*. "It is an episode which I shall always regret more than anything that has ever happened to me," Mays declared, "and yet I can look into my own conscience and feel absolved of all personal guilt. . . . Walter Johnson with all his terrific speed has hit batters on the head and yet they have not died. . . . Fairly often a batter gets hit on the head and seldom is he seriously injured."

Mays felt that Chapman either did not see the ball or was hypnotized by it as his teammate Chick Fewster had been in an earlier spring training incident. "During the same season," Mays' statement continued, "there were several pitchers in this league who have hit more batters than I have. . . . Because a terrible accident has happened does not relieve me from the responsibility I owe to continue pitching. . . . I have long since ceased to care what most people think about me. I have a few good friends I can depend on and that is all I need and all I want. In the meantime I have a wife and a family to support."

Mays went on to finish the 1920 season with a 26–11 record and was 27–9 in 1921. He registered 100 of his career total 207 wins after 1920, but the Ray Chapman incident left a shadow that he could never escape.

Little-Known Facts

Muleskinner Lancaster, Boston first baseman in the thirties and later a famous insurance agent, once hit a foul ball into the right-field stands that was caught by his own mother. . . . Only one major league ballplayer every died of boredom during a World Series, but baseball historians disagree on his name. . . . Ten players have hit four home runs in a single ball game, but superstition forbids any major league player from hitting five.

Conrad Horn

FORGET ABOUT METS-RED SOX, POOR BILLY BUCKS, AND ALL THAT OTHER LIGHT-WEIGHT 1986 STUFF—ANOTHER BOSTON-NEW YORK MATCHUP WAS THE STUFF OF LEGEND

Boston-New York: The Really *Exciting Series*

BILL CHUCK

♦ ♦ ♦

Boston versus New York. The rivalry encompasses art, culture, politics, commerce, and class. And, of course, baseball. Let's talk World Series. Clemens, Gooden, Wilson, Buckner? How about Wood, Mathewson, Speaker, Snodgrass? Nineteen eighty-seven was the seventy-fifth anniversary of Fenway Park and the strange, exciting World Series of 1912.

Let's set the scene. The year started with William Howard Taft as President of the United States. At least 325 pounds, Taft had a special bathtub built in the White House to meet his needs. It could fit four people (probably three Terry Forsters). Nineteen twelve was a presidential election year. Taft lost when Teddy Roosevelt entered the race as the "Bullmoose Progressive," split the Republican vote, and enabled Democrat Woodrow Wilson to be elected twenty-eighth President. In January, 25,000 textile workers in Lawrence, Massachusetts staged the now-famous "Bread and Roses Strike" that broke the American Woolen Company Sweatshop and established the International Workers of the World as a powerful union.

Time for baseball. In January, Charles Ebbets announced plans to build a new $750,000 stadium in Brooklyn for the Trolley Dodgers. Ground was broken in March. In February, the Yankees announced that they would wear new pin-striped uniforms. Spring training saw Cy Young announce his retirement. In April, the season began with a classic stadium opening. Built on the marshes of Boston (also known as "the Fens"), Fenway Park became the new home of the Red Sox. April 18, 1912 was to be opening day. It rained. A doubleheader was scheduled for the next day, Patriots Day. It rained once more. On April 20, the first game was played against . . . you guessed it, New York. The Sox won in eleven, 7–6. But simultaneously news was arriving of a far more ominous event: the sinking of the Titanic.

By May, Ty Cobb was suspended indefinitely for thrashing a fan who had sworn at him. American League President Ban Johnson reinstated Cobb only after the Tigers went on strike and refused to play. It didn't matter: The Tigers would finish sixth. The Philadelphia Athletics, who had won in 1910 and 1911 and would win again in 1913 and 1914, were to be a third-place club. By July, it became apparent that 1912 was the year of the Boston Red Sox: They set a league record with 105 wins that held up until the 1927 Yankees won 110. In the senior circuit, John McGraw was leading his Giants to the second of three straight National League pennants: They won by ten games over the Pirates.

Heinie Zimmerman of the Cubs won the National League batting title and, by some modern accounts, the Triple Crown. In the American League, Ty Cobb (who else?) won the batting crown with a .410 average, down ten points from his league-leading average of the previous year.

The National League champion Giants were led by pitching greats Christy Mathewson and Rube Marquard. Fred Merkle was at first, Fred Snodgrass in center, and Chief Meyers behind the plate. The Red Sox had one of the greatest fielding outfields of all time. Harry Hooper and Duffy Lewis flanked center fielder Tris Speaker, who played as if he were a softball player in short center and occasionally turned line drives into unassisted double plays. He hit .344 for his career and .383 for the 1912 season. But the Bosox story in 1912 was pitcher Joe Wood. Known as "Smokey Joe" for his smoking fastball, he had one of the best pitching years ever, a 34–5 record with 35 complete games, a 1.91 earned run average, and 10 shutouts. One of those shutouts, on September 6, was a famous 1–0 win over Walter Johnson. Johnson had had a record sixteen-game winning streak halted in August. This win marked Wood's fourteenth straight, and he eventually tied Johnson's streak.

It was the first time that Boston and New York met in the World Series. They should have met in 1904, but John McGraw wouldn't let his Giants play the then named Pilgrims, stating "we don't play minor leaguers." Ah, Boston versus New York.

It's now October and time for the World Series. Game One, New York. Pitching for the visitors, Smokey Joe Wood. For the Giants, Jeff Tesreau. Already the controversy begins. The Giants have 20-game-winners Mathewson and Marquard. Why a rookie spitballer? McGraw claims to be saving Mathewson for the Boston opener in Game Two. Observers believe that McGraw is conceding the win to Wood. Tesreau pitches well, leading 2–0 through five, but gives up one run in the sixth and three more in the seventh. Going to the bottom of the ninth, it's still 4–2. The Giants score one and put runners on second and third with only one out, but Wood strikes out Fletcher and Crandall to win, 4–3. "That was the biggest thrill I ever had in baseball, those two strikeouts," Wood would later say.

The Series returns to Boston for Game Two. The Red Sox are greeted by more than 30,000 fans, none more rabid than the "Royal Rooters." Numbering about 500, they're led by Boston Mayor John "Honey Fitz" Fitzgerald, the future grandfather of John Kennedy (the President, not the utility infielder). Prior to the game they give a car to Sox manager Jake Stahl as a token of their appreciation. The game starts at three, with Christy Mathewson pitching for the Giants and Ray Collins for Boston. Red Murray and Buck Herzog each get a single, double, triple, and two runs batted in for New York. The Giants, however, make five errors. The Sox have only one error, but it's a dropped fly ball by Duffy Lewis that allows the tying run to score. That's how it ends, tied 6–6 after eleven. Called on account of darkness.

After two games, Boston leads New York, one game to none.

October 10. The next game is also in Boston, the Giants' Rube Marquard pitching against Buck O'Brien. The Giants score one run in the second and another in the fifth to lead 2–0 going to the bottom of the ninth. Boston-New York weirdness then strikes. Duffy Lewis beats out an infield hit and scores on Larry Gardner's double to right: 2–1. Jake Stahl bounces to Marquard, who snags Gardner at third. Darkness is setting in, and a typical New England mist descends upon Fenway as Heinie Wagner beats out an infield hit. An out and a stolen base later, the Sox have runners on second and third with two outs. Hick Cady hits a liner to right. Stahl and Wagner race home with the tying and winning runs. But through the fog Josh Devore makes a dive for the ball and heads right to the clubhouse. Boston fans, elated, go home feeling that their beloved Sox have taken a two-game Series lead. After the game the writers get the call from the umps. Devore caught the ball. The Giants win, 2–1.

After three games, the Series is tied at one game apiece. Back in New York, there's a rematch of the opening-game pitchers. The results are the

Fred Merkle

same: Wood the winner, Tesreau the loser. Wood strikes out eight and drives in a run in a 3–1 win.

Back to Fenway. Trying to even the Series, the Giants send Christy Mathewson against Red Sox rookie Hugh Bedient, who is hot off a 20–9 season. Mathewson pitches brilliantly, giving up only five hits. Two of the hits, in the third, are back-to-back triples by Harry Hooper and Steve Yerkes. Then, second baseman Larry Doyle errs on a Tris Speaker grounder, producing another run. That's enough for Bedient, who allows only three hits for a 2–1 win.

The championship is in sight. After a Sunday off-day, Smokey Joe Wood is scheduled to pitch. Sox owner Jim McAleer pulls a Steinbrenner-type move and insists that the Game Three loser, Buck O'Brien, 4–9 in the regular season, pitch this key game. Manager Stahl protests, but McAleer wins. O'Brien doesn't. The Giants score five in the first, and Marquard coasts to a 5–2 win. The game is saved by what Hugh Fullerton in *The New York Times* calls a "miracle catch" by Fred Snodgrass. On the train ride back to Boston, Wood's brother, who lost a $100 wager on the game, gives O'Brien a black eye. Rough day.

After six games played, the Sox lead 3–2.

Well, it's back to Fenway for Game Seven, er, I mean Six, I mean . . . well, what game was it? The Royal Rooters want to know. You see, fans bought tickets in strips of three games. The location of the seventh game is to be decided by a coin flip. Tickets for this fourth Boston game are sold on a first-come, first-serve basis. This means the seats reserved for the Royal Rooters are sold by a very naive ticket clerk. Led by Honey Fitz, the Rooters march in shortly before the game is to start, waving their miniature red stockings and singing the song "Tessie." They try to take their seats. Unsuccessful, they swarm the field to protest just as Wood marches to the mound to clinch the title. The officers from the left-field stands fail to move the loyal fans who had followed their Sox in Boston and New York. They're moved by mounted officers from the right-field stands. Five mounted policemen disperse the crowd, but in the process, the Rooters knock down the then-low left-field bleacher fence. The game is delayed as the outfield fence is repaired. By the time the game starts, Smokey Joe's arm has tightened up. In the worst-played game of the World Series, the Giants score six in the first, knock out Wood as easily as the Rooters knocked out the fence, and bury the Sox, 11–4. The headlines the next day proclaim the Giant success. The nation waits and worries as Teddy Roosevelt wages his successful battle against an assassin's bullet.

The Giants have Christy Mathewson for the finale, but the Sox have American League President Ban Johnson. On the coin flip deciding the location, Johnson calls "tails" and the Red Sox are at home. Each of the first seven games was viewed by over 30,000 fans, but this game has a crowd of only 17,000. There had been a rally by the Rooters following the last game vilifying the Red Sox ownership and, unbelievably, cheering the Giants management. Boston-New York. Only in a Boston-New York series would the home team fans boycott the final game of the World Series! The Giants score a run in the third against Bedient. Josh Devore walks on four pitches and scores on a long double to left-center by Red Murray and beyond the grasp of Speaker. In the sixth Hooper makes a barehanded catch falling into the stands to save a run. In the Red Sox seventh, Jake Stahl hits a Texas Leaguer between three Giant fielders. After Matty walks Heinie Wagner on four pitches, Olaf Henrikson pinch hits for Bedient. Matty goes to 0–2, but at 2–2 Henrikson crashes a double down the third-base line and the game is tied. The Series is tied at 3–3, the game at 1–1. On the mound for the Giants, their best, Christy Mathewson. Now pitching in relief for the Sox, their best, Smokey Joe Wood. The score is tied at the end of nine.

In the tenth, Red Murray and Fred Merkle each double. The Giants have the lead and Wood is injured by a batted ball off his pitching hand. It's the bottom of the tenth and the Giants lead, 2–1. But this is Boston-New York. Clyde Engle leads off the inning pinch-hitting for Wood. He lofts a soft fly ball to center. Fred Snodgrass etches his name in the pages of World Series infamy: He drops the ball. In Los Angeles, Fred Snodgrass's mother is in a movie theater, following the game on an electronic scoreboard. When the muff is shown, she faints and is carried out of the theater. Snodgrass redeems himself by making a magnificent catch of a Harry Hooper liner. With one out, Yerkes walks. Mathewson against Tris Speaker. Matty fools him and gets Speaker to loft a foul pop down the first-base line. At this point we can only speculate as to what happened. There are some who claim that Mathewson called for Chief Meyers, the catcher, to catch this ball. Some suggest that Speaker or the Boston bench yelled first baseman Merkle off the ball. Merkle quits cold. As described in *The Times,* perhaps he is suffering from "financial paralysis" calculating the difference between the winning and losing shares. The ball drops. One should not give a Tris Speaker a second life. He rips a vicious single to right to tie the score, 2–2, and advances to second on the throw as Yerkes goes to third. Lewis is intentionally passed and the bases are loaded with one down. With the score tied, the infield and outfield are drawn in. Larry Gardner hits a long fly to Devore, who catches it over his head and makes a desperate throw to the plate too late. Yerkes has scored the championship run. The Boston Red Sox win Game Eight, 3–2, and the championship, four games to three.

Hugh Fullerton writes in *The New York Times,* "Boston fans are mentioning his name only in whispers, and deepest gloom prevails [in New York] wherever baseball is discussed." It is called the "$30,000 muff," the difference between the winning and losing shares (not for each player, for the teams). There is no tendency for the Giant players to blame either Snodgrass or Merkle, but others say Snodgrass's muff cost each New York player $1283, the difference between winning and losing. The winning player's share was $4,024.68.

The 17,000 Sox fans are jubilant. The Sox are paraded and saluted the next day at Faneuil Hall. They're given an extra day's pay, for the last game was played one day after the season had officially ended. The Giants take the train home. Mathewson travels alone.

Mathewson was 0–2 with a 1.57 ERA. Marquard was 2–0 with a 0.50 ERA. Wood was 3–1 with a 3.68 ERA. The Sox hit .220, Speaker .300; the Giants .270, Herzog .400. But the story of this series was the poor fielding. The Sox made fourteen errors. The Giants made seventeen errors. Doyle and Fletcher made four each. Merkle, already called "Bonehead," made three. Fred Snodgrass made one. But it was the error that would forever haunt him. John McGraw, no softy, gave him a $1,000 raise for the next season in recognition of the good year he had. Alas, when Snodgrass died in 1974, his obituary in *The New York Times* headlines, "Fred Snodgrass, 86, Dead, Ballplayer Muffed 1912 Fly." It makes you think of Bill Buckner, doesn't it? (And just as unfairly. Snodgrass redeemed himself, remember, and the 1986 Red Sox blew their lead before Buckner bobbled Mookie Wilson's grounder.)

By October 19, there was no mention of the Series in the newspaper. But seventy-five years later, we look back to that Boston victory over their rivals from New York, and await yet another.

"Please Don't Let Them Knock Me Off This Roof!"

BOB RULAND

♦ ♦ ♦

The other day John Holway asked me how it came to be that I happened to be on that Flatbush rooftop on Sunday, October 5, 1941.

This is a good question, seeing as how it was well known to one and all that at that time I was a fourteen-year-old Giants fan who did not generally care to mingle with Yankee or Dodger fans. It was my opinion that the former group are snobs while the latter seem to be somewhat boisterous.

Well, anyway, the answer is that my father was a NYPD cop who got assigned to guard this roof in back of Bedford Avenue. Since it over-looked Ebbets Field and a World Series was in progress, the landlord did not wish to have a large number of freeloaders congregate thereupon, thus causing it to cave in and create a variety of problems. Therefore only tenants of this four-story walkup were permitted to gain access thereto. Naturally, in my own personal case I enjoyed a special status.

When we arrived I quickly came to realize that the big scoreboard in right center blocked much of the view. One had to choose between the two ends of the building. The one on the right revealed only left and center fields. I decided to take up a position to the left where I could see down the right-field line, including home plate.

Shortly after I sat down in back of this low parapet, I was joined by two occupants of the fourth-floor rear. One was a tall thin fellow with a large Adam's apple who wore a flat peacap. The other guy was short and fat and appeared not to have shaved for several days. He wore a derby with a dent. I never learned their names.

256

As the fourth game of this series got ready to start, I could tell from the manner in which they spoke that they were Dodger fans of long standing. I therefore considered it wise to conceal my true identity. So I told them I was from St. Louis and was rooting for the Browns. This resulted in some very mournful looks. It was some years later that I confessed this venial sin to the SABR priest, Father Beirne, who for penance instructs me to apologize to Bill Borst and Ron Gabriel 'for this transgression. I now do so.

Anyway, they seemed to be pretty agreeable folks who told many Brooklyn stories, including one about how they watched from this very roof in 1920 when the Clevelands clobbered the Robins. It seemed that was what the local fans called them in those days on account of the manager's name was Wilbert Robinson.

I will not dwell at any length on the details of the first eight innings. You can look them up in the various record books. As is well known throughout baseball circles, the Dodgers went into the top of the ninth with a 4–3 lead and with the Yankees unable to figure out how to deal with Hugh Casey's curves. When the first two batters could not even get the ball out of the infield and Tommy Henrich now had two strikes against him, it was a lead-pipe cinch that the Brooklyns would now tie the Series at two apiece.

Throughout these events we were able to keep track of the ongoing developments, due largely to a Philco radio which my new acquaintances had connected with a long extension cord running down the fire escape and into their flat below. I therefore heard Red Barber speak of such things as "cat-bird seat," "rhubarbs," "pea patches," and this and that. He was now saying that "anything can happen in Ebbets Field and usually does." Just then what he said proved to be very accurate because I saw Henrich swing and miss on the 3–2 count and so it seemed that all assembled might leave. But I also saw him drop the bat and take off very rapidly toward first base. Why was he doing this, I thought?

While we tried to learn the answer from the radio, which could not be heard because of much yelling, the crowd from the other end of the building was racing to where we were standing to get a better view. I was not prepared for what now happened and was pushed by this surging group of individuals to the top of the aforementioned parapet. Amid much shoving, snarling, and no little amount of cursing, I found this painful and disconcerting because I looked down at the alley below with many clotheslines in between. My dime-store graph-paper notebook I used to keep score flipped over the edge and I was now clutching only the eraser part of my pencil, which had been broken in two from the crush of various persons. It was all somewhat alarming.

About the time I had cause to believe that I would now soon join the notebook on the pavement below, I became aware of two things, each of which was somewhat comforting. The first of these was that the two Brooklyn fans from the fourth floor-rear had grabbed my ankles, which I doubt they would have done if they knew my true Giant identity.

The other thing I found heartening was the sound of my father yelling at the crowd. He threatened that if they did not deport themselves in a more orderly fashion it might become necessary for him to bash a skull or two. He was concerned that the falling of any citizens from this roof would create much paperwork for him besides causing him to be bawled out by his sergeant.

When things calmed down a bit, we were aware that catcher Mickey Owen had failed to hold the third strike. I learned, many years later, that the ball rolled all the way to where future SABR vice president Jack Kavanagh sat (next to Casey Stengel, but that's another story) watching. Jack was one of Larry MacPhail's ushers at the time and is still somewhat reluctant to discuss this unusual development.

But I fear I digress. What occurred next is also now history. I know only that lo these many years later it is how the observers react and the things which they say that I remember forever. Things like these:

FAT PERSON: "Owen is a bum! He should of stood in St. Louis!"

RED BARBER: "DiMaggio lines it to left. . . . Henrich moves to . . . second with the tying run."

THIN PERSON: "Look at Camilli! I can tell from the way he . . . gestures he is yelling swear words."

ME: "Who does he swear at?"

THIN PERSON: "At the world! That is at who!"

RED BARBER: "Count 0 and 2 on Keller. . . . There's a long drive over Walker's head against the screen in right. The Yankees go ahead 5–4."

FAT PERSON: "Why does Leo not remove Casey?"

RED BARBER: "You could boil an egg on the back of Casey's neck."

THIN PERSON: "Leo does not dare go near the mound. He fears for his life."

RED BARBER: "Ball four! Dickey draws his third walk today."

FAT PERSON: "Leo is a bum! He too should of stood in St. Louis!"

RED BARBER: "Gordon lines one over Wasdell's head in left . . . another double and two more runs come in."

THIN PERSON: "It is MacPhail who is a bum! Better he should of stood in Cincinnati."

RED BARBER: "Rizzuto takes ball four."

FAT PERSON: "Babe Phelps would never of left that ball get away."

THIN PERSON: "Like I say: It was MacPhail who brung all these bums here."

And on and on like that.

So, anyway, when it was all over and done with, the guys from the Bronx scored four times, the Dodgers were out 1-2-3 in the bottom of the ninth, and were now down 3–1 in the Series instead of tied. It was all very difficult to comprehend.

It was all very quiet on the roof now. As the various residents filed down the staircase to their respective flats, I heard the fat person suggest to his friend, "Leave us retire to Mulligan's saloon, where we may weep in our beers." I then heard the thin person say, "I will go by Mulligan's but I do not weep. I am a Yankee rooter!"

"Since as of when?" he inquires.

"Since as of now!" he responds.

Alas, to this very moment, I do not believe his statement to be true.

ABOUT THE CONTRIBUTORS

Paul D. Adomites is the editor and publisher of *The Cooperstown Review of Books.*

During his childhood in a Detroit suburb, **Larry Amman** was entertained by his father's dinnertime tales of seeing Ty Cobb in action.

Don Bell is a freelance writer and world traveler from Sutton, Quebec.

Henry Berman, M.D., is president and CEO of Group Health Northwest, an HMO headquartered in Spokane, Washington. He is the author of three books, the most recent of which is *Choosing the Right Health Plan.* His Bill James Fantasy League baseball team won a world championship in 1992.

Peter C. Bjarkman's most recent books are the two-volume *Encyclopedia of Major League Baseball Team Histories, The Baseball Scrapbook,* and *The History of the NBA.*

Darryl Brock is the author of *If I Never Get Back,* a fictionalized version of the 1869 Red Stockings' great season.

Bill Chuck is an administrator at Boston's Emerson College.

Debbie Dagavarian-Bonar is Director of Testing and Assessment at Edison State College in New Jersey.

Richard Derby worked for British Petroleum for twenty-three years. When his job was eliminated, he started a baseball memorabilia shop, called Yannigans, in Westlake, Ohio.

Rich Eldred is currently researching the origins of the Boston Red Sox.

Jay Feldman, a frequent contributor to *Sports Illustrated* and other magazines, lives in Davis, California.

Cappy Gagnon, the definitive authority on Notre Dame major leaguers, is the only known French-surnamed softball player to make an unassisted triple play as a left-handed third baseman.

Jeremy Giller is a freshman at Williams College who joined SABR when he was nine years old.

Peter M. Gordon has worked as both a theater director and a teacher and is currently the program manager of WLIW on Long Island. Jim Buklarawicz assisted him with his statistics.

John Holway is the author of *Voices from the Great Black Baseball Leagues,* from which this article is excerpted.

Jim Kaplan is the co-author, with *New York Times* columnist Ira Berkow, of *The Gospel According to Casey: Casey Stengel's Inimitable, Instructional, Historical Baseball Book.*

Lawrence S. Katz is an attorney in Sterling Heights, Michigan. His upcoming book on baseball in the prewar era will be published in 1994.

Jack Kavanagh is the author of several baseball books. He is a retiree who writes for the fun of it and hopes that his readers are as much entertained as informed by his work.

Richard Kendall is a middle-school social studies teacher in Buffalo, Wyoming.

John McCormack, a former international lawyer for Texas Instruments, now plays contract bridge and writes for SABR.

Joseph M. Overfield has written for the *Niagara Frontier, Baseball Digest,* and *Baseball Research Journal.*

Jim Reisler writes for the *Morristown Daily Record* in New Jersey.

Lawrence S. Ritter is the author of the classic *The Glory of Their Times.*

Upon retirement in 1986, **Bob Ruland** joined SABR, which he has served in a variety of positions, including Treasurer. He is currently Secretary and a member of the Executive Board. He still cherishes his boyhood memories of the New York Giants.

Jamie Selko is an award-winning Army intelligence linguist in Germany.

Robert E. Shipley is a systems analyst for the Department of Defense in Philadelphia.

James K. Skipper Jr. is the retired chairman of the Sociology Department at the University of North Carolina at Greensboro.

Duane A. Smith is a professor of history at Colorado's Fort Lewis College.

Lyle Spatz is a regional economist for the U.S. Department of Commerce.

John Thom is a business communications consultant in Los Angeles.

Larry Thompson is a U.S. diplomat stationed at the American Embassy in Guatemala City.

John Thorn is an author and the president of Total Baseball.

Jules Tygiel is a historian on the faculty of San Francisco State University.

David Q. Voigt, a historian, is the author of the three-volume *American Baseball.*

Pete Williams is an associate professor of English at County College of Morris in Randolph, New Jersey.

Plug Into the SABR Network!

SABR members receive *The National Pastime* and *The Baseball Research Journal*—the annuals that most of the articles in this book came from—along with a membership directory, a monthly newsletter, *The SABR Bulletin*, and specialty publications like *Nineteenth Century Stars*, *Minor League Stars*, reprints of great old baseball books, and much more.

You don't have to be a researcher to be welcomed into the Society. If you enjoyed this book, you'll *love* SABR.

To join, send this form or a facsimile, with $35 (U.S.), $45 (Canada and Mexico), or $50 (overseas) to:

> SABR
> Dept. T
> P.O. Box 93183
> Cleveland, OH 44121

(Check or money order, U.S. funds or foreign equivalent, please.)

Name _____

Street _____

City_____ State/Province _____ Zip _____

Phone (_____) _____